Manchester by Area

Essentials

Time Out Digital Ltd
4th Floor
125 Shaftesbury Avenue
London WC2H 8AD
Tel: + 44 (0)20 7813 3000
Email: guides@timeout.com
www.timeout.com

Published by Time Out Digital Ltd, a wholly owned subsidiary of Time Out Group Ltd.
Time Out and the Time Out logo are trademarks of Time Out Group Ltd.

© **Time Out Group Ltd 2016**
Previous editions 2007, 2011.

Editorial Director Sarah Guy
Group Finance Controller Margaret Wright

Time Out Group Ltd
Founder Tony Elliott
President Noel Penzer
Publisher Alex Batho

10 9 8 7 6 5 4 3 2 1

This edition first published in Great Britain in 2016 by Ebury Publishing
20 Vauxhall Bridge Road, London SW1V 2SA

Ebury Publishing is part of the Penguin Random House group of companies whose addresses
can be found at global.penguinrandomhouse.com

Distributed in the US and Latin America by Publishers Group West (1-510-809-3700)

For further distribution details, see www.timeout.com

ISBN: 978-1-84670-360-7

A CIP catalogue record for this book is available from the British Library.

Printed and bound in China by Leo Paper Products Ltd.

Manchester Shortlist

The **Time Out Manchester Shortlist** is one of a series of guides that draws on Time Out's background as a magazine publisher to keep you current with everything that's going on in town. As well as Manchester's key sights and the best of its eating, drinking and leisure options, it picks out the most exciting venues to have opened in the last year and gives a full calendar of annual events. It also includes features on the important news, trends and openings, all compiled by locally based editors and writers. Whether you're visiting for the first time in your life or the first time this year, you'll find the *Time Out Manchester Shortlist* contains all you need to know, in a portable and easy-to-use format.

The guide divides Manchester into eight areas, each containing listings for Sights & Museums, Eating & Drinking, Shopping, Nightlife and Arts & Leisure, and maps pinpointing their locations; a further chapter rounds up the best of the rest. At the front of the book are chapters rounding up these scenes city-wide, and giving a shortlist of our overall picks. We also include itineraries for days out, plus essentials such as transport information and hotels.

Our listings give phone numbers as dialled within Manchester. To dial them from elsewhere in the UK, preface them with 0161. To call from outside the UK, use your country's exit code followed by 44 (the country code for the UK), 161 (without the initial zero) and the number given.

We have noted price categories by using one to four pound signs (**£-££££**), representing budget, moderate, expensive and luxury. Major credit cards are accepted unless otherwise stated.

All our listings are double-checked, but places do sometimes close or change their hours or prices, so it's a good idea to call a venue before visiting. While every effort has been made to ensure accuracy, the publishers cannot accept responsibility for any errors that this guide may contain.

Venues are marked on the maps using symbols numbered according to their order within the chapter and colour-coded as follows:

- ❶ Sights & Museums
- ❶ Eating & Drinking
- ❶ Shopping
- ❶ Nightlife
- ❶ Arts & Leisure

Time Out **Manchester** Shortlist

EDITORIAL
Editor Ruth Allan
Copy Editor Cath Phillips
Proofreader John Watson

DESIGN & PICTURE DESK
Art Editor Christie Webster
Group Commercial Senior Designer
    Jason Tansley
Picture Editor Jael Marschner
Deputy Picture Editor Ben Rowe
Picture Researcher Lizzy Owen

ADVERTISING
Account Managers Deborah Maclaren,
    Helen Debenham at the Media
    Sales House

MARKETING
Senior Publishing Brand Manager
    Luthfa Begum
Head of Circulation Dan Collins

PRODUCTION
Production Controller
    Katie Mulhern-Bhudia

CONTRIBUTORS
This guide was researched and written by Ruth Allan, with additional contributions
from Jessica Hardiman, John Thorp, Simon Binns, Alex Mays and Greg Thorpe.

PHOTOGRAPHY
pages 2 (top left), 3 (bottom left), 5, 7, 8, 12, 13, 22, 23 (left), 33, 35, 37, 38, 39,
42, 46, 51, 52, 58, 60, 73, 84, 85, 89, 93, 106, 115, 128, 130, 142, 146, 152, 173
Marketing Manchester; 2 (top right), 43 Antony Potts; 2 (bottom left), 36 Mark Waugh/
Marketing Manchester; 3 (top left), 141 Ben Page Photography/Marketing Manchester;
11 Tupungato/Shutterstock.com; 14 Paul Adams; 20, 82, 83 © The Vain Photography/
Carl Sukonik; 23 Mike Peel/Wikimedia Commons; 24, 86, 123 Jack Kirwin; 29 Ben
Blackall; 30, 124 Paul Karalius; 34 Olivia Lennon; 40 Manchester City Council; 45 Jonny
Draper Photography; 50, 74 Alastair Wallace/Shutterstock.com; 59 Diana Jarvis/Visit
England/Marketing Manchester; 61, 121 © Jason Lock Photography; 64 Mark Waugh/
Manchester Press Photography Ltd; 79 James Brown 93ft; 88 Adrian Houston Limited; 98,
99 John Clarke; 100 Preston in Paris Photography; 103 © Akse; 105 M.V. Photography/
Shutterstock.com; 108 (right) Devin Ainslie; 126 Rept0n1x/Wikimedia Commons; 127
Katja Bohm; 132 Paul Jones; 139 Nick Harrison; 144, 145 Percy Dean; 148 Menachem
Abrams; 150 Ian Tilton; 161 Stillwave.co.uk; 168 Patyo1994/Wikimedia Commons;
169 © eli pascall-willis/Alamy Stock Photo; 183 Andreas Andrews

The following images were supplied by the featured establishments: 2 (bottom right), 3 (top
right and bottom right), 17, 44, 49, 64, 69, 77, 80, 81, 92, 94, 95, 108 (left), 109, 110,
112, 113, 133, 134, 154, 158, 164, 174, 176, 177, 178, 180

Cover photograph: View Pictures/UIG/Getty Images

MAPS
JS Graphics (john@jsgraphics.co.uk).

About **Time Out**

Founded in 1968 by Tony Elliott, Time Out has expanded from humble London
beginnings (the original London Time Out magazine was a single fold-out sheet of
A5 paper) into the leading resource for those wanting to know what's happening in
the world's greatest cities. As well as our influential what's-on weeklies in London
and New York, we publish nearly 30 other listings magazines in cities as varied as
Beijing and Tel Aviv. The magazines established Time Out's trademark style: sharp
writing, informed reviewing and bang up-to-date inside knowledge of every scene.
   Time Out made the natural leap into travel guides in the 1980s with the City Guide
series, which now extends to over 50 destinations around the world. Written and
researched by expert local writers and generously illustrated with original photography,
the full-size guides cover a larger area than our Shortlist guides (which are aimed at
the short-break travel market). Many of these cities, and others, are now also covered
on our website, www.timeout.com.
   Throughout this rapid growth, the company has remained proudly independent.
This independence extends to the editorial content of all our publications. No
establishment has been featured because it has advertised, and no payment
has influenced any of our reviews.

Don't Miss

New Cathedral Street

WHAT'S BEST
Sights & Museums

The blending of history and modern development in Manchester is a constant and very visible process, and the last couple of decades have seen as furious a programme of rebuilding as the city has experienced since the cotton mills and their attendant slums sprang up in 19th-century 'Cottonopolis'. Today's Manchester appears to alter its appearance on an almost daily basis, with road works and large-scale scaffolding a seemingly permanent fixture in the city centre.

Perhaps one of the reasons for this is that the anchor of history holds steady here – which allows confidence in change. Manchester is no stranger to upheaval, after all, having witnessed and absorbed abrupt incursions of interlopers from Roman legions to Bonnie Prince Charlie's Jacobite rebels. In fact, quite often the city has been the one leading the rebellion, this being the place that saw the birth of everything from the Suffragette movement and Robert Owen's socialism to Marx and Engels' *Communist Manifesto*.

To put it another way, Manchester is a city that walks with a swagger. Even during the dark days of post-industrial gloom, it possessed a remarkable self-belief – an attitude that undoubtedly saw it emerge, at the turn of the millennium, as one of the UK's strongest cities.

Some of the credit, if that's the appropriate word, must go to the IRA bombing of 1996, which led to the development of Exchange Square. The city's new, modern heart was born, which in turn led to the rest of the city smartening up its act.

Newly reconfigured St Peter's Square and the ever-expanding pedestrianised Spinningfields business and leisure district are two examples of the wave of change that has rippled across the city's core.

The enviable sweep of history still remains with old favourites such as the Whitworth Art Gallery (p118), Central Library (p53) and Victoria Station (p63) on the receiving end of multi-million pound refits. And entirely new attractions, such as the HOME arts centre (p125), MediaCityUK (p140) and the Etihad Campus (p146), have arrived in very modern form to wrench the city into the 21st century.

Modern public spaces

Located just where you'd expect, New Cathedral Street connects old and new Manchester, and opens up the old sightline between the cathedral and St Ann's church (now bordered by glossy shops). In the background looms Ian Simpson's Beetham Tower (p128). Meanwhile, the complete overhaul of St Peter's Square – including the moving of war memorials, renovation of Central Library and creation of a new, controversial passage between the Town Hall and Library (another project conceived by Simpson) – is probably the most significant change in recent years. Like it or not, there's no denying that the grand public square and new tramlines are an improvement.

A planned route connecting the city centre with the Imperial War Museum North and the Trafford Centre should have a particularly positive impact on the city's western side when it opens around 2020.

Other new public spaces include the waterside plaza at MediaCityUK and yet more at Spinningfields, which had expanded to nearly half-a-million square metres of upmarket

SHORTLIST

Best architecture
- Imperial War Museum North (p142)
- John Rylands Library (p57)

Best restoration projects
- Central Library (p53)
- Victoria Station (p63)
- Whitworth Art Gallery (p118)

Best for people-watching
- St Ann's Square (p73)
- Spinningfields (p73)

Best-kept secrets
- Elizabeth Gaskell House (p153)
- Greater Manchester Police Museum (p90)
- St Mary's (p60)
- Victoria Baths (p155)

Most impressive history
- Chetham's Library (p57)
- Manchester Cathedral (p58)
- Town Hall (p63)

Most beautiful stained glass
- Manchester Cathedral (p58)
- Manchester Jewish Museum (p149)

Best for kids
- Manchester Museum (p115)
- MOSI (p129)

Most emblematic
- Salford Lads Club (p136)
- Manchester United FC (p166)

Most impressive views
- Imperial War Museum North tower (p142)
- National Football Museum (p59)
- Town Hall tower (p63)

Most impressive art
- Manchester Art Gallery (p57)
- Whitworth Art Gallery (p118)

Bags packed, milk cancelled, house raised on stilts.

You've packed the suntan lotion, the snorkel set, the stay-pressed shirts. Just one more thing left to do – your bit for climate change. In some of the world's poorest countries, changing weather patterns are destroying lives.

You can help people to deal with the extreme effects of climate change. Raising houses in flood-prone regions is just one life-saving solution.

Climate change costs lives.
Give £5 and let's sort it *Here & Now*

www.oxfam.org.uk/climate-change

Be Humankind Oxfam

MOSI

shopping, restaurants and bars at last count. Decent green space still comes at a premium, though, and a drive to turn the centre into a residential area has led to inevitable clashes, with much of the Northern Quarter's artistic community upping sticks for Salford and other, less pricey corners of the city. The lack of green space, healthcare and schools still conspires to make loft-style living the preserve of the young and unencumbered.

All change

While regeneration slowed slightly during the recession, the builders are now back in business. One of the most exciting developments is an entirely new district called St John's. The planned site starts at the bottom of Quay Street, and runs west to Salford and along to MOSI (Museum of Science and Industry, p129),

taking in the former Granada TV studios and *Coronation Street* set.

While plans are still being finalised, a new-build £78-million arts complex called the Factory has the go-ahead as the future home of Manchester International Festival and its associated artistic productions. There will also be a vintage-style hotel called the Grande, alongside new skyscrapers and repurposed old buildings such as the listed Bonded Warehouse. The hope is that this building will become a hub for small-scale creative industries, like a mini Northern Quarter. Time will tell how that pans out.

Other future changes include £3 million worth of new exhibition space at the MOSI, as well as ongoing rumblings in north Manchester around the £800-million NOMA development (p147), whose only attraction at present is the eco-friendly 'sliced egg' HQ of the

Cooperative Bank. Elsewhere, existing resources such as Great Northern Warehouse and Salford Quays have blossomed as new retailers have moved in. Look out for festivals and foodie events both there and in the city's thriving suburbs of Chorlton, Didsbury and Monton.

Old favourites

What the city has got, in terms of historic attractions, is pretty impressive. The biggest wow factor comes from the refurbished Central Library, whose flagstone floors and chambers have lost none of their impact in spite of a radical internal overhaul. The structure, which is loosely based on Emperor Hadrian's Pantheon in Rome, shimmers inside with interactivity and state-of-the-art research zones. Elsewhere, the John Rylands Library (p57), a staggering neo-Gothic monument on Deansgate, is equalled by the high drama of Pugin's Manchester Monastery (p154). The city's libraries raise their own flag for architectural endeavour, from medieval Chetham's (p57) to the quiet refuge of the Portico.

Manchester's large attractions are rather good at winning awards. The Whitworth Art Gallery, for example, was crowned Art Fund's Museum of the Year in 2015, with director Maria Balshaw earning a CBE for her efforts both here and at the Manchester Art Gallery. The Daniel Libeskind-designed Imperial War Museum North, meanwhile, continues to add to its collection of prizes for architecture.

The city's niche museums aren't to be overlooked either: the Gallery of Costume feels like stepping into your well-dressed great aunt's wardrobe, while museums dedicated to transport, police and the Jewish community may be small but are nevertheless fascinating.

It's certainly a city that, to the outsider, can seem perplexing: architecturally disparate, unlovely in parts, Manchester's charms are often buried beneath a layer of shoulder-shrugging effrontery. Yet as any current resident will tell you, this is a city that rewards those who wait and inspires loyalty from its supporters. Among them, famous names include Manchester's in-house 'brand' designer, Peter Saville;

Manchester Monastery

campaigner, poet and University of
Manchester chancellor Lemn Sissay;
and Sir Ian McKellen, grand marshal
of Manchester Pride.

Neighbourhoods

Much of the centre is heavily
commercial, packed with big-name
stores and chain cafés, which makes
the Northern Quarter the number
one destination for alternative
shopping and dining. Chinatown,
meanwhile, has some of the city's
most exciting options for eating out.

The medieval quarter, from St
Ann's Square to the cathedral, is
home to the city's most pleasing
architecture. Castlefield is where
epochs collide most impressively,
from the Roman settlement where
Manchester began to the canals
that are the enduring footprints
of the Industrial Revolution.

Salford Quays has been
transformed. Just a decade ago, it
was a museum-less concept waiting
to spark. It is now home to Imperial
War Museum North and the Lowry,
watersports on the Quays, and
MediaCityUK, home of the BBC
in the North.

North Manchester is mainly
residential, but offers plenty of
parkland – including Heaton Park
(p148), the jewel in the city's green
crown, containing Grade I-listed
Heaton Hall and other, less-heralded
gems such as Boggart Hole Clough.
Beyond affluent South Manchester,
the path heads towards Cheshire and
fertile National Trust territory.

Manchester often requires a
little effort on the part of the visitor
to unearth its sometimes hidden
charms; consequently, it offers an
element of discovery in the simplest
journey. The compact centre makes
walking an attractive option. A
much-underrated activity, as in
many UK cities, is strolling and
observing the upper levels of
buildings; look above the chain-store
façades and unexpected architectural
delights are often revealed. Try the
old warehouses around Ancoats,
or the grandeur of King Street.

Guided walks (search for tour
options on the Visit Manchester
website) can add context and
historical facts, while more niche
tours are available from independent
operators such as Manchester
Modernist Society and the Skyliner
architecture blog. Modernism was a
big thing in Manchester, and you'll
find delightful examples south of
Piccadilly Station, within the former
UMIST university campus on
Sackville Street.

Otherwise, the established
attractions are uniformly good.
Even those that divide opinion, such
as the National Football Museum, are
fascinating buildings, and much of
the city's sightseeing can be done for
free. The good folk of Manchester
are unlikely to hand anything to
you on a plate, but should you be
prepared to make the first move, it's
a city whose rich history and more
recent renaissance make it one of
Britain's most rewarding, if not
quite conventional, urban centres.

DON'T MISS

French

Eating & Drinking

Manchester always knew it could do music, football and politics – and if you gave it half a chance, it would tell you – but food was different. Critics claimed that restaurants were years behind those in the south; Manchester was nothing more than a mass of takeaways and chain eateries.

But following what can only be described as a food revolution, it's a different world today. There has been a rampant growth in the numbers of restaurants and bars in the Northern Quarter, and a boom in street food and coffee purveyors, not to mention a thriving craft beer scene. Throw in a couple of world-class chefs (Aiden Byrne at Manchester House, and the French's exec, Simon Rogan) and things have taken an about-turn, with Manchester now leading where it once followed. The city is home to

restaurants that others ape – such as the Almost Famous burger chain and the Parlour (winner of many national 'Sunday roast' awards) – and is able to support upmarket chains such as Iberica Spanish restaurant and Hawksmoor steakhouse (previously confined to London).

Obviously, long before any of the changes happened, the city was already mouthing off about it. Manchester, as journalist and professional northerner Stuart Maconie once said, is a city that fancies itself rotten – so why not let it wine, dine and show off to you?

Eating

Spurred by a shift in consciousness around sustainable eating and the arrival of big-name chefs, there has been a spike in the popularity of contemporary British cooking in the city. Restaurants such as the French (p66) and Manchester House (p68) use regionally sourced (and occasionally rooftop sourced, as in the case of the French) ingredients in reinterpretations of classic dishes. Venison tartare, sarsaparilla marshmallows and foraged herbs are the new order of the day.

Artistic creations on the plate are complemented by one of the most varied selections of international restaurants in the country. The best ethnic eateries aren't necessarily to be found among the gaudy neons of Curry Mile and Chinatown but are instead dotted around the Northern Quarter (Kabana, 52 Back Turner Street, 835 2447), Deansgate (Umezushi, p70) and Victoria Park (Seoul Kimchi, p160).

With so many styles of cooking within such close proximity, cross-pollination is inevitable, and it's not unusual for Mancunian menus to feature a fusion of local and international flavours. Rare-breed, Middle White pork lasagne is a stand-out dish at gourmet pub Tariff & Dale (p95) in the Northern Quarter. The glitzy Living Ventures group has created a Pacific Rim-meets-Manc fusion at Australasia (p64): the mango soufflé, served with a glass pot of mango tea, is a local classic; as are the crisp pork belly cubes with pineapple.

Though the city doesn't possess a Michelin-starred restaurant, there's plenty to enjoy, and one of Manchester's core strengths is its casual food. The Almost Famous brand, for example, was born in the heart of the Northern Quarter and its own-brand sauces are now sold near and far, while late night Mexican wrestling-themed bar Crazy Pedro's, just off Deansgate, takes pizza in a direction all of its own. Jamaican jerk chicken and rum salsa slice, anyone?

SHORTLIST

Best new
- Crazy Pedro's (p66)
- French (p66)
- Volta (p160)
- Hawksmoor (p67)
- Salut (p68)

Dine in style
- Rose Garden (p159)
- Damson MediaCity (p143)
- Manchester House (p68)
- Australasia (p64)
- The French (p66)

Gourmet pub food
- Parlour (p159)
- Clarence (p149)
- Tariff + Dale (p95)

Craft beer
- Port Street Beer House (p94)
- Font (p119, p156)
- Common (p101)
- New Oxford (p139)

Cool coffee
- Takk (p95)
- North Tea Power (p92)
- Proper Tea (p59)
- Pot Kettle Black (p68)

International hit list
- Yuzu (p111)
- San Carlo Cicchetti (p70)
- Habesha (p108)

To the pub
- Briton's Protection (p118)
- Molly House (p114)
- Marble Beer House (p157)

Best bar none
- Cloud 23 (p130)
- Under New Management (p140)
- Kosmonaut (p102)
- Gorilla (p123)

DON'T MISS

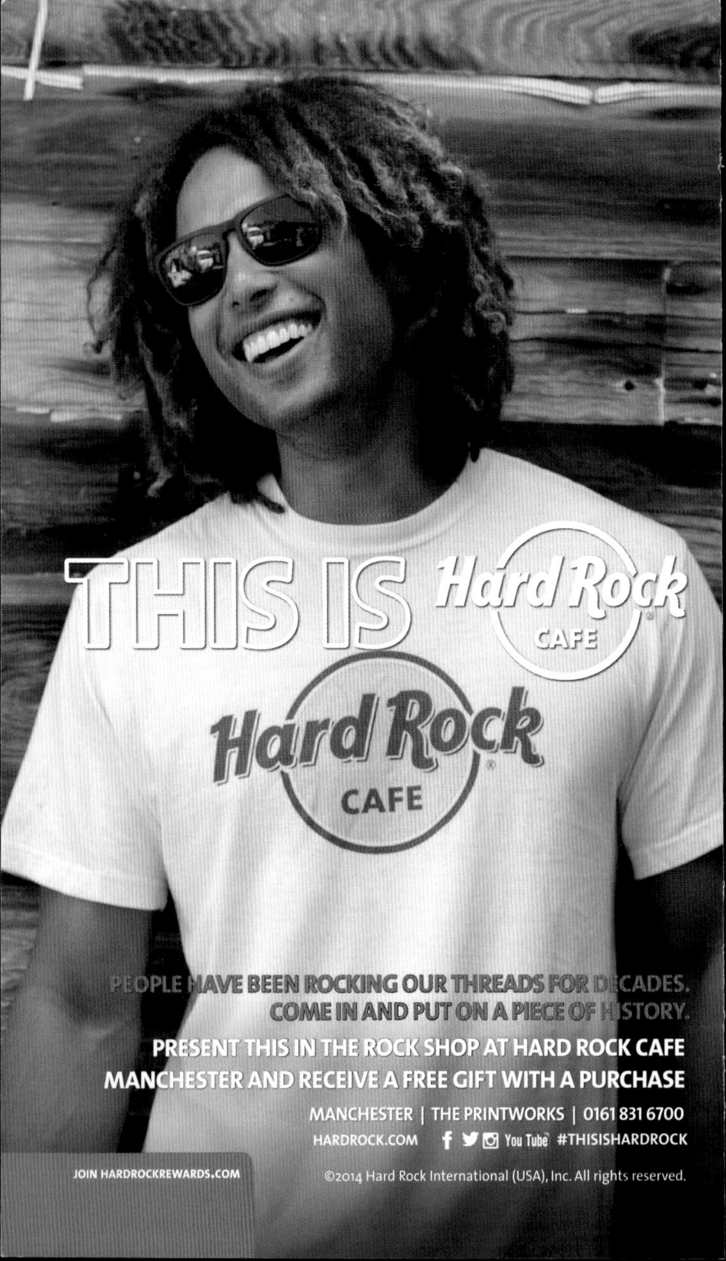

THIS IS Hard Rock CAFE
Hard Rock CAFE
PEOPLE HAVE BEEN ROCKING OUR THREADS FOR DECADES.
COME IN AND PUT ON A PIECE OF HISTORY.
PRESENT THIS IN THE ROCK SHOP AT HARD ROCK CAFE
MANCHESTER AND RECEIVE A FREE GIFT WITH A PURCHASE
MANCHESTER | THE PRINTWORKS | 0161 831 6700
HARDROCK.COM YouTube #THISISHARDROCK
JOIN HARDROCKREWARDS.COM
©2014 Hard Rock International (USA), Inc. All rights reserved.

Parlour p14

The city excels at pub food too. The best old-school examples are to found at the Victorian Chop Houses: Mr Sam's (p69), for example. The modern Wharf (p132) in Castlefield comes a close second.

However, Manchester's food scene is not confined to the centre. Talked-about restaurants pepper Manchester's suburbs: Lily's (p172) in Ashton is a must for vegetarians and fans of south Indian food; the Rose Garden (p159) in Didsbury has fine British food and wine; and pub/restaurant/brewery, the Clarence (p149), makes a tram ride out to Bury worthwhile. All produce classy food at a fraction of the price you might expect to pay in London or Paris.

Then there are those dining heroes who are a little too rock 'n' roll to get a look-in with the Michelin judging panel. Upmarket Italian restaurant San Carlo (p70), has a bank of paparazzi outside, waiting for the latest superstar to emerge while Rosso (43 Spring Gardens, 832 1400, www.rossorestaurants.com) is a rococo-style banking hall turned catwalk, where the Italian-inspired dishes are a bit of an afterthought. The average food does little to deter the crowds – football star and co-owner Rio Ferdinand is a regular visitor. To put it in the words of the late Tony Wilson, 'This is Manchester: we do things differently here.'

The Lowry

Pier 8
Salford Quays
M50 3AZ
www.thelowry.com

Gallery Opening Times:
Sun-Fri 11am-5pm;
Sat 10am-5pm
Entry is free, but please
make a donation.

THE LOWRY
ART & ENTERTAINMENT

The Lowry boasts an award-winning programme where you can find the best in drama, dance, opera, ballet, comedy, music and family shows. There's participatory activity for all ages, and the Galleries showcase the work of LS Lowry alongside that of artists of local, national and international renown. This unique building also contains a restaurant, coffee shop and theatre bars, all set against stunning backdrops.

Although the city centre is full of the usual array of chain coffee houses, a short wander away from Market Street reveals a more varied scene. From touristy Teacup (p95) to connoisseur's choice North Tea Power (p92) and hipster havens such as Takk (p95), the Northern Quarter is hooked on caffeine. Further afield, Caffè Lupo (p138) does the best coffee in Salford, while Slattery (p150) in Whitefield is worthy of a pilgrimage for those in search of a great cuppa and a slice of something sweet, as is Didsbury Village's French pâtisserie, Bisous Bisous (p158).

Manchester has its fair share of grim fast-food outlets, although 'fast' doesn't have to mean 'bad' – if you know where to look. The Arndale Market (p71) is a great place to start, with more than a dozen fast and healthy food merchants to choose from, including Viet Shack (summer rolls are around £3) and Panchos Burritos, plus a craft beer bar. For pudding on the go, ice-cream maker Ginger's Comfort Emporium has taken the top slot in the British Street Food Awards several times over. Look out for the vintage pink van at Mancunian festivals, or pop into their Afflecks café (p96).

Drinking

The Northern Quarter is the heart of the city centre bar scene, with numerous quirky watering holes. Common (p101), Kosmonaut (p102) and even the famous Night & Day Café (p102, a favourite haunt of bands such as Elbow), are places frequented by creative types for their fine selections of rare beers, and their playlists filled with obscure sounds. The Northern Quarter is not just for the cool kids, though, and if your tastes are more mojito than microbrew then you could do worse than the funky booths the Black Dog Ballroom (p101).

The area is also the home of the city's burgeoning craft beer scene. Sample around 20 handpulls and draught beers at Port Street Beer House (p94) before making your way to the Marble Brewery-owned 57 Thomas Street (p90) for a pint of Ginger Marble or Earl Grey IPA. Blackjack Brewery has taken over the Smithfield (37 Swan Street, 839 4424, www.the-smithfield-hotel. co.uk) and there are frequent brew-tap weekends at local breweries such as Cloudwater and First Chop. One of the best places to start is the craft-brewer run Beermoth off-licence, on Tib Street.

For cocktails, visit the 'sky bar' at the Hilton, Cloud 23 (p130), which offers an unequalled view of the city. Other options include Deansgate's adventurous Elixir (p66) and Mr Cooper's House & Garden (p178), in the Midland Hotel, which has made a name for itself by using herbaceous tinctures and blends. The 12th-floor bar at Manchester House (p68) is another fashionable haunt.

In addition to its raft of bars and cocktail dispensaries, Manchester and its environs are home to plenty of traditional pubs. The Briton's Protection (p118), on the edge of Deansgate, has the widest selection of whiskies for miles around, and an authentic snug in which to nurse your glass. The Peveril of the Peak (p119), largely unchanged since World War II, is a tiled wedge on the corner of Great Bridgewater Street. In Salford, the New Oxford (p139) might not be pretty but it is home to nearly 30 draught beers and ciders, while the Eagle Inn (p138) is a treat for music fans. Over in trendy Chorlton, the Marble Beer House (p157), the Beagle (p155) and the Font (p119) are all a few steps from each other, and offer the kind of pub crawl to please the most impassioned CAMRA member.

The Avenue

WHAT'S BEST
Shopping

Manchester has escaped with minor cuts and bruises from a UK-wide recession, brushing itself off in readiness for a new chapter in its retail history. Sure, there are plenty of famous brands to be found across the city centre and beyond, but where Manchester continues to distinguish itself is with homegrown brands such as menswear retailers Oi Polloi and Lissom & Muster.

The high end

King Street, once dubbed the 'Bond Street of the North', was one of the credit crunch's first casualties in Manchester. While King Street wasn't exactly knee-deep in tumbleweed, the number of empty shop windows starkly reinforced the fact that the times were now, definitely, a-changing. Thankfully,

King Street is making a comeback, with a new and eclectic mix of tenants moving in, such as local music hero Liam Gallagher's own-brand Pretty Green (p76). The street has more food and drink outlets now (a trend started by the opening of Jamie's Italian in 2012), but aside from the likes of Bravissimo, the White Company (p80), Barbour (p71) and Hermès, the centre of the high-end retail action has largely shifted to Spinningfields (see box p73).

This business district, a new-build enclave on the banks of the River Irwell, home to all manner of corporate and banking HQs, is centred around a lively new public space, Hardman Square. It's flanked at one end by the striking presence of the Civil Justice Centre, the largest (and surely most architecturally exciting) civil court to be built in

Britain in over 100 years. At its opposite boundary, running down from Deansgate, shopping street the Avenue serves the suited and booted of Spinningfields, hosting major stores from the likes of Mulberry (p76), Oliver Sweeney, Flannels (p72) and Armani.

Of course, Spinningfields isn't the only place where you can splash your cash: Selfridges (p78), Harvey Nichols (p75) and House of Fraser (p75) all offer an ingenious mix of clothing, household goods, technology and food designed to relieve you of your readies.

Independent streak

As well as the well-heeled, the city is home to one of the biggest student communities in Europe. They may not be rich, but their collective force creates a market for all things hip and quirky, and it's to the Northern Quarter that they flock.

This former run-down garment district is studded with independent boutiques and retro stores such as Junk (p97) and Cow (p96) and lifestyle shops and cafés such as Fig & Sparrow. Indie institution Afflecks (p96) continues to sell a huge choice of 'pre-loved' clothing, kitsch gifts and posters, while street- and skate-wear is covered by Black Sheep (36 Dale Street, 0333 600 0161, www. blacksheepstore.co.uk), Carhartt (59-61 Oldham Street, 831 9488, www. carhartt-wip.com) and the main branch of Note (61 Thomas Street, 478 3535, www.noteshop.co.uk). The area's biggest independent success story, however, is the Oi Polloi (p97) menswear and accessories store, which specialises in brands such as Margaret Howell and Fjällräven. (A sister shop opened in London in 2015.) In short: increasingly, more high-end names are beginning to move in, but the NQ is still the domain of affordable niche retailers.

S H O R T L I S T

Best new
- Lissom & Muster (p75)
- Rapha Cycle Club (p78)

Best department stores
- Harvey Nichols (p75)
- Selfridges (p78)

Best for culture vultures
- Craft & Design Centre (p96)
- Magma (p97)
- Spirited Wine (p78)

Best for street style
- Oi Polloi (p97)
- Note (left)
- Oxfam Originals (p98)

Music to your ears
- Johnny Roadhouse (p121)
- Beatin' Rhythm (p96)
- Piccadilly Records (p96)

Heaven for foodies
- Hanging Ditch (p72)
- Unicorn Grocery (p163)
- Siam Smiles Thai Supermarket (p112)

Great family fun
- Fred Aldous (p97)
- Oklahoma (p96)
- Museum of Science & Industry shop (p129)

Best for gifts
- Fig & Sparrow (p96)
- Moth (p162)
- Hotel Chocolat (p75)

Best bargains
- Office Sale Shop (p76)
- Cow (p96)
- TK Maxx (p78)

Arndale Centre

Something for all

Market Street, Manchester's
mainstream shopping hub, continues
to be packed, especially at weekends.
High-street brands such as H&M,
Debenhams and TK Maxx (p78), and
edgier neighbours such as All Saints
and Urban Outfitters (p79), line up
against the looming Arndale Centre,
itself home to an enormous Next
and Topshop (p78). Rebuilt after the
IRA bomb, the Arndale still has its
1970s tiled tower but now features
a glittering extension, making it
the country's biggest inner-city
shopping mall, with an annual
footfall of 40 million.

The Marks & Spencer store
nearby is connected to the Arndale
by a handy footbridge; opposite,
there's a neat row of shops including
branches of Paperchase and a large
Zara. The small boutiques, upmarket

shops and jewellers in the elegant
trio of the Barton, St Ann's and
Royal Exchange arcades are worth
exploring too, not least for unique
eyewear from Seen (p78) and funky
treads from Ran (p76).

The intimate layout of the city
centre means that nowhere is truly
exclusive. Shoppers can happily
hop between areas: skint but savvy
youngsters make a day of it at
Selfridges, while WAG wannabes
are as comfortable browsing the
graffitied rabbit-warren of the
Northern Quarter in a hunt for
vintage pieces as they are at the
cosmetic counters of Harvey Nichols.

Beyond the centre

For those who prefer to stay away
from the chaos of the city centre,
the suburbs do a very good job of
keeping up. Bohemian Chorlton is

Barton Arcade

popular with local residents, but also attracts outsiders looking for a leisurely afternoon stroll. Chorlton's Beech Road has a quirky (if small) selection of exclusive clothing shops and galleries, while nearby Manchester Road offers gift shops, delis galore and the vegan Unicorn Grocery (p163).

Also in South Manchester, both Didsbury Village and West Didsbury's Burton Road are home to bookshops, fashion retailers and imaginative delis. The outlying towns of Stockport, Bury and Bolton, meanwhile, appeal with a mix of high-street shopping and excellent markets.

In Salford Quays, the Lowry Outlet (p144) offers discounts of up to 70 per cent, and serves residents of the nearby modern apartments. As the adjacent film and television production complex at MediaCity

has filled up, the mall has seen new additions including Gap, Clarks and Marks & Spencer. Food and drink needs are covered by Booths supermarket (p143).

Out of town, too, and perennially popular, is the massive Trafford Centre (p163). Faux palm trees and Romanesque sculptures might not be to everybody's taste, but rain-free shopping, extended opening hours and free parking are all draws. A new tram connection is in the pipeline, making the Trafford Centre a genuine rival for Market Street's Arndale complex.

Locals are justifiably proud of one of the widest arrays of shops outside the capital, and many others flock to the city from elsewhere in the North West and beyond. From high street to independent, and from second-hand to glossy designer goods, Manchester does shopping very well.

Gorilla

WHAT'S BEST
Nightlife

Manchester's legendary nightlife
has eclecticism at its heart, and
the city has resisted boiling down the
best elements of its after-hours scene
to a generic cover-all template. So,
while Manchester is proud of its
musical history, it refuses to stifle
innovation with nostalgia. All
manner of nightlife options coexist
here, making it an exhilarating
city in which to step out.

The city's manageable size makes
it easy to hop between districts, yet
each retains a unique identity, from
the creative vibrancy of the once-
industrial Northern Quarter to the
leafy, bar-loving southern suburbs.
Manchester, it seems, is a city that
doesn't tolerate homogeny and
many of its most dynamic ventures
proclaim that they have sprung up as
antidotes to the status quo. Whether
it's established or brand-new bands,

clubbing or comedy that floats your
boat, or if you have no agenda but to
try things out, Manchester's nightlife
has something for you.

Clubs

The original modern city continues
to move with the times, and recent
years have seen several of its most
iconic spaces turned into live and
clubbing venues, now enjoyed by
audiences far from those they were
intended for. The city's cool Trof
group runs three of them, including
the former Deaf & Dumb Institute
(p122). Its vintage auditorium,
dating back to 1877, is home to
Manchester's largest glitter ball
and is a memorable place to dance
the night away.

Other Trof ventures include
rave-cave Gorilla (p123) on the site

of the old Greenroom theatre, and the Albert Hall (p81). This long-forgotten Wesleyan chapel hides in plain sight on Peter Street, only revealing its perfectly preserved stained-glass windows and lozenge-shaped balcony to those with much-sought-after tickets for its live shows and club nights.

The unusual Mayfield Depot (p106), a former train station, plays occasional host to super-promoters the Warehouse Project (see box p110). The revenue generated by the club phenomenon enables them to be bold with their choice of venue; they have previously housed raves in disused breweries, a bomb shelter under Piccadilly Station, and the gargantuan Victoria Warehouse near Old Trafford football stadium.

Looking for something a bit more old-school? Several decades after 'Madchester' and the baggy revolution that made the city the club capital of Europe, Manchester's most famous musical pedigree is still alive and kicking, thanks to Factory Records ventures such as FAC251: The Factory (p122), as well as an armada of nostalgia nights.

The underground techno and house scene, spearheaded by venues such as Soup Kitchen (p94), is well worth investigating. For hip hop and grime – and a dizzying list of other styles – check out Antwerp Mansion (p163), where you'll be rewarded for your efforts by an open-hearted crowd. Harmless but mediocre indie nights are everywhere, but thankfully easy to spot (and avoid) from their rampant drinks promotions and queues of bop-hungry students. Lovers of quality indie and rock 'n' roll should venture instead to South (p83), which bursts the city centre's image-conscious bubble with a roster of floor-stomping nights. Across town, Islington Mill (p140) invites you to leave your inhibitions at the door,

SHORTLIST

Best for gigs
- Deaf Institute (p122)
- Manchester Apollo (p165)
- Manchester Academy (p123)

Underground sounds
- Islington Mill (p140)
- Soup Kitchen (p94)
- Antwerp Mansion (p163)

Best for laughs
- Comedy Store (p132)
- Frog & Bucket (p102)
- Kings Arms (p138)

Most beautiful venues
- Manchester Cathedral (p58)
- Band on the Wall (p101)
- Albert Hall (p81)
- Manchester Apollo (p165)

Best-kept secrets
- Eagle Inn (p138)
- Under New Management (p140)
- Volta (p160)

Best for gay clubbers
- Cruz 101 (p114)

Most eclectic line-ups
- Deaf Institute (p122)
- Islington Mill (p140)

Best for all-night dancing
- Soup Kitchen (p94)
- Cruz 101 (p114)
- Gorilla (p123)
- Warehouse Project (p110)

Most glamorous
- Cloud 23 (p130)
- Manchester House (p68)
- Mr Cooper's House & Garden (p178)

Best out of town
- Volta (p160)
- Beagle (p155)

with a booking policy that makes progressive look conservative. Björk, Hot Chip and Death Grips have all played or DJed here.

Manchester's Northern Quarter has more nightlife to choose from than any other city district. Most of the bars keep late hours and are independently run; a refreshing antidote to the identikit chain bars of which even Manchester has its fair share. The quirky aural entertainments on offer here provide an apt warm-up for the state-of-the-art acoustics of Band on the Wall (p101). In addition to its staple music gigs, Band on the Wall plays host to a number of club nights, including the perennially popular Keep it Unreal with Mr Scruff.

If scruffy chic isn't your thing, and you want instead to air your designer labels, Cloud 23 (p130) and Manchester House (p68) bars offer a stylish and occasionally celebrity-studded experience with great views. Better yet, allow yourself to drift through Deansgate's late-night bar scene. The Liar's Club (p82) and Mojo (p83) know how to party, while Hawksmoor's (p67) dark wood-panelled bar is an atmospheric place to start the evening off.

Music

Two decades after the city-defining 'Madchester', Manchester's home-grown music scene has finally shifted to a more genre-defying mix of influences. While some local acts on the rise scorn the 'Manchester band' tag for fear of pigeonholing, others acknowledge that it need not mean consignment to the Factory Records' cast-off bin. Manchester-bred artists such as Elbow and Everything Everything bring sounds from the city to international ears, but to experience the true scope of the 'Manchester sound' there's no better place than Manchester itself,

and no better place to start than the wealth of unsigned acts playing in smaller venues such as Fuel Café Bar (p163) or Gullivers.

Further up the career scale, the city-centre champion of the independents, Soup Kitchen (p94), hosts local and touring bands who have yet to fill a venue the size of the ornate Manchester Apollo (p165). For stellar acts, there's Manchester Arena (p82), scaling the live experience up (and down) to a distant view of the likes of Pharrell Williams or Fleetwood Mac.

Size of venue and fame of band are not always synonymous, however; scene stalwart Night & Day Café (p102) occasionally supplements its usual unsigned bands with hip names that sell out faster than you can say 'I'm with the band'. Aforementioned club and live venue the Deaf Institute welcomes acts of the calibre of Florence and the Machine and the xx, while the Trof group's other venues, Albert Hall and Gorilla, show equally impeccable taste in the booking department. For a different, yet equally Mancunian, music experience, head to Matt & Phred's Jazz Club (p102) in the Northern Quarter – but book ahead as weekends get busy.

Music festivals

Perhaps as a result of modern bands' near-constant touring schedules, Manchester's music festival scene is not what it was. Aside from annual events such as the avant-garde Future Everything festival in February, and the indie carnivals of Sounds From the Other City and Dot to Dot in May, many festivals are now a one-venue event. The likes of Night & Day and Fuel Café Bar offer forward-thinking guitar-driven and electronic-music-focused 'one-dayers' on a regular basis. Larger festivals usually offer wristbands that allow multiple entries for a smallish outlay (leaving you with ample change for your beer money), although the more popular sell out well in advance. The festival scene is fairly fluid: existing events wither away and new ones appear with confusing regularity. It's best to keep an eye on bar posters or online to ensure you don't miss out.

Gay & lesbian

Manchester's Gay Village – the area around Canal Street immortalised by writer Russell T Davies (*Doctor Who*) in TV series such as *Queer as Folk* and *Cucumber* – is now so established that veteran bars such as Napoleons and the New Union are tourist draws in their own right. Previous fears of over-development within the Village have, thankfully, proved unfounded, but that may be more down to the recession putting the brakes on new-builds than to inspired planning.

Whatever the reason, this famous stretch of the Rochdale Canal is packed with drinkers most weekends, and at the first hint of good weather. Although some revellers are undeniably the tourists and hen parties it had been feared might discourage regulars, the sense of community remains palpable and there really is something for everyone. Cavernous venues Via (p114) and G-A-Y (p114) both provide something special for clubbers, as well as alfresco drinking during the day. And while karaoke options are plentiful, there's room for credible clubbing experiences, such as the funky house nights at Cruz 101 (p114); niche bars such as Vanilla (p114); and even the odd boutique hotel. The annual Pride festival in August is among Europe's largest celebrations. As such, it's a good idea to book accommodation well in advance.

Comedy

Manchester is enjoying an energetic resurgence in the comedy department thanks to two central locations – the flagship Comedy Store (p132) and old favourite the Frog & Bucket (p102) – plus a host of often free nights at pubs such as the Kings Arms (p138) and the Castle Hotel (p90).

The two main venues offer a complete night out – acts at the Comedy Store can be enjoyed over dinner, and the Frog & Bucket invites cheesy post-show dancing. If your Comedy Store budget stretches to a ticket but not a meal, try Cask (p132) on nearby Liverpool Road – a cosy bar that allows you to bring in food from the chip shop next door.

Fancy yourself as a stand-up? Mondays at the Frog & Bucket play host to Beat the Frog, with respect and other prizes for any amateur act who can perform five minutes of original comedy before the frog banishes them from the stage. Tickets are less than £5 and students or competitors (book your slot in advance) can come along for free. Since the Frog & Bucket kick-started the careers of laughter legends such as Peter Kay and Dave Gorman, you never know what it might lead to.

Big names such as Sarah Millican often play Salford's Lowry or the Apollo and, occasionally, the Dancehouse or Gorilla. Few, however, can match the appeal of University of Salford graduate Peter Kay, who packed out the 21,000-capacity Manchester Arena for a record-smashing 40 nights in 2009.

Even he started somewhere, and a comedy night dedicated to the best new talent can be found in the heart of student territory at the Pub/Zoo on Grosvenor Street. Its XS Malarkey night has been running for nearly 20 years and is so confident of its own longevity that it offers lifetime membership with discount privileges.

Bridgewater Hall

Arts & Leisure

Manchester is emerging from nearly 20 years of cultural construction and renovation. The magnificent Bridgewater Hall (p124) was among the first of the newbuilds, followed by Salford's Lowry centre (p145). The most recent addition is the HOME purpose-built arts centre (p125), which includes cinemas, art galleries, theatres and cafés; while a £78-million permanent home for Manchester International Festival (p37) and its biennial series of artistic world premières has recently received the green light too.

The success of Manchester International Festival, and the emergence of cultural hubs such as HOME and MediaCityUK in Salford, has shored up Manchester's cultural confidence, with festivals forming a large part of the city's offering. Leading the pack in July is MIF,

followed by food and drink, comedy, science and literature events. Music festivals are still popular (this is Manchester, after all), although there are fewer large-scale operations such as Park Life and Pride, and more independent events and one-day festivals such as Salford's Sounds from the Other City.

Look out for active events at the city's cultural spaces, such as early-morning yoga at the Whitworth art gallery or urban dance classes at Zion Arts. Late-night opening at venues such as Manchester Art Gallery and Central Library, typically on a Thursday, is another welcome trend. Certain venues have upped the ante to the extent that the likes of HOME and the Lowry offer so much under one roof that it's easy to lose a whole day sampling their individual cultural wares.

Whatever your passion, it's the unmistakable infusion of Mancunian flavour that makes downtime here so good. Even the industrial heritage settings – the neoclassical grandeur of the Portico (p59), the glass-roofed atrium of the Craft & Design Centre (p96) – are unique.

Film

There's great enthusiasm for film here. The Manchester International Film Festival takes over the multiplexes during the summer months, while sci-fi, horror and extreme sports seasons, run by promoters such as Grimm Up North, see screenings in offbeat spaces such as the Dancehouse (p125) or Victoria Baths (p155). Manchester is also a mainstay for movie locations, even doubling for New York in big-budget movie *Captain America*.

When it comes to venues, forget the bland anonymity of the multiplex: HOME (p125) is king. Its five screens show the widest selection of arthouse, independent and foreign language films in town, while visits from international

directors (Danny Boyle is its patron) offer an additional dimension. But it remains to be seen whether HOME will remain a focal point for the city's cultural glitterati after moving to a new, purpose-built venue on the fringe of the city centre.

Theatre

Due for a large revamp in 2016, the Royal Exchange (p87) is the home of new playwriting talent in the city. Its annual Bruntwood Playwriting Competition reveals a dedication to new work that's being replicated elsewhere, most notably at Contact Theatre (p125) and summer's 24:7 Theatre Festival.

Other theatrical venues of note include Bolton's Octagon (p151) and the Lowry (p145), which, while it rarely commissions work, acts as a receiving house for some of the UK's biggest touring shows. Formerly housed in Central Library, the renowned Library Theatre Company has been absorbed by HOME. Early productions under the artistic direction of Young Vic graduate Walter Meierjohann have been well received.

HOME

Literature

Readers and writers in the city have rarely had it so good. Novelist Jeanette Winterson and the Poet Laureate, Carol Ann Duffy, regularly hold public debates and events (courtesy of the two universities at which they are employed; see box p127), while the city's Literature Festival continues to grow, boosted by developments such as the new International Anthony Burgess Foundation (p125), the £10,000 Manchester Writing Prize and the refurbished Elizabeth Gaskell House (p153). Edgier action comes courtesy of the city's burgeoning spoken word scene, which has seen nights such as Bad Language at the Castle Hotel bring the likes of Jo Bell to a wider audience. The Contact Theatre and Zion Arts continue their award-winning work with younger and marginalised audiences; the city's own Comma Press has recently become a National Portfolio organisation (in recognition of its pioneering work in translating stories from other languages, and promoting local talent such as Emma Jane Unsworth). Carcanet is a publisher of note in poetry. It all adds up to a rich, if sometimes a little underground, writing scene.

Dance

The Palace and Opera House are sister venues run by the same organisation and put on reliable touring shows from the English National Ballet. The Lowry, meanwhile, excels at contemporary dance, bringing choreographers and dancers including Matthew Bourne and Carlos Acosta to Manchester, plus works by the Birmingham Royal Ballet and contemporary international touring companies. For more experimental work, head to Contact Theatre, Dancehouse or

DON'T MISS

SHORTLIST

Most high-profile event
- Manchester International Festival (p37)

Coolest festivals
- Sounds from the Other City (p34)
- Parklife (p35)

Grand dame of classical music
- Hallé (p32)

Best for cutting-edge dance & theatre
- Contact Theatre (p125)
- HOME (p125)

New playwriting champ
- Royal Exchange Theatre (p87)

Eclectic arts
- Islington Mill (p140)

Best cinema
- HOME (p125)

Loveliest hidden gems
- Chetham's Library & School of Music (p57)
- Portico Library (p59)
- Victoria Baths (p156)

Best participatory sports
- Chill Factore (p164)
- Great Manchester Run (p34)

Biggest rivals
- Manchester City Football Club (p150)
- Manchester United Football Club (p165)

Best spiritual retreat
- Manchester Buddhist Centre (p104)

Lushest park
- Fletcher Moss (p153)

HOME, whose intimate spaces mean you can get up close to the newest moves in contemporary and urban dance.

Classical music

Under Mark Elder, the Hallé orchestra, which will chalk up 160 years in 2018, is enjoying the kind of critical and popular success unseen since its 1960s Sir John Barbirolli heyday. The Bridgewater Hall (p124), performing home of the Hallé, celebrates its 20th birthday in 2016. The Hallé has a second home in an atmospheric, deconsecrated church in Ancoats, renamed Hallé St Peter's (p147) in honour of its new tenants.

The orchestra's success has no doubt been helped by the friendly rivalry between Mark Elder and the equally charismatic former head of the BBC Philharmonic (now conductor laureate) Gianandrea Noseda. Noseda's artistic direction was formidable: when he led the Phil through its first complete cycle of the Beethoven symphonies in 30 years, the performances were uploaded on to the BBC's website. Some 1.4 million quick-fire downloads later, the Phil realised it had someone rather special fronting its orchestra. The Phil has now moved to Media City and is under the guidance of new chief conductor Juanjo Mena. The orchestra's musicians are involved in the community, and often perform in Salford's churches and mills. Keep an eye on the website for free tickets to recordings.

The public profile of the Royal Northern College of Music (p126) is aided by regular performances by its students, as well as popular crossover shows by everyone from Evian Christ to Philip Glass as part of events such as the Future Everything festival (p33). The University of Manchester's Quatuor Danel quartet – arguably one of the best quartets in Europe – regularly plays at the Martin Harris Centre. Manchester International Festival is also having a positive impact on classical music. The event manages to produce genuinely moving concerts that reflect the entire musical spectrum currently at play in the city – Manchester Camerata joining forces with local stars Elbow, for example, and new choral works by Arvo Pärt performed among gallery goers at the Whitworth.

Sports & leisure

This city of sporting prowess seamlessly produces world-class athletes and stages international events. The two football clubs, City (p150) and United (p165), ignite passionate debate wherever you go, and the region plays host to four rugby league clubs, one of rugby union's top teams (Sale Sharks) and Lancashire Cricket Club, based (for now, at least) at Old Trafford.

But there's also room for specialist events. Manchester Velodrome (p151) houses a 3,500-seat track for what might be considered a minority sport (track cycling), and yet the venue's winter season races regularly pull in 3,000 punters. Its Revolution events – spectator-friendly, with a 'night at the races' feel – are often packed. The Etihad Campus (formerly known as Sport City) has hosted everything from the National Badminton Championships to the Paralympic World Cup.

Another draw here is the ease with which visitors can indulge in healthy pursuits. If trekking through the urban landscape leaves you yearning for space and fresh air, then head north to Heaton Park (p148) or south to 1,000-acre Tatton Park (p154), one of the jewels in the National Trust's crown.

WHAT'S ON
Calendar

Manchester Pride p35

The following are the pick of the annual events that happen in Manchester. Further information about events can be found nearer the time from flyers and seasonal guides available from tourist information centres (p189), or www.visitmanchester.com.

January

Early Jan **Chamber Music Festival**
Royal Northern College of Music, Oxford Road
www.rncm.ac.uk
World-class classical sounds.

Jan or Feb **Chinese New Year**
Chinatown
www.visitmanchester.com
Fireworks and the Golden Dragon Parade enliven the city's Chinatown.

February

Early Feb **National Squash Championships**
Etihad Campus, p146
www.nationalsquashchamps.net
England's finest players battle it out for the national title.

Mid Feb **Queer Contact**
Contact Theatre, p125
www.contactmcr.com
Celebration of queer and LGBT performance. See box p109.

Late Feb **FutureEverything**
Various locations
www.futureeverything.org
Electronic and experimental music, and similarly forward-looking arts, with international and local artists in this city-wide 'festival as laboratory'.

Grimmfest p36

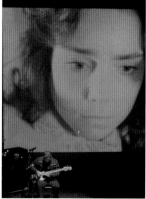

March

Early-mid Mar **Manchester Irish Festival**
Various locations
www.manchesteririshfestival.co.uk
Two-week annual festival culminating in one of the UK's largest St Patrick's Day parades.

Mid Mar **¡Viva! Spanish & Latin American Festival**
HOME, p125

www.vivafilmfestival.co.uk
Ten days of films, art and theatre from Spain and Latin America.

May

Early May **Sounds From the Other City**
Various venues, Chapel Street, Salford
www.soundsfromtheothercity.com
A one-day celebration of new music and art.

Mid May **Morrisons Great Manchester Run**
City Centre
www.greatrun.org
Pre-booking is essential for Europe's biggest 10K.

Late May **Spring Festival of Markets**
New Cathedral Street, City Centre
www.manchester.gov.uk/markets
Specialist food, drink, plants and gifts.

June

Early June **Parklife**
Heaton Park
www.parklife.uk.com
A weekend of diverse, modern music, and festival fun and frolics.

Late June **Manchester Day Parade**
Deansgate, City Centre
www.manchesterday.co.uk
A wonderfully exuberant street celebration of Mancunian pride.

July

July **Greater Manchester Fringe Festival**
Various locations
www.greatermanchesterfringe.co.uk
Month-long event celebrating the very best of Manchester's alternative scene.

Early-mid July **Manchester International Festival (biennial: 2017, 2019)**
Various locations
www.mif.co.uk.
See box p37.

Late July **RHS Flower Show at Tatton Park**
Tatton Park
www.rhs.org.uk/tatton
Horticultural heaven, over five days.

Late July-early Aug **Manchester Jazz Festival**
Various locations
www.manchesterjazz.com
Popular festival featuring bands in indoor and outdoor venues.

Late July-early Aug **Dig the City**
Various locations
www.digthecity.co.uk
Week-long festival featuring street food, fashion and plenty of gardens.

August

Ongoing Manchester Jazz Festival (see July); Dig the City (see July).

Late Aug **Manchester Pride**
Gay Village
www.manchesterpride.com
Weekend of floats, parades and parties.

Manchester Pride

Christmas Lights Switch-on p38

September

Mid Sept **Manchester Food & Drink Festival**
Various locations
www.foodanddrinkfestival.com
Food markets, celebrated chefs and restaurant events.

Late Sept **Buy Art Fair**
Spinningfields
www.buyartfair.co.uk
Commercial contemporary art fair. Attracts big-name and emerging artists.

Late Sept-Nov (2017) **Asia Triennial Manchester**
Various locations
www.asiatriennialmanchester.com
Events showcasing South Asian art.

Late Sept-Jan **Warehouse Project**
Various locations
www.thewarehouseproject.com
Three months of underground raves with the biggest names in dance and electronica, culminating in a New Year's Day closing party. See box p110.

October

Ongoing Warehouse Project (see Sept); Asia Triennial Manchester (see Sept).

Early Oct **Grimmfest**
Various locations
www.grimmfest.com
Horror, gore and sci-fi films, and related spooky events.

See it here first

Artistic world premières at Manchester International Festival.

For years, Manchester's global contribution to culture was largely based on three things: politics, football and music. That changed in 2007 when the city launched the ambitious – and often audacious – **Manchester International Festival** (p35), a biennial arts bonanza that revolves around new commissions and big names. Kraftwerk, Marina Abramovic, Björk, Kenneth Branagh and Adam Curtis are just a few of those who have contributed.

Nearly a decade down the line, the festival shows no signs of slowing down. In fact, it continues to accrue glorious reviews. In 2013, for example, arch-thesp Kenneth Branagh captured attention as Macbeth. In the same year, there was a haunting performance by Maxine Peake in *The Masque of Anarchy,* while Adam Curtis's politically charged *It Felt Like A Kiss*, co-produced with Punch Drunk, was a triumph in 2009.

Björk, who describes the festival as having a 'fertile mindset', premiered her *Biophilia* album here in 2011 (and returned in 2015). Damon Albarn's circus-opera, *Monkey: Journey to the West* started its life at the Palace in 2007. The mesmerising *Tree of Codes*, a ballet collaboration between choreographer Wayne McGregor, visual artist Olafur Eliasson and composer Jamie xx, was a highlight of 2015.

The festival continues to evolve: over the coming years, the festival team will move into a new home, a new £78-million arts centre called the Factory in the St Johns Quarter.

Founding artistic director Alex Poots left in 2015. John McGrath, from the National Theatre Wales, is his replacement – and his CV suggests that the combination of the new and unexpected that makes this event so special looks set to continue.

Mid Oct **Dashehra Diwali Mela**
Albert Square
www.dashehradiwali.co.uk
Bhangra, Bollywood, dance, food and
fireworks combined.

Mid-late Oct **Manchester
Literature Festival**
Various locations
www.mlfestival.co.uk
Two weeks of literary delights.

Mid Oct **Great Northern
Contemporary Craft Fair**
Spinningfields
www.greatnorthernevents.co.uk
Annual show from the UK's brightest
designer-makers.

Late Oct **Manchester
Science Festival**
Various locations
www.manchestersciencefestival.com
The Science Festival features more
than 200 events, from walks and demos
to comedy and stargazing.

November

Ongoing Warehouse Project (see Sept);
Asia Triennial Manchester (see Sept).

Early Nov **Greater Manchester
Comedy Festival**
Various locations
www.greatermanchesterfringe.co.uk
A ten-day event showcasing comedy.

Mid Nov **Christmas Lights Switch-on**
City Centre
www.manchester.gov.uk

Mid Nov-late Dec **Manchester
Christmas Markets**
Various locations
www.manchester.gov.uk/markets
Stocking-fillers, glühwein and food.

December

Ongoing Warehouse Project (see
Sept); Manchester Christmas
Markets (see Nov).

Christmas Markets

Itineraries

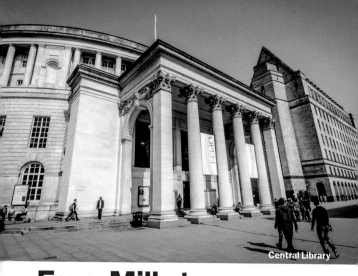
Central Library

From Mills to Madchester

Is it a characteristic defiance, a certain insecurity or just sloppiness that leads to Manchester being so coy about its astonishing past? The city has been midwife to the Industrial Revolution, the Football League, to communism and, most recently, the discovery of graphene. The first TUC congress was held here; Ernest Rutherford split the atom; and Alan Turing oversaw the beginnings of the computer age in the city. And yet these achievements are largely overlooked. A little craning of the neck and a certain amount of initiative is needed, but in a city centre as compact as Manchester's, the past can be explored with minimal effort. It should take an hour to complete this walk, which goes from one side of the city centre to the other, and across 2,000 years of history.

Start on **Miller Street**, in the shadow of the **Co-operative Insurance Tower**. This modernist delight was the tallest building in the UK when it opened in 1962. The tower is located at the junction with Rochdale Road, and while it may take a heroic feat of imagination to picture it now, this is where modern Manchester – indeed, the modern world – was born in 1780, when Richard Arkwright built his first cotton mill, thus kickstarting the Industrial Revolution.

Perhaps somewhat symbolic of the unsentimental greed of the capitalist revolution that it inspired, the site lay unrecorded, buried for years beneath a car park, but it was latterly brought back to attention when Channel 4's *Time Team* programme excavated the site in 2005.

A stark contrast is offered by **1 Angel Square** (p147), also on Miller Street, which while not officially open to the public, is worth admiring as the centre of the city's £800-million North Manchester (NOMA) regeneration scheme. It holds the title of the UK's most eco-friendly construction and houses the Co-operative Group HQ, which moved here from the neighbouring tower in 2013.

Just to the north, the rising towers of what is now called the **Green Quarter** loom above the old slum district – of Red Bank. Friedrich Engels – himself the beneficiary of his family's cotton wealth – paid several visits to this area (as well as to Little Ireland, behind Oxford Road Station). His observations led to the writing of his *Conditions of the Working Classes in England* in 1844.

Walk downhill from here and turn left on to Corporation Street. Soon you'll see the glass bubble of Victoria Station's new roof on the right, with **Balloon Street** on the left. The street is named in honour of pioneering aeronaut James Sadler, who made the city's first balloon ascent near here in 1785. The derelict block on the right – **City Buildings** – was the site of the home of Ann Lee, who would go on to establish the utopian Shaker movement in late 18th-century America. In her day, the road was called Toad Lane; today, it is **Todd Lane**, and this row of buildings forms a peculiar-looking island that harks back to Victorian times between the shiny surfaces of the National Football Museum and Victoria Station.

Follow the tramlines along Corporation Street, underneath the striking glass **Arndale Bridge**, and note the **red pillar box** on the right. This is the postbox that was somehow left standing when the IRA bomb exploded a few feet away in 1996.

Take the next left turn now, where the experience of **Market Street** will drive away all thought of history for five gaudy minutes. Just past the Market Street Metrolink stop, you'll reach the corner of **Piccadilly Gardens** (p106). Look up to your right. Now home to a Santander bank, this building was the Royal Hotel in 1888, and an innocuous plaque records that the Football League was formed here in April of that year.

Walk down **Mosley Street**, past Manchester Art Gallery and across **Princess Street**. Immediately to your right is the site of John Dalton's laboratory, where Dalton helped to establish the principles of modern atomic theory. Carry on to the end of **St Peter's Square**. This area was completely reorganised in 2015 by architect Ian Simpson (who designed Beetham Tower, which you'll see looming ahead).

The end of St Peter's Square nearest the Midland Hotel marks the site of the demolished **St Peter's Church**, while the cenotaph that was placed here as a marker has been moved back in the direction of Manchester Art Gallery. Turn right, past the beautiful rotunda of the **Central Library** (p53), and stroll a short way along Peter Street to reach what is now the **Radisson Blu Edwardian** (p178), one of the city's plusher hotels. This was formerly the Free Trade Hall, one of the numerous reminders of the city's radical past that has been transformed into a distinctly more capitalist present. Around this site, back in 1819, a public protest for parliamentary reform degenerated into bloodshed – the infamous Peterloo Massacre – when sabre-wielding troops galloped into a crowd of around 60,000, killing 11 and injuring 400 (the blue plaque on the wall refers to this as being the crowd's 'subsequent dispersal').

Various musical anecdotes can be relayed about the **Free Trade Hall**. From 1858 to 1996, the spot was home to the Hallé orchestra, Britain's longest-established symphony orchestra, which is now situated five minutes away in the Bridgewater Hall (p124). Bob Dylan received his infamous 'Judas' heckle here shortly after going electric in 1966, while in the upstairs Lesser Free Trade Hall, in 1976, the Sex Pistols played two momentous gigs. The show's promoters, Howard Devoto and Pete Shelley, would go on to form the Buzzcocks, while also in attendance were future members of Joy Division, Simply Red, the Fall, the Smiths and Anthony H Wilson.

Turn back the way you came and take one of the next two right turns, either of which will lead you to the **Manchester Central Convention Complex** (p59), formerly the Victorian-era Central railway station. Bear right and follow **Lower Mosley Street**, with the Bridgewater Hall on your left, then cross the road at the traffic lights and note the housing development on your left at the next crossroads. Another example of Manchester's viciously unsentimental attitude towards its heritage, the site of the **Haçienda** – in its day perhaps the most famous club in the world – now resides beneath the block of flats that bears its name. To be fair, when open, the club would go out of its way not to advertise its presence; at the height of the 1990s Madchester rave scene it was identified by a small brass plaque.

From here, go right down **Whitworth Street West** towards Deansgate for the short walk to Castlefield. The best route is to turn right at the Deansgate traffic lights, walk beneath the railway bridge and go left down **Liverpool Road**. Note the signs to your left pointing out the remains of Roman Manchester. Here lie the disappointingly remnants of the four **Roman forts** built between the first and fifth centuries; most of the remains were destroyed during the Industrial Revolution, as the Rochdale canal and the still-standing railway viaducts were ploughed through. **Beetham Tower** (p128) looms close over the site, an imposing reminder of the distance travelled in the two millennia since.

Manchester Central Convention Complex

Corn Exchange

Manchester in…

…an hour

As 60 minutes isn't very long, we'll give you a choice. One option is to indulge yourself at **Exchange Square**, the city's retail-cum-cultural epicentre. This fantastic public space was created in the wake of the 1996 IRA bombing, and is now being redesigned to make way for the city's second cross-centre tramline.

Tuck in at the food court in the former **Corn Exchange** (p61), where smoked mozzarella is a must at Salvi's Italian deli. There's also a huge branch of **Selfridges** (p78) to explore. In the distance looms the hulking **Arndale** shopping centre and the **Printworks** entertainment complex. Give the defiantly quirky **Paramount Book Exchange** on Shudehill (no.25, 384 9509, www.paramountbooks.co.uk) a try if you have time.

Alternatively, leave Exchange Square via Shambles Square. On your way, you'll pass two of the city's oldest public houses – the **Old Wellington Inn** (p68) and **Sinclair's Oyster Bar** (p70). Incredibly, this is the third home for both places: they were moved here in 1971 to make way for redevelopment, and then shifted again during the post-bomb rebuild.

Manchester's often overlooked 600-year-old **Cathedral** (p58) is next door on Cateaton Street. Its visitor centre houses the excellent Proper Tea café, owned by TV presenter Yvette Fielding; beyond it is **Chetham's Library & School of Music** (p57). The library's ancient texts should hold the interest of any bibliophile for a little while. Enjoy a browse in the reading room, former haunt of a certain K Marx. The School of Music puts on free lunchtime

Volta

concerts. If, after all that, you've still got a few minutes to spare, hot-foot it up Corporation Street and on to Cross Street, where you can nip into **Mr Thomas's Chop House** (no.52, 832 2245, www.tomschop house.com) for the famous corned beef hash and a crafty pint.

…an afternoon

It's always edifying to combine a cuppa with some culture, so start proceedings in the café of the **John Rylands Library** (p57) at the end of Deansgate, where, over a brew, you can peer up at the building's unrestrained neo-Gothic architecture.

Deansgate itself is a major stretch of listed Mancunian real estate, central to the city's emergence as a railway and canal capital, which links the north and south. There are dozens of drinking dens dotted along this key artery: if you're in need of further refreshment, try the **Knott** (p131), a bar offering tasty ales and hearty food.

Halfway up the old thoroughfare sits **St Ann's Square**, an elegant 18th-century civic space. The square and its surrounding streets were designated a Conservation Area by Manchester City Council in the 1970s. If you're not grabbed by the neoclassical **St Ann's Church** (p60), which sometimes stages music recitals, you may be more inspired by the big-brand stores here. Wander up and down the Barton Arcade, perhaps stopping for a cuppa at **Pot Kettle Black** (p68), and visit the former Kendal's department store. Now a **House of Fraser** (p75), the shop is still referred to locally by its old name. **King Street**, parallel to St Ann Street, offers higher-end boutiques, with the likes of Whistles, Hermès and Vivienne Westwood.

As afternoon turns to evening, a couple of nearby cultural options slide into focus: the **Opera House** (p87) and the **Royal Exchange** theatre (p87). Before a performance at either, head to **Harvey Nichols** (p75) for a long cocktail, as the sun (if you're lucky) begins to dip.

Rose Garden

...24 hours

Mornings in Manchester are usually relatively calm: even Market Street and the Arndale are quiet before lunch. However, there's more interesting shopping and street life elsewhere: have a roam around the **Northern Quarter**'s offbeat fashion outlets, the shops of **Afflecks** (p96), and the studios of the **Craft & Design Centre** (p96). Check out the **Centre for Chinese Contemporary Art** (p90) in the same building, while morning coffee is a must at **Fig & Sparrow** (p96) or **North Tea Power** (p92).

As you wander back into the city centre, a couple of cultural spaces beckon. The striking **Bridgewater Hall** (p124) stages lunchtime concerts a couple of times a week, and has an airy café-bar. Eating options also abound at **HOME** (p125), an impressive new complex that includes five cinema screens, typically showing independent films, alongside performance spaces and an art gallery. To balance the modern with the ancient, trip along to Deansgate and visit the excellent **People's History Museum** (p59), which dispenses a history lesson as seen through Mancunian eyes. Even if you're not hungry yet, it's worth crossing the River Irwell, a short walk from the museum, for the Lowry Hotel's afternoon tea: the **River Bar & Grill** (p140) offers gliding waiters, exquisite cakes and champagne to wash it all down.

If you're quick, there'll be enough time for a little fresh air and green grass. Head for **Fletcher Moss Gardens** (p153) in Didsbury, before an early-evening pint at one of the nearby countrified inns and an aesthetically pleasing contemporary British meal at the **Rose Garden** (p160). For something a bit more rock 'n' roll, this strip is also home to the **Volta** bar and restaurant (p160), owned by local DJ duo Luke Cowdrey and Justin Crawford. There'll be no need for a late-night taxi, at least not if you're sleeping at the **Didsbury House Hotel** (p182), a vivacious little Victorian boutique conversion.

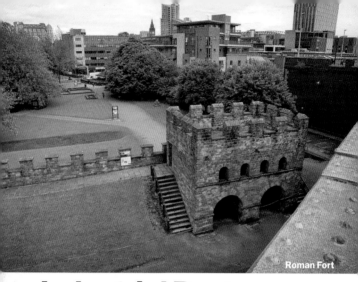
Roman Fort

Industrial Past, Cultural Future

From its early beginnings as a Roman fort to today's reinvented post-industrial city, Manchester is the sort of place that doesn't stand still for long. This walk begins at one end of **Deansgate** and, via a circuitous route that requires around two hours (and features a few watering holes), takes in one of the city's oldest settlements alongside one of its newest, in an apt demonstration of the ever-changing nature of this city.

Start your walk at **Beetham Tower** (p128). The brashest symbol of Manchester's modernity, and the city's tallest building, it provides a handy landmark by which to navigate. The tower packs in top-end apartments, a Hilton hotel and a 23rd-floor cocktail bar; it's also not a bad place to sample a high-rise high tea (11.30am-5pm daily, around £23 per person), should the mood take you.

Refreshed, head down **Liverpool Road**, where, between the White Lion pub and the Oxnoble (p131), you'll find a small park. Cut across it into Castlefield and you'll step back in time: here, you'll find the replica of a **Roman fort**. The original was built in AD 79 and named 'Mamucium', Latin for 'breast-shaped hill' (it was also known as 'Mancunium'); it's where modern Manchester first began. Mamucium was abandoned in AD 410; its stone remains led to locals christening the area the 'Castle-in-the-field'.

Today, Castlefield's peaceful cobbled streets and gentle canals belie its once frenetic nature: the Bridgewater and Rochdale canals, as well as a railway (more on that later), made this a clanking, dirty hub of Industrial Revolution commerce. The area inevitably fell into decline during the grim, post-industrial years, but thankfully, in 1972, it was designated the UK's first 'urban heritage park'. Its cleaned-up canals and cobbles now make it one of the best places to head for when the sun shines. If you have time, stop off at the ever-popular **Dukes 92** (p131), a canalside pub that peddles decent pints and hearty grub in one of the best alfresco settings in the city.

When you've finished off that pint, head back towards Liverpool Road via the **Castlefield Arena**. Although mostly quiet, the arena is occasionally used during the summer for music, art and sports events.

Head along **Potato Wharf** to get back on to Liverpool Road. Opposite and to your left is a sandstone Georgian terrace, the rather unassuming site of the world's oldest passenger railway station. It was here, in 1830, that 700 people gathered to witness the first Manchester to Liverpool run, which promised to cut the travel time between the two cities to an almost inconceivable (for that time) hour-long journey. The inaugural run didn't go quite according to plan, with political protests and even a tragic death (of William Huskisson, President of the Board of Trade, who fell into the path of the oncoming train). But, despite this, the railway did what the Liverpool & Manchester Railway Company had hoped: it changed British industrial transport forever. The station is now part of the **Museum of Science & Industry** (MOSI, p128); train-spotters can hop on board a steam train here and travel along a short stretch of the original tracks.

Turn right and head back up Liverpool Road. Ahead, you'll see the Victorian **Upper Campfield Hall**, which has been hosting lively markets for more than 130 years (check www.castlefieldmarket.org.

uk for details). For now, though, turn left on to **Lower Byrom Street**, passing the main entrance of MOSI, which is set to expand its gallery provision for adults in 2017 (it's already the city's biggest draw for those with kids) and has recently undergone a £9 million revamp.

Continue along Lower Byrom Street and, on the left, you'll spot the back of the former **Granada TV studios**. Work starts in 2016 on turning the modernist-era Granada offices into a 200-room 'event hotel' called the Manchester Grande, while the wider area is set to be rebranded as **St Johns**. The centrepiece of the new quarter will be a purpose-built, £78-million arts complex that will be a permanent home for the Manchester International Festival (p37). Granada Studios was the famous location of the *Coronation Street* soap opera set for nearly 50 years, but the Rovers Return and cobbled streets are just a memory today after ITV Granada shifted its base to Media City, over in Salford Quays, in 2011. Eagle-eyed fans may still spot a few remnants here and there.

Cross the road and head up a set of stone steps into the often overlooked **St John's Gardens**, one of the few green spaces in the city centre. Built in 1769, the church that once stood here was demolished in 1931; beneath your feet lie the remains of 22,000 people. Emerge on to **St John Street**, stopping to admire its rows of Georgian terraces, and head straight on, back on to Deansgate.

On this spot, you're standing directly above the mid-point of the city's forgotten waterway, the **Salford Junction Canal**. Once connecting the Rochdale Canal and the River Irwell, the waterway closed in the 1930s and was mostly filled – sadly, the warren of underground tunnels that lie beneath the city's streets are seldom open for guided

walks (check www.visitmanchester. com for details of occasional tours).

From Deansgate, turn left down **Quay Street**, passing the Grade II-listed **Opera House** (p87) on your right. Continue down Quay Street, turning right before the Irwell Bridge to walk along the **River Irwell**.

On the opposite bank, you'll see the scruffy **Mark Addy** pub (834 7271, www.themarkaddy.com). A converted landing station, the pub is named after a 19th-century Salford hero who is reckoned to have saved around 50 people from drowning in the highly polluted waters of the River Irwell. Addy, a landlord whose pub was close to the river, was awarded numerous commendations for his actions (including the Albert Medal, now housed in the Salford Museum & Art Gallery; p138). But he may have paid the ultimate price for his heroism: it's thought he contracted tuberculosis after jumping into a particularly fetid stretch of water to rescue a young boy. A better bet for food and ale is the **Dockyard** pub (p66), which is part of Spinningfields' new riverside development and run with passion by local entrepreneur Steven Pilling.

At the bridge, walk up the steps to return to street level. Turn right on to Bridge Street to find a pair of Manchester's most intriguing buildings. On the corner is the **People's History Museum** (p59), which reopened in 2010 following a £12.5-million redevelopment. Its Corten steel entrance wing, immediately to your right, links to the glorious Grade II-listed Pump House inside.

Rising up beyond the museum is the **Civil Justice Centre**. Known locally as the 'filing cabinet' because of its unusual cantilevered design, its western face features the largest suspended glass wall in Europe, which allows you to see the inner workings of the courts – the intention being that it would reflect the transparency of the British legal system.

Follow this glass wall and then turn left into **Spinningfields**, Manchester's business and leisure district. **Hardman Square**, the small open area at its centre, plays host to all manner of enjoyable events each year, from outdoor film screenings to the city centre's only festive ice rink. There are a number

St Johns p47

of chain eateries surrounding the square, which cater to both office workers and visitors.

Leave Hardman Square and turn right on to the **Avenue**, the city's most high-end shopping street, whose residents include DKNY, Oliver Sweeney and Mulberry. Spanish restaurant **Ibérica** (p67) is perfect for *croquetas* and a chilled glass of fino, while the **Oast House** pub (829 3830, www.theoast house.uk.com) is something of a waymarker as a result of its unmissable oast tower and massive beer garden. The Avenue is topped off, at its Deansgate end, by the Armani store, whose angular, contemporary lines juxtapose somewhat sharply with its nearest neighbour, the neo-Gothic **John Rylands Library** (p57). The clash between architectural styles is softened somewhat by the library's new-ish glass extension; a visual link between old and new.

Back on Deansgate, turn left and head towards **House of Fraser** (p75), on the corner of Deansgate and King Street West. No ordinary department store, the 175-year-old,

six-storey building was, for almost 70 years, better known as Kendal's. Harrods bought the store in 1919 and promptly renamed it, but after protests it reverted to the original moniker. Sadly, when House of Fraser took over the store in 2005, the name was consigned to history – although locals still call it Kendal's. The towering art deco building has been used variously as an air-raid shelter and venue for Miss Great Britain, while its make-up counters have appeared on TV programmes from *Corrie* to *Ashes to Ashes*.

Today, Kendal's provides you with two ways to end your walk: in the chichi surroundings of **Tom's Champagne Bar** (third floor) or in the **San Carlo Cicchetti** restaurant (ground floor; p70), Italian tapas dishes mirror the excellent meals churned out by its bigger brother, **San Carlo** (p70), across the road.

Kendal's is an appropriate place to finish this walk, as it reflects, in miniature, the constant reinvention of Manchester – a reinvention that almost always comes with a self-conscious nod to the past.

John Rylands Library

Manchester by Area

Exchange Square p57

City Centre

Numerous factors have contributed to the almost entire regeneration of Manchester's city centre during the last 25 years, including the devastating IRA bomb of 1996 and the opportunities presented by hosting the 2002 Commonwealth Games. Moreover, Manchester has taken advantage of unprecedented opportunity to remodel itself; a process that has happened in stages. After an interlude as a shopping centre, the **Corn Exchange** has become a food court; the **Royal Exchange** has had a £30-million facelift; and the much-maligned **Arndale Centre** has been overhauled, extended and is now a glittering palace of commerce. New public squares have been unveiled: **Exchange Square**'s concentric benches now provide a stopping point for shoppers, while **Cathedral Gardens** are home to a public park and playground – and the **National Football Museum**.

Manchester's renaissance carries on today. The **Spinningfields** pedestrianised business, shopping and eating district extends along the banks of the River Irwell. Home to numerous corporate headquarters, it also houses the **People's History Museum**, and big-name stores such as **Mulberry** along high-end shopping boulevard The Avenue. Eating and drinking around here comes in the shape of Spanish specialist **Ibérica**, **the Alchemist** cocktail bar, Aiden Byrne's fine-dining establishment **Manchester House** and many more.

Just across Deansgate, Peter Street has come into its own, with highlights that include the fully renovated, Grade II-listed **Great Northern Warehouse** entertainment complex (www.thegreatnorthern.com) and Edwardian Methodist church-turned-live-venue **Albert Hall**, which is a destination in itself.

Slotted between Victoria Station and the Corn Exchange, a corner of medieval Manchester lives on. The 15th-century building that houses **Chetham's Library** sits above the confluence of the rivers Irk and Irwell. Not far away squats **Manchester Cathedral**, close by Hanging Ditch. Local folklore has it that the ditch refers to the practice of tying a noose around the neck of a miscreant, then kicking them off the bridge. In truth, it marks the course of the River Irk, where 12th-century fullers (cloth cleaners) would hang out their cloth to dry. There's a feted wine shop of the same name to mark the spot.

Chetham's Library played a pivotal role during the Industrial Revolution. Manchester became the world's largest centre of manufacturing (nicknamed 'Cottonopolis'), and was rammed with impoverished mill workers. Friedrich Engels and Karl Marx regularly met at the library to discuss what they saw. Between them, they penned two central socialist texts: *The Condition of the Working Classes in England* and the *Communist Manifesto*.

Further south, Alfred Waterhouse's **Town Hall** is a reminder of Manchester's industrial ambition, and one of the city's most important buildings. Ford Madox Brown's wall murals are particularly notable, but even the corridors, with mosaic floors and vaulted ceilings, are remarkable.

Chetham's isn't the only atmospheric library in Manchester. The **John Rylands Library** is a neo-Gothic masterpiece, while the **Portico Library & Gallery** leans to the neoclassical.

Behind the Town Hall, **Central Library**, built in 1934, was once the largest public library in the UK. Modelled on Rome's Pantheon rotunda, this Mancunian landmark, and the adjacent **St Peter's Square**, have undergone a remarkable transformation. The library's revamp took four years (2010-14) and cost more than £40 million. Now fully accessible, it makes the most of its circular shape even if it's lost a bit of atmosphere in the process. Meanwhile, St Peter's Square has been transformed into a noble-feeling outdoor space to rival those of London.

Sights & museums

Abraham Lincoln Statue

Lincoln Square, Brazenose Street, M2 5LF. Metrolink St Peter's Square, or City Centre buses, or Deansgate or Oxford Road rail. Map p54 C4 ❶

An imposing if slightly incongruous presence amid the nearby office blocks, this statue was donated to the city in 1919 in recognition of the support that Lincoln received from the citizens of Manchester in his campaign against slavery. It was moved into the city centre in 1986, from its original location in Platt Fields Park.

Cathedral Gardens

M4 3BG. Metrolink Victoria, or City Centre buses, or Victoria rail. Map p55 D2 ❷

Cathedral Gardens is a rather wind-swept patch of open space wedged in between the National Football Museum, Chetham's Library, Victoria Station and the Corn Exchange. Its grass slopes (which are often worn down to bare earth), layered water features and playground are colonised every Saturday by hordes of teenage alt-rock tribes and pockets of clattering skateboarders, putting the space to vibrant if unpredicted use.

Central Library

St Peter's Square, M2 5PD (234 1983, www.manchester.gov.uk/centrallibrary). Metrolink St Peter's Square, or City Centre buses, or Oxford Road rail. **Open** 9am-8pm Mon-Thur; 9am-5pm Fri, Sat. **Admission** free. Map p55 D4 ❸

MANCHESTER BY AREA

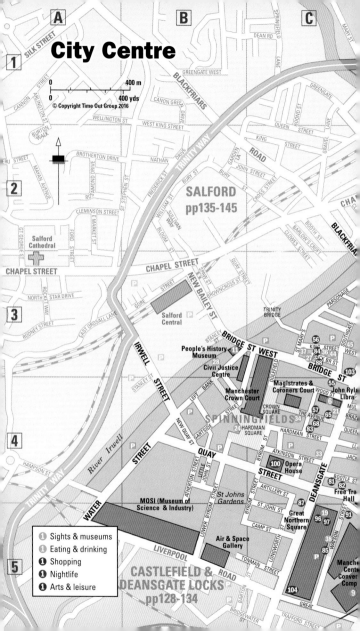

City Centre

A   **B**   **C**

1

SILK STREET

0   400 m
0   400 yds
© Copyright Time Out Group 2016

BLACKFRIARS

GREENGATE WEST

2

SALFORD
pp135-145

Salford
Cathedral

CHAPEL STREET

CHAPEL STREET

3

Salford
Central

People's History
Museum

Civil Justice
Centre

Manchester
Crown Court

BRIDGE ST WEST

BRIDGE ST

Magistrates &
Coroners Court

John Ryla
Libra

4

River Irwell

QUAY STREET

Spinningfields

Hardman
SQUARE

Hardman STREET

Opera
House

DEANSGATE

MOSI (Museum of
Science & Industry)

St Johns
Gardens

Free Tra
Hall

Great
Northern
Square

Air & Space
Gallery

5

LIVERPOOL ROAD

CASTLEFIELD &
DEANSGATE LOCKS
pp128-134

Manch
Cent
Conver

Legend:
- ● Sights & museums
- ● Eating & drinking
- ● Shopping
- ● Nightlife
- ● Arts & leisure

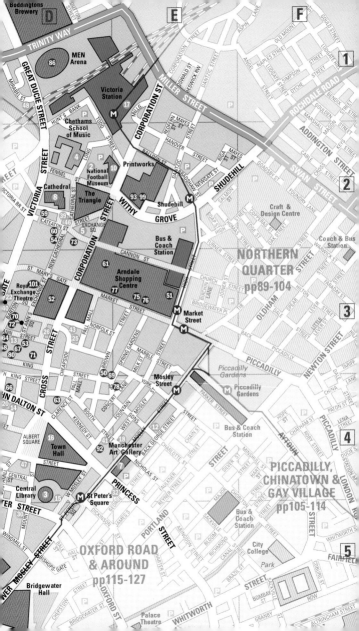

Central Library's classical-revival style disguises the fact that it was built only in 1934. One of the city's most recognisable landmarks, it reopened in 2014 following a spectacular £40-million renovation. It now has many interactive elements for kids, such as real-looking yet virtual 'puddles', as well as the latest computers and gaming consoles. Those with an interest in local history should seek out the screening booths in the British Film Institute's Mediatheque, designed for exploring films and television programmes in the BFI archives (particularly those that take the North West as their subject matter). See box p62.

Chetham's Library & School of Music

Long Millgate, M3 1SB (Library 834 7961, www.chethams.org.uk; School 834 9644, www.chethams.com). Metrolink Victoria, or City Centre buses, or Victoria rail. **Open** 9am-12.30pm, 1.30-4.30pm Mon-Fri. **Admission** free. **Map** p55 D2 **④**

Chetham's is a stunning 15th-century survivor that has lasted more or less intact to the present day, the former priests' college, cloisters and other rooms exuding an almost tangible sense of history. Founded in 1653, the library is the oldest public library in the English-speaking world. Within its impressive walls, Karl Marx and adopted Mancunian Friedrich Engels met to research the birth of Communist theory. Reading bays with lockable iron gates (a novel security measure introduced in 1740) are a feature. Ring ahead to check which rooms are available to visit.

The adjoining school of music is the largest of its kind in the UK and puts on around 100 public performances a year, as well as staging free lunchtime concerts most Tuesdays, Wednesday and Thursdays at 1.30pm. Entry (for concerts only) is via Hunts Bank; call the school on the day of the concert to confirm timings.

Exchange Square

M3 1BD. Metrolink Victoria or Shudehill, or City Centre buses, or Victoria rail. **Map** p55 D2 **⑤**

Relax on rows of amphitheatre-style seating (with decorative metal bars to spoil the fun of more adventurous skateboarders) arranged, like living-room furniture, around the Corn Exchange. A playful water feature is occasionally given the washing-up liquid treatment by mischievous youths. The square is surrounded by centres of shopping and entertainment (the Arndale, Selfridges, Corn Exchange, the Printworks) and enlivened by occasional public events, so there's no danger of anyone using it to get a rest, but it's an inventive communal space.

A new Metrolink station opens at Exchange Square in early 2016, opposite the Arndale Centre. It's part of the new Second City Crossing (2CC) line, due for completion by the end of 2017.

John Rylands Library

150 Deansgate, M3 3EH (306 0555, www.library.manchester.ac.uk/rylands). Metrolink St Peter's Square, or City Centre buses, or Deansgate rail. **Open** noon-5pm Mon, Sun; 10am-5pm Tue-Sat. **Admission** free. **Map** p54 C4 **⑥**

Despite giving the impression of near-medieval antiquity, this glorious Gothic building (part of the University of Manchester) is, in fact, little more than a century old, having opened in 1900. Among its many historical treasures is the world's oldest surviving fragment of the New Testament. Hands-on activities, touch-screen digital displays and a changing programme of exhibitions bring artefacts to life, while the guided tours are highly recommended. The extension (which was built in 2008) houses an airy café and gift shop, as well as the conservation centre.

Manchester Art Gallery

Mosley Street, M2 3JL (235 8888, www. manchestergalleries.org). Metrolink

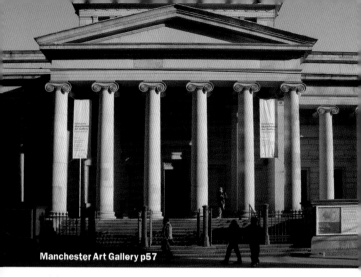

Manchester Art Gallery p57

*Market Street or St Peter's Square,
or City Centre buses, or Oxford Road
or Piccadilly rail.* **Open** 10am-5pm
Mon-Wed, Fri-Sun; 10am-9pm Thur.
Admission free. **Map** p55 E4 ⑦
Under director Dr Maria Balshaw,
Manchester Art Gallery has taken a
turn for the progressive, collaborating
with visionary academics and artists,
and taking a leading role in Manchester
International Festival's commissions.
There's a good mix of new and old
to explore. Highlights from the three
floors of the permanent collection
include some stunning Pre-Raphaelite
art (including Rossetti's *Astarte
Syriaca*), notable pieces by Turner, and
some superb Impressionist paintings
of early 20th-century Manchester
by the underrated Adolphe Valette,
Lowry's early art teacher. Temporary
exhibitions (often free) can be attention-
grabbing, sometimes making use of
non-gallery spaces, such as the foyer,
lifts and façade.

The Grade I-listed building itself,
designed in 1824 by Charles Barry (who
was also responsible for the Houses
of Parliament), had a £35-million
extension and refit a decade or so ago,
letting in more light, and opening a new
wing and interactive children's gallery.
A good café, restaurant and shop round
out the mix.

Manchester Cathedral

*Cathedral Yard, M3 1SX (833 2220,
www.manchestercathedral.org).
Metrolink Victoria, or City Centre
buses, or Victoria rail.* **Open** 8.30am-
6.30pm Mon-Sat; 8.30am-7pm Sun.
Easter, Aug, Christmas hours vary.
Admission free. **Map** p55 D2 ⑧
A church building of some kind has
existed on this site since the first millennium, and the present cathedral has
adapted to damage inflicted variously
during the Civil War, by a direct hit
from German bombers in 1941 and
by the IRA bomb of 1996. Of particular note is the beautiful wooden
roof, the Anglo-Saxon Angel Stone
(possibly a survival from an earlier
church on the site) and the stained-
glass Fire Window, which evocatively
bleeds flame-coloured light into the
Regimental Chapel. There's also a
book/gift shop, and a decent café,

Metrolink Victoria, or City Centre buses, or Victoria rail. **Open** 10am-5pm Mon-Sat; 11am-5pm Sun. **Admission** free. **Map** p55 E2 ⑩

It seems fitting that Manchester, a city that's known the world over for its footballing prowess, is home to this entertaining, interactive celebration of the sport. The museum holds both the FIFA and FA collections, including the hallowed ball used in that World Cup final (1966, if you must ask), while changing exhibitions add interest to permanent displays. The museum itself is housed inside Urbis, once Manchester's ill-fated 'museum of the city', a striking glass building that underwent an £8-million overhaul in readiness for its new incarnation. As well as displays on football-fan history and World Cup branding, there's an interactive toddler room, real-life penalty shoot-out game, and a very reasonabe café selling pies, sausage rolls and hot drinks. Free 20-minute tours run on the hour from 11am to 4pm. No booking required.

called Proper Tea, which is run by the team behind Teacup (p95) and by TV presenter Yvette Fielding.

Manchester Central Convention Complex

Off Lower Mosley Street, M2 3GX (834 2700, www.manchestercentral.co.uk). Metrolink Deansgate-Castlefield, or City Centre buses, or Deansgate rail. **Map** p55 D5 ⑨

This site was the city's third main station (Central Station) during the late 19th century, but it closed shortly after the railway line became obsolete in 1969. In 1986, the building was resurrected as G-Mex (Greater Manchester Exhibition Centre), hosting sports and trade events. It was also used as a concert venue – the Smiths and Oasis played here – before the Arena usurped that role. The place was rebranded and opened as Manchester Central in 2007. It hosts major international events and political conferences.

National Football Museum

Cathedral Gardens, M4 3BG (605 8200, www.nationalfootballmuseum.com).

People's History Museum

Left Bank, Spinningfields, M3 3ER (838 9190, www.phm.org.uk). Metrolink St Peter's Square, or City Centre buses, or Salford Central rail. **Open** 10am-5pm daily. **Admission** free. **Map** p54 B3 ⑪

Reopened in 2010 following a £12.5-million development, the People's History Museum is dedicated to telling a 200-year tale of British democracy. Dry and dusty, it isn't: interactive exhibits bring political history to life, while a contemporary wing, fused to the Grade II-listed Pump House, also features a sunny riverside café.

Portico Library & Gallery

57 Mosley Street, entrance on Charlotte Street, M2 3HY (236 6785, www. theportico.org.uk). Metrolink Piccadilly Gardens, or City Centre buses, or Piccadilly rail. **Open** 9.30am-4.30pm Mon, Fri; 9.30am-5.30pm Tue-Thur; 11am-3pm Sat. **Map** p55 E4 ⑫

Manchester Cathedral p58

Tucked unobtrusively away at the side of the Bank pub, and accessed via a buzzer system, the Portico recently celebrated 200 cerebral years of book lending (you have to be a member to borrow from the collection) and arts events. Its tightly packed library, with creaking floorboards, leather-backed chairs and archaic section headings ('polite literature' is one) takes you right back to 19th-century Manchester – and it remains a peaceful haven. Art exhibitions take place beneath a gorgeous Georgian glass-domed ceiling, and literary events are held throughout the year. Drinks and cakes are available during opening hours, plus various lunch options (omelettes, sandwiches) on weekdays.

St Ann's Church

St Ann Street, St Ann's Square, M2 7LF (834 0239, www.stannsmanchester. com). Metrolink St Peter's Square, or City Centre buses, or Victoria rail. **Open** 10am-5pm Tue-Sat. **Admission** free. **Map** p55 D3 ⑬
Manchester Cathedral (p58) and this church (built in 1712) have long been the two focal points of what survives of old Manchester; indeed, the tower of St Ann's is said to mark the geographical centre of the old city. Despite now being swallowed up by the various surrounding temples of commerce, it remains a likeable and visible presence, hosting services and regular free concerts. See the website for details.

St Mary's Church

Mulberry Street, M2 6LN (834 3547, www.hiddengem.catholicfaith.co.uk). Metrolink St Peter's Square, or City Centre buses, or Deansgate or Oxford Road rail. **Open** 8am-6pm daily.
Admission free. **Map** p55 D4 ⑭
The aptly named Hidden Gem – founded in 1794 and claimed to be the oldest post-Reformation Catholic church in the country – is approached either from the drably unimaginative Brazenose Street or, more enticingly, via a pair of decorated alleyways from John Dalton Street. Outside, an impressively sculpted stone arch haloes the entrance door; inside, Royal Academician Norman Adams' beautiful *Stations of the Cross* series of paintings adorns the walls. It's a busy functioning church, so visitors should

Modern manners

The city's Victorian legacy has taken a turn for the new.

Manchester may have given rise to some shiny showpieces in recent times – Beetham Tower, One Angel Square, the National Football Museum – but the city's historic assets haven't been forgotten. Heritage, it seems, is valued more than ever in design guru Peter Saville's 'original modern' city, and major refurbishment projects have transformed some of the city's most eye-catching 19th-century and early 20th-century buildings.

Victoria Station (p63), which opened in 1844 and is adjacent to the city's largest live-music venue (Manchester Arena), has had a £44-million facelift that has transformed the grim and draughty interchange into a 21st-century space – thanks largely to a striking new glass roof. Sympathetic renovation has preserved the building's glass dome, mosaics, war memorial, wall map, and the glass-and-iron canopy that runs the length of the façade.

Just around the corner, the **Corn Exchange** (*pictured*) ends a 20-year identity crisis after a £30-million conversion into an eating and drinking destination. It's now home to, among others, Wahaca, local Italian Salvi's Cucina and burger chain Byron. Some will wonder if the offer is too sanitised for such a stunning building, which had its beginnings in 1837.

Heading south, the **Whitworth Art Gallery** (p118) has doubled in size following a £15-million redevelopment that has connected the original 1899 frontage with a modern glass extension at the rear, which overhangs and overlooks Whitworth Park. Exhibitions include artists of the stature of Cornelia Parker, as well as selections from the gallery's internationally recognised textile collection. It was a deserving winner of the Art Fund's Museum of the Year award in 2015.

Cotton mills are playing a major role in the city's vibrant post-industrial renaissance too. The hulking brick buildings of Ancoats, which once drove Manchester's cotton-making dominance, are being restored into cool urban apartments, as well as cultural spaces like **Hallé St Peter's** (p147).

Finally, either side of the city's largest train station, Piccadilly, change is afoot. There are plans to redevelop both the abandoned railway station/former parcel sorting centre **Mayfield Depot** (p106) and baroque **London Road Fire Station** at Fairfield Street, which has been largely abandoned since 1986. Fans of crumbling architectural relics are advised to view as soon as possible.

Born again

The revamped Central Library offers much more than books.

Manchester's **Central Library** (p53) is an icon of the city's cultural landscape. An imposing circular building, neoclassical in style with a two-storey columned portico and high-level colonnade that takes inspiration from the Pantheon in Rome as well as US libraries, it was designed by architect E Vincent Harris and opened in 1934.

Nearly eight decades later, the library underwent a comprehensive four-year renovation, to the tune of £50 million. It reopened in March 2014 as a building that redefines the conventional concept of a library. Juxtaposing tradition with innovation and old-school architecture with modern media, the complex now houses a music library, a BFI Mediatheque, a children's library and an archive centre. There are sections relating to the history of the city's LGBT community and to Manchester Broadsides, which were printed songs used to spread the news and entertain pre-1900.

The renovation was not without controversy – a great number of supposedly obsolete items, including outdated reference books and damaged artefacts that would prove too costly to repair, were pulped due to lack of space in the library's new format – but it has not damaged the building's soul.

The jewel in the crown is the Wolfson Reading Room, where furniture (much of it also designed by Harris) was refurbished and the oculus dome was given some much-needed TLC. Elsewhere, the stained-glass windows in the ornate Shakespeare Hall were cleaned and restored to their former brilliance. The hall takes its name from the large window depicting Shakespeare and scenes from his plays, by Arts and Crafts artist Robert Anning Bell.

Located in St Peter's Square, an area that's enjoyed a great deal of rethinking in the past decade, the Central Library has been reborn as one of the city's finest assets.

show discretion if just sightseeing. Check ahead for times of services.

St Peter's Square

M2 5PD. Metrolink St Peter's Square, or City Centre buses, or Oxford Road rail. **Map** p55 D4 ⑮

Ian Simpson Architects' overhaul of St Peter's Square (to be completed in 2016) has not been without controversy. But following the reopening of Central Library in 2014, Simpson's blank-canvas approach (removing pretty much everything from the Square and pushing it to one end) started to make sense. The grubby Peace Garden was a victim of his vision, but the result sees the Cenotaph (1924, designed by Edwin Lutyens) and Memorial Cross enjoying more space, and the rest of the square laid out with public seating, views and trees that make Manchester feel like a city that appreciates its early 20th-century heritage. In fact, it's the ideal spot from which to take in the Alfred Waterhouse-designed Town Hall (1877), the elegant colonnades of the Town Hall Extension (1934-38) and the baroque Midland Hotel (1903).

Town Hall

Albert Square, M60 2LA (234 5000, café 827 8767, www.manchester. gov.uk/townhall). Metrolink St Peter's Square, or City Centre buses, or Oxford Road rail. **Open** 10am-5pm Mon-Fri; 10am-4pm Sat. **Admission** free. **Map** p55 D4 ⑯

Alfred Waterhouse's imposing neo-Gothic building (completed in 1877 and now Grade I-listed) remains a proud symbol of Manchester. Its lofty halls – home to a range of statuary, city council staff and civil-wedding ceremonies – are usually, but not always, open to the public. Visitors are normally free to visit the ground-floor Sculpture Hall (which hosts occasional art exhibitions and has a permanent café) and the first-floor Great Hall, which features a noted series of 12 murals depicting the history of the city by Ford Madox

Brown, and famous floor mosaics of Manchester's mascot, the worker bee. The building is still home to numerous council offices, but much of the rest of the complex, including the extensively renovated Town Hall Extension, is closed to the public for security reasons. However, guided tours are available, including visits to the 280ft clock tower and its bell, Great Abel. Check the website for details.

Victoria Station

Todd Street, Station Approach, M3 1PB. Metrolink Victoria, or City Centre buses, or Victoria rail. **Map** p55 E1 ⑰

Manchester's second station was in need of a bit of TLC. Aside from the lovely tiled map of the Lancashire & Yorkshire Railway on the entrance walls, the rest of the building, including its wood-panelled ticket offices, iron-clad Victorian façade and its roof, had reached breaking point. Thankfully, a £40-million restoration scheme, including a new ceiling, plus refurbishment of the original façade, station mosaics, first-class lounge and more, has just been completed. Regional rail services and the Metrolink run from here, and the Manchester Arena can be accessed from the main plaza.

Eating & drinking

1847

58 Mosley Street, M2 3LQ (236 1811, www.by1847.com). Metrolink Piccadilly Gardens or St Peter's Square, or City Centre buses, or Oxford Road rail. **Open** noon-3pm, 5-10pm Mon-Fri; noon-10.30pm Sat; noon-8pm Sun. **££. Vegetarian. Map** p55 E4 ⑱

Veggie meets fine dining at this Scandi-inspired hideaway. Own-made gnocchi with squash, burnt leek and feta terrine; beer-battered halloumi with mushy pea emulsion; and cucumber-gin sponge and sorbet are the kind of elegant combinations you can expect here. Service can be a bit patchy, but

Almost Famous

the wine list is a gem. Early-evening deals make this a popular choice with, among others, the city's academic and LGBT fraternities.

Almost Famous

Great Northern Warehouse, Peter Street, M3 4EJ (no phone, www.almost famousburgers.com). Metrolink Deansgate-Castlefield or St Peter's Square, or City Centre buses, or Deansgate rail. **Open** noon-11pm Mon-Thur; noon-midnight Fri, Sat; noon-9pm Sun. **£-££. Burgers. Map** p54 C5 ⓳

Almost Famous led the burger revival in Manchester (the original branch is in the Northern Quarter) and remains one of the best 'dirty food' purveyors in town. Sup a vodka and elderflower tonic cocktail (aka 'Bitch Juice') while chomping Triple Nom and Blood Butter burgers laden with fried pickles, American cheese and secret-blend house sauces with apt yet controversial names (Suicide, Redneck). Decor features big posters and low lighting. No reservations.

Ape & Apple

28-30 John Dalton Street, M2 6HQ (839 9624, www.joseph-holt.com). Metrolink St Peter's Square, or City Centre buses, or Oxford Road rail. **Open** noon-11pm Mon-Thur; noon-midnight Fri, Sat; noon-9pm Sun. **Pub. Map** p55 D4 ⓴

A pub of solid Victorian stock, but with a bright modern interior, this is the city-centre bastion for local brewer Holt, which still manages to produce an excellent bitter for around £2.50 a pint. There's a separate dining room upstairs and a quaint beer garden out back. The menu runs from sandwiches and burgers to chicken tikka masala.

Australasia

1 The Avenue, M3 3AP (831 0288, www.australasia.uk.com). Metrolink St Peter's Square, or City Centre buses, or Deansgate rail. **Open** noon-midnight daily. **£££. Pan Asian. Map** p54 C4 ㉑

This is one of the city's most uniquely Mancunian establishments, a magnet for WAG-types and business people to celebrate in beach-hued surrounds.

Choose wine or cocktails via an iPad, and tuck into some of the freshest sushi in town. House specials include crispy pork belly with pineapple curry, soft-shell crab seaweed wraps, and succulent slices of sweet potato from the Japanese robata grill, with mango soufflé for dessert. Book well ahead and ask for one of the booths.

Barburrito

65 Deansgate, M3 2BW (839 1311, www.barburrito.co.uk). Metrolink Market Street or St Peter's Square, or City Centre buses, or Victoria rail. **Open** 11am-8pm Mon-Wed; 11am-9pm Thur; 11am-11pm Fri; 11am-10pm Sat; noon-8pm Sun. **£**. **Mexican**. **Map** p55 D3 ㉒

This growing Mexican fast-food chain started out in Manchester, and its focus remains on a smooth, build-your-own burrito experience. Other outlets include the original Piccadilly Gardens branch, but this one is a favourite for its user-friendly booths. Pick your meat (pulled pork, spicy shredded beef – or vegetarian) and beans, add rice, then spice (the salsas range from mild to 'mule driver') and you're good to go. Endless soda refills make it hard not to come here weekly. There are plenty of halal options too.

BrewDog

35 Peter Street, M2 5BG (832 1922, www.brewdog.com). Metrolink St Peter's Square, or City Centre buses, or Oxford Road rail. **Open** noon-1am Mon-Sat; noon-midnight Sun. **Bar**. **Map** p54 C4 ㉓

Manchester's social heartland is home to this industrial-style craft-beer bar. Choose from a range of BrewDog classics – such as Punk IPA, Dead Pony Club and the spirit-strength Sink the Bismarck! – or go for bottles from cult international breweries such as Denmark's Mikkeller and USA craft gurus AleSmith. With a large smoking terrace and a prime location next to the Albert Hall (p81), the Dog is ideal for a pre- or post-gig pint.

Carluccio's

3 Hardman Square, M3 3AQ (839 0623, www.carluccios.com). Metrolink St Peter's Square, or City Centre buses, or Salford Central rail. **Open** 8am-11pm Mon-Fri; 9am-11pm Sat; 9am-10.30pm Sun. **££**. **Italian**. **Map** p54 B4 ㉔

The Spinningfields branch of the Italian-lover's chain of choice caters largely to lunch-breakers from nearby offices. At evenings and weekends, though, particularly in the warmer months, the restaurant is a haven for families, thanks to a child-friendly menu and the much-loved cloudy Sicilian lemonade. There's a popular alfresco seating area too.

Chaophraya

19 Chapel Walks, M2 1HN (832 8342, www.chaophraya.co.uk). Metrolink St Peter's Square, or City Centre buses, or Victoria rail. **Open** noon-11.30pm Mon-Sat; noon-10pm Sun. **£££**. **Thai**. **Map** p55 D3 ㉕

Chaophraya might be decorated with the standard array of orchids, bamboo and Buddha statuettes that characterises many Thai eateries, but the food is anything but usual. From tried-and-tested favourites such as *gaeng khiew waan gai* (green chicken curry) to uncommon fare such as *pla song pee nong* (sea bass in tamarind and chilli sauce), dishes are packed with genuine flavour. Chaophraya's ways with vegetables also make this a solid choice for meat-free friends.

Corbieres

2 Half Moon Street, M2 7PB (834 3381). Metrolink St Peter's Square, or City Centre buses, or Victoria rail. **Open** 4pm-midnight Mon-Thur; noon-midnight Fri, Sat; 2-11pm Sun. **Bar**. **Map** p55 D3 ㉖

Corbieres is one of those perplexing places that you go into for one drink and end up leaving five hours later, somewhat the worse for wear and wondering where the time went. Maybe it's something to do with its subterranean location. It also claims to have the best jukebox in Manchester – witness the groups of dancing drinkers that regularly fill the place near closing time.

Crazy Pedro's

55-57 Bridge Street, M3 3BQ (359 3000, www.crazypedros.co.uk). Metrolink St Peter's Square, or City Centre buses, or Victoria rail. **Open** noon-4am Mon-Sat; 5pm-4am Sun. **£**. **Pizza/bar**. **Map** p54 C3 ㉗

This riotous, late-opening Mexican wrestling-themed bar is located where football ace George Best had his fashion boutique in the 1970s – the pizzas are almost as legendary as the venue's former incumbent. Nacho Libre is a particular treat (searing salsa, tortilla chips, cheese, jalapeños, fresh guacamole), while drinks include everything from craft beer in cans to one of the city's largest collections of tequilas. Enter with caution.

Dockyard

Left Bank, Irwell Square, M3 3ER (359 4549, www.dockyard.pub). Metrolink Victoria, or City Centre buses, or Salford Central rail. **Open** 11am-11pm Mon-Sat; 11am-10.30pm Sun. **Pub**. **Map** p54 B3 ㉘

Located in Spinningfields in what used to be Café Rouge, this is the second outlet – after Salford Quays (p144) – for this popular modern pub. Cask ales, craft beers, pies and a capacious, glass-fronted space combine to create a winning formula.

Elixir

123 Deansgate, M3 2BY (222 8588, www.elixir-manchester.co.uk). Metrolink St Peter's Square, or City Centre buses, or Victoria rail. **Open** 4pm-1am Mon-Thur, Sun; noon-2am Fri, Sat. **Bar**. **Map** p54 C4 ㉙

This upmarket bar with its steampunk-meets-brothel decor sells some of the city's finest cocktails. Unfortunately (or fortunately, depending on your

perspective), Manchester's hen parties can't get enough of it – and why not? The house special is a vintage birdcage filled with sweets and eight miniature cocktails to share. Best employed as an occasional remedy.

French

Midland Hotel, 16 Peter Street, M60 2DS (236 3333, www.the-french.co.uk). Metrolink St Peter's Square, or City Centre buses, or Oxford Road rail. **Open** 6.30-9pm Tue; noon-1.30pm, 6.30-9pm Wed-Sat. **££££**. **Modern British**. **Map** p55 D5 ㉚

The Parisian grand dame of the city's restaurant scene has taken a U-turn and now serves exclusively British creations by Simon Rogan, one of the country's finest chefs. He's known for his restaurants in the Lake District (L'Enclume, Rogan & Co) and Fera at London's Claridges. The menu here is similar: expect regional ingredients – some grown on the roof of the hotel, no less – transformed using a combination of modern and classical techniques. Try Rogan's 'kebab' (raw ox, micro leaves, kohlrabi, mustard and coal oil) and his sarsaparilla-marshmallow sandwich with a hefty shot of cordial on the side.

Rogan also oversees the Midland's Mr Cooper's House & Garden restaurant (www.mrcoopershouseand-garden.co.uk) – a cheaper option than the French, with appealing cocktails and an inventive bistro-style menu.

Gaucho

2A St Mary's Street, M3 2LB (833 4333, www.gauchorestaurants.co.uk). Metrolink Market Street, or City Centre buses, or Salford Central rail. **Open** noon-11pm Mon-Fri; noon-11.30pm Sat; noon-10.30pm Sun. **£££**. **Argentinian**. **Map** p54 C3 ㉛

Argentinian cuisine doesn't often top 'must-try' lists, but the Manchester outpost of the smart, London-centric chain shows it's worth attention. Meat-lovers adore the pure Argentinian beef steaks, served with a lively chimichurri sauce, with traditional sides and super-sweet desserts. The immaculate if pricey wine list includes many bottles sourced from Gaucho's own vineyards, and there's a swanky bar. Finished in crystal and lilac leather, this former Methodist church is a treat through and through.

Grill on the Alley

5 Ridgefield, M2 6EG (833 3465, http://blackhouse.uk.com/grill-on-the-alley). Metrolink St Peter's Square, or City Centre buses, or Salford Central rail. **Open** noon-10.45pm daily. **£££.** **Grill.** Map p55 D4 ③②

Mancunians don't often get a chance to barbecue, so the Grill's dry-aged steaks and fresh fish, cooked over an open flame to seal in moisture, are a delight. Sample the famous beer-fed and massaged Kobe beef or a locally sourced steak, then complete the feast with a dessert cocktail as a pianist plays. This atmospheric diner remains a local favourite, despite competition from Gaucho and Hawksmoor. There's another branch on New York Street.

Hawksmoor

184-186 Deansgate, M3 3WB (836 6980, www.thehawksmoor.com). Metrolink St Peter's Square, or City Centre buses, or Victoria rail. **Open** noon-3pm, 5-10pm Mon-Thur; noon-3pm, 5-10.30pm Fri, Sat; noon-9.30pm Sun. **£££.** **Steakhouse.** Map p54 C4 ③③

Dark panelled walls and frosted windows in this former Victorian courthouse make for an easy transition from day to night at the first branch of the cult British steakhouse to open outside London. Beef is sourced from the Ginger Pig farm in Yorkshire, with cuts sold per portion (fillet, sirloin) or by weight. Other options include burgers or lobster, with sides of macaroni cheese and triple-cooked chips, and a giant Ferrero Rocher-style dessert. There's plenty for boutique-vineyard aficionados and a lively bar.

Ibérica

14-15 The Avenue, M3 3HF (358 1350, www.ibericarestaurants.com). Metrolink St Peter's Square, or City Centre buses, or Deansgate rail. **Open** 11.30am-11pm Mon-Wed, Sun; 11.30am-late Thur-Sat. **£££.** **Spanish.** Map p54 C4 ③④

A flagship bar and restaurant in contemporary Spinningfields for this Spanish specialist – another first outside of London. The princely space includes red-tasselled lampshades dangling from a triple-height ceiling and more mirrors than the Palace of Aranjuez. The suckling pig is excellent, as are the corn fritters with cabrales cheese and scrambled egg. Wines by the glass include a number of hard-to-find regional favourites.

Katsouris Deli

113 Deansgate, M3 2BQ (819 1260, www.katsourisdeli.co.uk). Metrolink St Peter's Square, or City Centre buses, or Salford Central rail. **Open** 7am-4.30pm Mon-Fri; 8am-5.30pm Sat; 9am-4pm Sun. **£.** **Deli-café.** Map p54 C4 ③⑤

Katsouris has descended from Bury Market to bring city-centre punters the sandwiches they deserve. The salad bar offers healthy options, but it's the cakes and roast-meat sandwiches that really appeal. The chicken piri-piri sandwich is an entire world of flavour for around £5.

Koreana

40A King Street West, M3 2WY (832 4330, www.koreana.co.uk). Metrolink St Peter's Square, or City Centre buses, or Salford Central or Victoria rail. **Open** noon-2.30pm, 6.30-10.30pm Mon-Thur; noon-2.30pm, 6.30-11pm Fri; 5.30-11pm Sat. **££.** **Korean.** Map p54 C3 ③⑥

In business since 1985, and much loved by both customers and critics, Koreana still manages to have the feel of an undiscovered gem. Korean food has spicier flavours than Cantonese cuisine, and starters, soups and mains are traditionally served simultaneously. Try one of the several set menus, where

MANCHESTER BY AREA

you can feast on pork, squid and a kim-chi hotpot (with fermented vegetables and chillies) for a reasonable price.

Manchester House

Tower 12, 18-22 Bridge Street, M3 3BZ (835 2557, www.manchesterhouse. uk.com). Metrolink Victoria, or City Centre buses, or Salford Central rail. **Open** noon-2.30pm, 7-9.30pm Tue-Thur; noon-2.30pm, 6-10pm Fri, Sat. **££££**. **Modern British**. **Map** p54 C3 ③

With a sky bar and tasting menu by executive chef Aiden Byrne, Manchester House celebrates the city's inimitable sense of style with aplomb. As the flagship bar/restaurant of Manchester's most prolific and showy restaurant group, Living Ventures, no expense has been spared on the indus-trial-chic interior and open kitchen. Byrne's carefully crafted dishes, with their dry ices and sorbet domes, hark back to the heyday of Heston Blumenthal. The likes of squab pigeon with a foie gras 'cherry', or prawn cock-tail with passion-fruit ice, can't fail to create a talking point. Drinks are pricey, but food is excellent value at lunch.

Ocean Treasure 235

Great Northern, 2 Watson Street, M3 4LP (839 7613, www.oceantreasure235. co.uk). Metrolink Deansgate-Castlefield or St Peter's Square, or City Centre buses, or Oxford Road rail. **Open** 2pm-midnight Mon-Fri, Sun; 2pm-1am Sat. **££**. **Chinese**. **Map** p54 C5 ③

Ocean Treasure may be part of Manchester 235 casino, but don't let that put you off. Its a local favourite for Cantonese cooking, where you can tuck into clay pots, halal meat with XO sauce, or dim sum. The barbecue pork in a fluffy white bun, and chicken and seaweed rolls with wasabi, are high-lights at one of the few spots on this side of town for a late-night feast.

Old Wellington Inn

4 Cathedral Gates, M3 1SW (839 5179). Metrolink Victoria, or City Centre buses,

or Victoria rail. **Open** 11am-11pm Mon-Sat; noon-10.30pm Sun. **Pub**. **Map** p55 D2 ③

It's impossible to separate the Old Wellington Inn and Sinclair's Oyster Bar (p70) – two historic icons of the Mancunian spirit – joined as they are at the hip. Having survived all that was thrown at them by the Luftwaffe, they were threatened by the wrecking ball in the late 1970s before inspired engi-neering intervened to allow both pubs to be raised several feet and various concrete monstrosities built around them. Ironically, it was this concrete that saved the pubs from another bomb – this time, courtesy of the IRA in 1996. In the aftermath, the pubs were moved 300 yards to their current position, an upheaval that has only served to enhance their charmingly wonky appearances.

The Wellington is a free house (owned by Nicholson's) dating from the early 1500s, while Sinclair's is a couple of hundred years younger and part of the Samuel Smith stable. The pair share an immense outdoor drinking area.

Pot Kettle Black

14 Barton Arcade, Deansgate, M3 2BW (no phone, www.potkettleblack ltd.co.uk). Metrolink Market Street or Victoria, or City Centre buses, or Victoria rail. **Open** 8am-7pm Mon-Fri; 9am-6pm Sat; 10am-5pm Sun. **£**. **Café**. **Map** p55 D3 ④

Tucked away inside Grade II-listed Victorian Barton Arcade, Pot Kettle Black is a special spot for coffee. It's run by professional rugby league players Jon Wilkin and Mark Flanagan, who apply the same quality control to coffee as they do to their sport. Keep an eye out for thesps on a break from rehearsals at the Royal Exchange Theatre, and the boys themselves. The toasted caramel piccolo (Workshop blend) is a winner.

Salut

11 Cooper Street, M2 2FW (236 2340, www.salut.co.uk). Metrolink St Peter's

Square, or City Centre buses, or Oxford Road rail. **Open** 11am-6.30pm Mon, Tue; 11am-11pm Wed-Sat; noon-9pm Sun. **Wine bar. Map** p55 D4 ④

Enjoy 42 wines by the glass at this modern wine bar – perfectly preserved using Enomatic machines – and hundreds more by the bottle. Northern Italian reds such as Amarone and Chianti are almost always on tap, and wine flights are available for those who can't make up their minds. Staff are knowledgeable. Snacks include pork pies, nachos, and pecorino cheese with honey and walnuts.

Salvi's Cucina

19 John Dalton Street, M2 6FW (222 8090, www.salvismanchester.co.uk). Metrolink St Peter's Square, or City Centre buses, or Oxford Road rail. **Open** 10am-11pm Mon-Sat; 11am-10pm Sun. **££. Italian. Map** p55 D4 ④

Mozzarella is the star at Maurizio Salvi's homely Cucina restaurant and bar. Batches of smoked and plain cheese are flown in from Mondragone near Naples every Tuesday and Friday, to be served in this rustic eatery (and also sold individually at his deli bar situated around the corner in Exchange Square). Tuck into calzone or the likes of black spaghetti with clams, baby squid and mussels.

Sam's Chop House

Chapel Walks, M2 1HN (834 3210, www.samschophouse.co.uk). Metrolink St Peter's Square, or City Centre buses, or Victoria rail. **Open** 11.30am-11pm Mon-Thur; 10am-midnight Fri, Sat; 10am-10pm Sun. **££. British. Map** p55 D3 ④

If you fancy traditional British cooking, this beautiful old pub is the place to go. It was once frequented by painter LS Lowry – there's a statue of the artist inside – but you don't come here for the Victorian tiles or arty connections. The dumplings, roast beef, corned beef hash, and steak and kidney pudding are almost unrivalled. Don't forget to leave room for dessert: the sticky toffee pudding is divine;

Sam's Chop House

or try Lowry's favourite, rice pudding served with mixed berry jam.

San Carlo

King Street West, M3 2WY (834 6226, www.sancarlo.co.uk). Metrolink St Peter's Square, or City Centre buses, or Salford Central rail. **Open** noon-11pm daily. **£££. Italian. Map** p54 C3 ④

Big, busy and perennially popular, San Carlo has been providing traditional Italian fare for almost two decades. It's part of a nationwide chain, but doesn't compromise on either quality or flair. Sure, pizza and pasta feature on the menu, but the real draws are simple, well-executed dishes such as a sublime fish platter, pan-fried chicken, and *tonno alla siciliana* (tuna medallions in olive oil, white wine and butter). Despite creating its own competition with several other branches in Manchester, San Carlo remains one of the city's best bets for a good dinner out. A deserving favourite of football players and visiting celebs.

San Carlo Cicchetti

Ground floor, House of Fraser, 60 Deansgate, M60 3AU (839 2233, www.sancarlocicchetti.co.uk). Metrolink Market Street or St Peter's Square, or City Centre buses, or Victoria rail. **Open** 8am-11pm Mon-Fri; 9am-11pm Sat; 9am-10pm Sun. **££. Italian. Map** p54 C3 ④

It may be located across the road from big brother San Carlo (above), but this Venetian *cicchetti* bar is a destination in its own right. Tucked unobtrusively into the corner of a 175-year-old department store, its discreet waiter service and marble-topped tables contrast nicely with an informal tapas bar that runs one length of the L-shaped space. Whether you sit or stand, you can order small plates such as lobster ravioli, breaded baby mozzarella, and crostini. Open for breakfast, lunch and dinner, and frequented by well-heeled shoppers and those in the know, this is a gem, perfect for a post-shopping coffee or dinner à deux.

Sinclair's Oyster Bar

2 Cathedral Approach, M3 1SW (834 0430). Metrolink Victoria, or City Centre buses, or Victoria rail. **Open** 11am-11pm Mon-Sat; noon-7pm Sun. **Pub. Map** p55 D2 ④

See p68 Old Wellington Inn.

Tampopo

16 Albert Square, M2 5PF (819 1966, www.tampopo.co.uk). Metrolink St Peter's Square, or City Centre buses, or Oxford Road rail. **Open** noon-11pm Mon-Sat; noon-10pm Sun. **££. Asian. Map** p55 D4 ④

Despite its subterranean location, Tampopo has a very light and airy feel, and the shared benches and tables give the restaurant a real buzz when full. The menu incorporates tastes from Japan, Malaysia, Indonesia and other East Asian destinations to deliver a 'most wanted' of the region's cooking. There are also branches in the Trafford Centre and Corn Exchange.

Umezushi

4 Mirabel Street, M3 1PJ (0871 811 8877, www.umezushi.co.uk). Metrolink Victoria, or City Centre buses, or Victoria rail. **Open** noon-10pm Tue-Thur; noon-11pm Fri, Sat; noon-9pm Sun. **££-£££. Japanese. Map** p55 D1 ④

This innovative sushi restaurant doesn't really have a menu. Rather, the passionate owners serve whatever is fresh that day, be it Fleetwood brill or cobia. Sides such as roasted red-bream head or miso aubergine make the most of the catch of the day, while sushi comes in myriad shapes and sizes. The tasting menu is a great place to dip your toe in the water. A minimalist, woody setting and off-the-beaten-track location make Umezushi feel like a find. The drinks menu includes one of the best ranges of *nihonshu* (sake) in the whole country.

Wing's

Heron House, 1 Lincoln Square, M2 5LN (834 9000, www.wingsrestaurant.co.uk).

Metrolink St Peter's Square, or City Centre buses, or Oxford Road rail. **Open** noon-midnight Mon-Fri; 4pm-midnight Sat; 1-11pm Sun. **£££**. **Chinese**. **Map** p54 C4 ㊾

Manchester has a number of grand Cantonese restaurants, with Yang Sing (p111) and Wing's jostling for most luxurious – even though the latter is located in a somewhat brutalist brick building. This is where Man United managers sometimes go for a spot of post-match analysis. Service is on point, while the duck pancakes and old-school sweet and sour favourites nothing short of heavenly. Seating is mostly private booths, while decor consists of signed plates from famous guests over the years. Expect a bill worthy of the target audience.

Shopping

For an overview of shopping districts in the city centre, see box p73.

Agent Provocateur

Unit GA, Manchester Club, 81 King Street, M2 4ST (833 3735, www. agentprovocateur.com). Metrolink St Peter's Square, or City Centre buses, or Victoria rail. **Open** 10.30am-6.30pm Mon-Sat. **Map** p55 D3 ㊿

One word: gorgeous. (For men, the one word is 'phwoar'.) But there's nothing sleazy about AP's beautifully constructed lingerie. The shop's interior suits the ethos perfectly, with lush carpet, glass cases featuring jewelled riding crops and the familiar blush-pink and black colour scheme. The changing room is worth a visit for the candlelit four-poster, birdcages and chandeliers offering a brief glimpse of what your life might be like if you buy those pricey knickers.

Arndale Market

Arndale Centre, 49 High Street, M4 3AH (832 3552, www.manchester.gov.uk/ markets). Metrolink Market Street,

or City Centre buses, or Victoria rail. **Open** 9.30am-6.30pm Mon-Sat; 11am-5pm Sun. **Map** p55 E3 ㉛
See box p74.

Aston's of Manchester

12 Royal Exchange Arcade, M2 7EA (832 7895, www.astonsofmanchester. co.uk). Metrolink Market Street, or City Centre buses, or Victoria rail. **Open** 9.30am-5.30pm Mon-Sat. **Map** p55 D3 ㉜

There are very few good reasons not to give up smoking, but this shop is one of them. Its smell immediately transports you to Havana, and the place offers every esoteric kind of cigarette, including a vast range of flavoured tobaccos, pipes, and Habanos in painted boxes. Even if you smoke only once a year, you may be tempted by the glittering Zippo displays, the Swiss army knives or the giant-size rolling papers. Now why ever would they be of interest?

Barbour

5 St Ann's Passage, M2 6AD (832 7234, www.barbour.com). Metrolink St Peter's Square, or City Centre buses, or Victoria rail. **Open** 10am-5.30pm Mon-Sat; noon-5pm Sun. **Map** p55 D3 ㉝

The retailer of functional British clothing may have roots in the North-East, but it's a global brand now, with an outlet in one of Manchester's most picturesque and historic malls. Stroll along the tiled path between St Ann's Square and King Street and take in the saddle bags, waxed jackets, scarves and polo shirts, which look as at home on Market Street as they do on the moors.

Burberry

New Cathedral Street, M1 1AD (833 9065, http://uk.burberry.com). Metrolink St Peter's Square, or City Centre buses, or Victoria rail. **Open** 10am-7pm Mon-Sat; 11am-5pm Sun. **Map** p55 D2 ㉞

The must-have British design house has a shiny outlet in Manchester's home of luxury, New Cathedral Street. Pick up some perfectly cut mens- and womenswear, the much-aped

Burberry tartan or invest in a classic trench coat. Accessories are a strength thanks to the vision of chief creative Christopher Bailey (who originally hails from nearby Halifax).

Doherty Evans & Stott

64 Bridge Street, M3 3BN (835 3245, www.dohertyevansstott.co.uk). Metrolink Market Street, or City Centre buses, or Victoria rail. **Open** 10am-6pm Mon-Fri; 9.30am-5.30pm Sat. **Map** p54 C4 **55**

Located in premises that previously housed Richard Crème's boutique L'Homme (he was David Beckham's dresser and a legendary local face) and Vivienne Westwood's Anglomania, this site has a fashion heritage that this gentlemen's outfitters complements. Choice buys include handmade brogues by British leather brand Crockett & Jones and, of course, their trademark Italian-made suits.

Elite Dress Agency

35 King Street West, M3 2PW (832 3670, www.elitedressagency.com). Metrolink St Peter's Square, or City Centre buses, or Salford Central or Victoria rail. **Open** 10am-5pm Mon-Sat; 11am-4pm Sun. **Map** p54 C3 **56**

The Elite Dress Agency has been clothing Manchester's best-turned-out for years. It carries a rapidly changing stock of barely worn designer clothes; aficionados can snap up the likes of DKNY, Prada and Miu Miu for a fraction of the original price, or seek out more obscure US or European pieces, alongside Jimmy Choos and last season's it-bags. Packed rails and regular sales mean it's almost impossible to leave empty-handed.

Flannels

The Avenue, Crown Square, M3 3FL (0844 332 5787, www.flannels.com). Metrolink Deansgate-Castlefield, or City Centre buses, or Salford Central rail. **Open** 10am-6pm Mon-Sat; 11am-5pm Sun. **Map** p54 C4 **57**

This Manchester-based independent chain, stocking the cream of each season's fashion crop, resides in the city's designer destination, Spinningfields. Adored by footballers (and their wives), Flannels leans towards high glamour – Kenzo, D&G, Roland Mouret and Gucci – though such tastefully restrained labels as Prada, Tom Ford and Moncler also feature heavily. Take your gold card, and an understanding partner. If you're feeling less flush, head to the Flannels outlet in Salford's Lowry Outlet mall (p144).

Fred Perry

11 Police Street, M2 7LQ (832 9874, www.fredperry.com). Metrolink St Peter's Square, or City Centre buses, or Victoria rail. **Open** 10.30am-6pm Mon-Wed; 10.30am-7pm Thur-Sat; 11am-5pm Sun. **Map** p55 D3 **58**

Everyone knows the name of this label, the brainchild of football player Tibby Wegner and tennis star Fred Perry. Their first product was a must-have sweatband way back in the 1940s; yet, by fusing fashion with sportswear, Fred Perry continues to have universal appeal, adorning everyone from modern Mancs to Mods and Britpop stars such as Liam Gallagher and Damon Albarn. This outlet sells mostly menswear, including 'Fred Perry' shirts and Harrington-style jackets.

Hanging Ditch

42 Victoria Street, M3 1ST (832 8222, www.hangingditch.com). Metrolink Victoria, or City Centre buses, or Victoria rail. **Open** 11am-7pm Mon-Wed; 10am-10pm Thur-Sat; 1-7pm Sun. **Map** p55 D2 **59**

This wine merchant is run with passion by Ben Stephenson, son of famous local architect Roger Stephenson, and takes its name from the historic 'hanging ditch' that connected the city's two main rivers, the Irk and the Irwell. Dad designed the tiny space with great imagination, and a veritable library of wine covers the rear wall. Buy a bottle

Shopping central

From Hermès scarves to handmade boots, the city centre has all you could covet – and more.

Exchange Square attracts some of the biggest names in fashion: shops on its **New Cathedral Street** include Michael Kors, Burberry, Ted Baker and hip denim brand 7 For All Mankind, all book-ended by a vast Zara and an M&S. Department stores Harvey Nichols (p75) and Selfridges (p78), meanwhile, loom large on either side.

From here, it's easy to explore the boutiques that surround **St Ann's Square**. This bustling plaza is home to the Royal Exchange Theatre and three shopping arcades: the diminutive **St Ann's Passage**, the jewel-like Victorian **Barton Arcade** and the soon-to-be-revamped **Royal Exchange Arcade**. The Whisky Shop and independent footwear retailer Ran (p76) are worth a visit, as is Rapha Cycle Club (p78) for upmarket cycling kit.

Take a breather in the flagstone plaza behind St Ann's Church before bobbing through the ginnel beside Space NK on to **King Street**, Manchester's original shopping destination, which is now slowly recapturing its glory days. The cobbled street has a jumble of architectural styles that mixes Tudor frontages with Georgian townhouses – a good setting for upmarket brands such as Hermès, the Kooples, Tommy Hilfiger and L'Occitane.

Manchester's wealthy business area, **Spinningfields**, is bracketed by the Civil Justice Centre (aka 'the filing cabinet') and **The Avenue**, a pedestrianised street attracting well-heeled Mancunians with its parade of high-end shops.

As these include Armani, Mulberry (p76) and Flannels (p72), it's clear that the precinct has usurped King Street as the city's luxury retail quarter. There are some excellent restaurants in this part of town too, namely Australasia (p64), Manchester House (p68) and Ibérica (p67).

The art deco House of Fraser (p75; pictured) – formerly known as Kendals and, for a brief period in the 1920s, Harrods – sits at the Deansgate end of the street, offering five floors of fashion and beauty, and one of Manchester's finest Italian restaurants, San Carlo Cicchetti (p70).

Back to Market Street and the 1970s behemoth that is **Manchester Arndale**, housing every major high-street brand you'll ever need. A 2006 extension of the centre took its footprint to 1.5 million square feet, and you'll find major offerings from Topshop, Next, Apple and Waterstone's.

Trading places

Spend some time (and money) at Manchester's markets.

Manchester's Christmas markets are a huge draw, but there's more to the city's independent trading scene than festive keepsakes and mulled wine. Street food has taken off in a big way, and its associated markets and events are worth seeking out, combining food trucks and pop-ups with live music and the best of the city's craft ale scene. **Guerrilla Eats** (www.guerrillaeats.co.uk) and **Beat Street Manchester** (www.beat streetmcr.co.uk) are ones to watch.

Arndale Market (p71) has a fine mix of shops, from fabrics to fruit and veg. The food section has become something of a destination recently: Microbar, operated by Boggart Brewery, has a rotating range of ales and ciders, while food operators VietShack (Vietnamese street food) and Pancho's (burritos) have drawn attention from national food critics.

Outside the city centre, there's **Levenshulme Market** (Mar-Dec 10am-4pm Sat, www.levymarket. com). Run as a social enterprise, it has around 50 stalls dealing in food, drink, homewares, plants and gifts. Another must is **Altrincham Market** (10am-10pm Tue-Sat, 10am-6pm Sun), which reopened in 2014 after a complete overhaul. The beautiful 19th-century Market House (*pictured*) is now a swanky food hall with bench-style seating. Top picks include Honest Crust Pizza, single-estate hot chocolates and truffles from Sam Joseph, and wines from Reserve Wines.

If size is a priority, then **Bury Market** (www.burymarket.com) – the biggest market in the North-West, and just a 20-minute drive from the city centre – should fit the bill. With a history stretching back 500 years, and what some consider the best black pudding in the country, the market draws 250,000 shoppers every week.

For more information, see www. manchester.gov.uk/markets.

and drink it in-store, or sample the current by-the-glass options. It's a little pricier than elsewhere, but very classy.

Harvey Nichols

Exchange Square, M1 1AD (828 8888, www.harveynichols.com). Metrolink Victoria, or City Centre buses, or Victoria rail. **Open** 10am-8pm Mon-Fri; 9am-7pm Sat; 11am-5.30pm Sun. **Map** p55 D2 ⑥⓪

This beacon of luxury opened as part of the 2003 Exchange Square development. The first floor displays beautifully crafted womenswear and shoes – the likes of Gucci, Alexander McQueen and Roberto Cavalli, as well as exclusive fashion brands such as Christian Louboutin – while the second floor has choice menswear and a jewel of a food market, leading to a brasserie with surprising views. There are also beauty products galore, a Dermalogica counter, hair salon and an absolutely fabulous nail bar. It's a one-stop shop for the well-heeled, and a sublime browsing experience for everyone else.

Hotel Chocolat

Arndale Centre, New Market Lane, M4 3AJ (819 2533, www.hotelchocolat.co.uk). Metrolink Market Street or Shudehill, or City Centre buses, or Victoria rail. **Open** 9am-8pm Mon-Fri; 9am-7pm Sat; 11.30am-5.30pm Sun. **Map** p55 D3 ⑥①

Chocolate. In beautiful, minimalist, black packaging, sprinkled with such enticements as swirls of cream, dried raspberries and orange peel. It's a long way from the corner shop's sweetie counter – and so are the prices. Much of the cocoa is sourced from their own Saint Lucia plantation. There's another branch in the Trafford Centre.

House of Fraser

60 Deansgate, M60 3AU (0344 800 3744, www.houseoffraser.co.uk). Metrolink Market Street or St Peter's Square, or City Centre buses, or Victoria rail. **Open** 9am-8pm Mon-Sat; 11am-5pm Sun. **Map** p54 C3 ⑥②

The venerable old auntie of department stores clocked up 180 years of trading in 2015. But House of Fraser (or Kendal's, as it's better known by locals) should be praised for moving with the times. The unfailingly stunning window displays of this listed art deco store signpost six floors of on-trend fashion, homewares and cosmetics. A real draw is the lingerie department, stocking the likes of Seafolly and Triumph. There's also POP Swedish kidswear and a real world of wonder for chic little ones on the top floor, including Barbour Kids and Kenzo. The superb San Carlo Cicchetti Italian restaurant (p70) lies to the rear of the store.

Lissom & Muster

14 Tib Lane, M2 4JA (832 7244, www.lissomandmuster.com). Metrolink St Peter's Square, or City Centre buses, or Victoria rail. **Open** 10am-5.30pm Tue-Sat. **Map** p55 D4 ⑥③

Lose yourself among beautiful, hand-crafted things at this shrine to quality. British-made brogues, silk ties, Larke sunglasses, Manchester-made Private White VC Harrington jackets and saddle bags made by Chapman in Cumbria are displayed in ways that do their provenance justice. A male bias dominates the stock, but there's plenty for women who appreciate the finer things in life. Hand-woven blankets and candles are particular treats.

Mappin & Webb

12-14 St Ann Street, M2 7LF (832 2551, www.mappinandwebb.com). Metrolink Market Street or St Peter's Square, or City Centre buses, or Victoria rail. **Open** 9.30am-5.30pm Mon-Sat; 11am-5pm Sun. **Map** p55 D3 ⑥④

A proper – and proper pricey – jewellers, Mappin & Webb proves that diamonds really are a girl's best friend. And so are watches, earrings, pendants, engagement rings… Glittering glass cases, smooth staff and a hushed, plush atmosphere set the tone.

Mulberry

The Avenue, M3 3FL (839 3333, www. mulberry.com). Metrolink Deansgate-Castlefield, or City Centre buses, or Salford Central rail. **Open** 10am-6pm Mon-Sat; 11am-5pm Sun. **Map** p54 C4 ⑥⑤

Stocked with classic clothing, iconic accessories and quality luggage, Mulberry is a destination for both men and women seeking classic British style. Inhale deeply and savour the scent of baby-soft leather, often dyed in zesty colours and shimmering metallics. Treat yourself to a gorgeous bag – as long as your bank balance can take it: must-have handbags are often named after the celebrities who inspired them and come with price tags to match.

Neal's Yard

29 John Dalton Street, M2 6NY (835 1713, www.nealsyardremedies.com). Metrolink St Peter's Square, or City Centre buses, or Oxford Road rail. **Open** 9.30am-6pm Mon-Sat; 11am-5pm Sun. **Map** p55 D4 ⑥⑥

This eco-cosmetics company with old-fashioned service looks at home on one of the most historic streets in town. Ask one of the staff (who are often alternative practitioners themselves) for advice on the scented products – actors such as Thandie Newton swear by them. Bestsellers include Wild Rose Beauty Balm and the Bee Lovely range made from beeswax.

Office Sale Shop

3 St Ann's Place, M2 7LP (834 3804, www.office.co.uk). Metrolink Market Street or St Peter's Square, or City Centre buses, or Victoria rail. **Open** 10am-6pm Mon-Sat; 11am-5pm Sun. **Map** p55 D3 ⑥⑦

While most sale shops trade by the motto 'you get what you pay for', here, all stock is of generally good quality. The only difference between this and the main Office shop is that shoes have been dramatically marked down due to being end-of-line, last season or marginally scuffed. The place is forever overflowing with canny shoe-lovers of both sexes, loading up on £15 platforms and bargain baseball boots.

Oliver Sweeney

The Avenue, M3 3HF (834 0086, www.oliversweeney.com). Metrolink Deansgate-Castlefield, or City Centre buses, or Salford Central rail. **Open** 10am-7pm Mon-Sat; 11am-5pm Sun. **Map** p54 C4 ⑥⑧

This modern store, with its glazed façade and lime-green decor, looks futuristic, but the wares are traditional. Perfectly placed for Spinningfields' suited and booted, Oliver Sweeney stocks high-quality men's shoes and boots, and accessories such as belts and scarves. There's a comfortable central seating area for trying things on.

Pretty Green

81 King Street, M2 4AH (819 2856, www.prettygreen.com). Metrolink St Peter's Square, or City Centre buses, or Victoria rail. **Open** 10am-7pm Mon-Sat; 11am-5pm Sun. **Map** p55 D3 ⑥⑨

Liam Gallagher may be best known for his music, but the former Oasis singer recently revealed an unexpected aptitude for high-fashion menswear. The musician set up label Pretty Green in 2009, and has already opened stores outside London. The Manchester outlet is dominated by Gallagher's presence, with an outsize photo portrait plastered on the wall. Vanity snaps aside, though, there's much here to recommend: Mod-style shirts, sharply tailored jackets and racks of casual polo shirts epitomise a style that offers both class and attitude – perfect for a little Oasis-style swaggering.

Ran

7 & 8 St Ann's Arcade, M2 7HW (832 9650, www.ranshop.co.uk). Metrolink St Peter's Square, or City Centre buses, or Victoria rail. **Open** 9.30am-6pm Mon-Sat; 11am-5pm Sun. **Map** p55 D3 ⑦⓪

This hard-to-find pair of shops house an eclectic mix of shoes and clothes,

Fashion forward

Manchester designers and brands are much in demand.

Manchester has a sterling fashion pedigree. Famous designers such as Ossie Clark, Matthew Williamson and Henry Holland were born in or near the city, while brands such as Bench, Ringspun, Gio Goi and Joe Bloggs started here in the 1980s and '90s. Fast-forward to the 21st century, and new brands are beginning to make their mark.

The biggest recent success story is low-cost, online womenswear retailer **Boohoo** (www.boohoo. com). Founded by Mahmud Kamani and Carol Kane in 2006, the brand is a key player in the 16-24 age range. Tucked away on the Northern Quarter's Dale Street, Boohoo's HQ is as much a testament to the company's hometown as it is to its fashion-forward ethos.

In fact, the Northern Quarter is a hotspot for unusual and inventive fashion, a reputation that's bolstered by the success of high-end menswear shop **Oi Polloi** (p97), which now has its own line under the Cottonopolis moniker, as well as a major online presence and London outlet. Elsewhere in the area, the folk at menswear shop **Wood** (p101) are also paving a new path with their own line, Cyrus Wood, while skate shop **Note** (www. noteshop.co.uk) has two outlets in the neighbourhood. Note's own designs often pay homage to their roots through the use of a 'worker bee' emblem – the city's mascot.

Manchester also has a thriving street style that's kept afloat by 're-loved' pieces crafted from vintage fabrics at **Retro Rehab** (p99), 1950s styling at **Rockers England** (p99) and, of course,

Afflecks (p96), the famous four-floor fashion emporium that still reigns supreme when it comes to affordable, alternative fashion. At the other end of the spectrum sits one of the city's best-known labels, **Gorgeous Couture** (www.gorgeous couture.com), a hit with celebrities such as Amanda Holden for its body-conscious glamour and sleek range of made-to-measure and off-the-peg jersey dresses.

Fashion-conscious gents on the prowl for high-quality classic pieces should check out traditionally minded **Lissom & Muster** (p75), which stocks local designer clothing brand Private White VC (run by Nick Ashley, son of Laura). Private White garments, made by hand in Salford, span everything from luxury knitwear to waxed cotton jackets. They even make uniforms for the staff at the Whitworth Art Gallery.

mostly for men. Fila Vintage, Silas and J Shoes are brands of note. A friendly, personal service definitely makes Ran worth the hunt.

Rapha Cycle Club
5 St Ann's Alley, M2 7LP (834 6748, http://pages.rapha.cc/clubs/manchester). Metrolink St Peter's Square, or City Centre buses, or Victoria rail. **Open** 8am-8pm Mon-Sat; 10am-6pm Sun. **Map** p55 D3 ㉑
Luxury cycle clothing brand Rapha's café and shop is the place to pick up your bib shorts, manufactured to the highest standards in Italy. Despite being a London brand, Italian style runs through the collections, thanks to lines created in homage to the Giro d'Italia and iconic racers such as Marco Pantani. A compact café rounds off the chichi scene.

Seen
6 St Ann's Arcade, M2 7HN (835 2324, www.seen.co.uk). Metrolink St Peter's Square, or City Centre buses, or Victoria rail. **Open** 10am-6pm Mon-Sat. **Map** p55 D3 ㉒
Seen is located in one of Manchester's most historic shopping arcades. Walking in here is like visiting a boutique gallery: this is eyewear, but not as you know it. The collection includes Belgian brands such as Theo and handmade artisanal frames from the Italian-owned, African-influenced LGR.

Selfridges
1 Exchange Square, M3 1BD (0870 837 7377, www.selfridges.com). Metrolink Victoria, or City Centre buses, or Victoria rail. **Open** 10am-8pm Mon-Fri; 9am-8pm Sat; 11am-5.30pm Sun. **Map** p55 D2 ㉓
It would be a crime not to guide the discerning visitor to Selfridges: five floors of loveliness, desirability and luxury. The basement includes a state-of-the-art beauty hall and dessert bar, and there's a full-blown Italian restaurant from San Carlo on the second floor. Fantasise your way through

the Hermès and Chanel concessions, before moving up through Marc Jacobs, Acne, Rag & Bone and Isabel Marant to the top floor, where less expensive brands (Cos, Top Shop, Sandro, Sweaty Betty)reign supreme. Not to be missed. There's an equally excellent branch in the Trafford Centre.

Spirited Wine & Bistro Vin
63 Deansgate, M3 2BB (834 7328, www.spiritedwines.co.uk). Metrolink Market Street or Victoria, or City Centre buses, or Victoria rail. **Open** *Shop* 10am-8.30pm Mon-Sat; noon-8pm Sun. *Wine bar* 10am-10pm Mon-Sat; noon-8pm Sun. **Map** p55 D3 ㉔
An independent-thinking wine chain with outlets in London, Cardiff and, now, Manchester. Upstairs, in the Victorian Barton Arcade, a small wine bar serves cheese and charcuterie boards, and 20 wines by the glass. Strengths in the shop include Scottish whisky and English sparkling wines.

TK Maxx
51-55 Market Street, M1 1WA (832 2337, www.tkmaxx.com). Metrolink Market Street, or City Centre buses, or Piccadilly rail. **Open** 9am-8pm Mon-Sat; noon-6pm Sun. **Map** p55 E3 ㉕
For designer bargains, TK Maxx is unbeatable. Dedicate at least two hours to searching through the endless racks of last-season and surplus-stock designer finds. There's clothing for men, women and children, underwear, handbags and a brilliant homewares section, where the high-quality stock changes regularly and Egyptian cotton sheets are ten a penny (nearly). The shoe department is an essential fashionista spot, with up to 80% off Lulu Guinness and Kurt Geiger.

Topshop
Arndale Centre, M4 3AQ (615 8660, www.topshop.com). Metrolink Market Street, or City Centre buses, or Victoria rail. **Open** 9am-8pm Mon-Fri; 9am-7pm Sat; 11am-5.30pm Sun. **Map** p55 E3 ㉖

Seen

OK, nearly every town has a Topshop, but Manchester's branch of the high-street staple is particularly impressive. This huge store stocks the catwalk-inspired trends that make the brand famous, along with smaller concessions, affordable accessories and an enormous choice of shoes. Men aren't forgotten, with an in-store branch of Topman offering the freshest jeans and printed T-shirts. Arrive early in the morning to bag the most in-demand garments, or late in the evening to avoid the fashion-conscious crowds.

Urban Outfitters

42-43 Market Street, M1 1PW (817 6640, www.urbanoutfitters.com). Metrolink Market Street, or City Centre buses, or Victoria rail. **Open** 9am-8pm Mon-Sat; noon-6pm Sun. **Map** p55 E3 **77**

This cavernous, glass-fronted store may sit on Manchester's main shopping row, but its stock is far from typical of the high street. Students and hipsters flock here for three floors of cool concessions, costume jewellery, vintage clothing and quirky homewares, all accompanied by a booming, on-trend soundtrack. Expect to feel decidedly out of place if you're over 25.

Vivienne Westwood

47 Spring Gardens, M2 2BG (835 2121, www.viviennewestwood.com). Metrolink St Peter's Square, or City Centre buses, or Victoria rail. **Open** 10am-6pm Mon-Sat; noon-5pm Sun. **Map** p55 E4 **78**

Viv is from nearby Glossop, so it's only right that she should have a dedicated boutique here. And it does her justice. Carved mahogany display cases reveal glittering Westwood orb jewellery; the latest collections are hung beside huge gilt mirrors; and there's a chaise longue on which to try the latest shoe ranges. The pricey but stunning main collection is sold alongside the diffusion line T-shirts, and every self-respecting Manc fashionista owns a tartan Westwood bag.

MANCHESTER BY AREA

Alchemist.

Waterstone's

91 Deansgate, M3 2BW (837 3000,
www.waterstones.com). Metrolink
Market Street or St Peter's Square,
or City Centre buses, or Victoria rail.
Open 9am-8pm Mon-Sat; 10.30am-
5pm Sun. **Map** p55 D3 ❼

Committed bibliophiles may miss the
good old days of musty corridors and
rickety library steps – yet Waterstone's
still dominates the high street. Its
Deansgate store is a vast temple to the
published word, and has a particularly
good arts section. There's a quiet, table-
service café, helpful staff and three
floors of shiny, ink-scented stock to
get lost in. Its newer Arndale store has
a great kids' section, with colouring-in
tables, reading benches and toys.

White Company

21-23 King Street, M2 6AW (839 1586,
www.thewhitecompany.com). Metrolink
St Peter's Square, or City Centre buses,
or Victoria rail. **Open** 9.30am-5.30pm
Mon-Fri; 9am-6pm Sat; 11am-5pm Sun.
Map p55 D3 ❽

Who would have thought that such a
simple idea could end up manifesting
itself so successfully? The concept is in
the name – everything sold in this shop
is white. Towels, sheets, nighties –
every type of household linen, in fact –
but all made and presented so stylishly
that it's hard to imagine why anyone
ever wanted avocado towels to match
their bathroom suite. Tasteful items of
furniture are also on sale.

Nightlife

42nd Street

2 Bootle Street, M2 5GU (831 7108,
www.42ndstreetnightclub.co.uk).
Metrolink Deansgate-Castlefield, or
City Centre buses, or Deansgate rail.

Open 11pm-2.30am Tue, Thur; 10.30pm-2.30am Fri, Sat. Map p54 C4 ③
An unreconstructed indie club peddling the predictable soundtrack of Manchester tunes past and present, plus assorted Britpop and other guitar-based anthems. Friendly and popular with students, 42nd Street is busy most nights that it's open.

Albert Hall

22 Peter Street, M2 5QR (0844 858 8521, www.alberthallmanchester.com). Metrolink St Peter's Square, or City Centre buses, or Oxford Road rail. Open varies. Map p54 C4 ②
This Wesleyan chapel was among the largest of its kind in Europe when it was built in 1910, and today it's the city's most spectacular live-music venue. There's a horseshoe-shaped balcony, stained-glass windows and skylights, plus multi-tiered seating,

winding staircases and highly ornate original coving. Acts on the calendar are floor-fillers from Underworld to Everything Everything. A real must – if you can get a ticket. See box p86.

Alchemist

3 Hardman Street, M3 3HF (817 2950, www.thealchemist.uk.com). Metrolink St Peter's Square, or City Centre buses, or Victoria rail. Open 10am-midnight Mon-Wed; 10am-1am Thur; 10am-2am Sat; 10am-11pm Sun. Map p54 C4 ③
Cocktails are the biz at this bar, where the mixologists take their craft very seriously. House classic is the Smokey Old Fashioned; a bubbly rum option is aptly named the Bubble Bath, while meringue-topped floaters are blowtorched before your eyes. Regular drinks (beer, wine and spirits) are excellent too. Decor is 18-carat: there

really is a touch of magic about the place. Forget the food, though, which is all rather fried. There's another branch on New York Street.

Liar's Club

19A Back Bridge Street, M3 2PB (834 5111, www.theliarsclub.co.uk). Metrolink St Peter's Square, or City Centre buses, or Victoria rail. **Open** 5pm-4am daily. **Map** p54 C3 ③④

This tiki bar knows how to party, making this the perfect place to get acquainted with the locals. Sister venue and late bar Crazy Pedro's (p66) is upstairs in the same block, but Liar's, with its palm-fringed dancefloor, is arguably the most fun. Try one of over 100 rums or sup a sharing cocktail from an actual treasure chest.

Manchester 235

Great Northern Warehouse, 2 Watson Street, M3 4DT (828 0300, www. manchester235.com). Metrolink Deansgate-Castlefield or St Peter's Square, or City Centre buses, or Deansgate rail. **Open** 24hrs daily. **Map** p54 C5 ③⑤

Inhabiting a slightly tired-looking leisure development, Manchester 235 is a luxury bar and casino complex, with a showpiece Modern British restaurant at its heart under the auspices of celebrity chef James Martin. Although live music was a thing in its early days, the venue has become a serious gambling haunt (as the opening hours suggest). However, it's a fun choice for a quirky night out.

Manchester Arena

Victoria Station, M3 1AR (950 5000, www.manchester-arena.com). Metrolink Victoria, or City Centre buses, or Victoria rail. **Open** varies. **Map** p55 D1 ③⑥

The largest concert venue in the city centre plays host to performers that command a crowd: typically major pop acts, household-name comedians (Peter Kaye) and (mostly) middle-of-the-road rock bands – although the likes of Vampire Weekend can sometimes be spotted here too.

Liar's Club

Milton Club

244 Deansgate, M3 4BQ (850 2353, www.themiltonclub.co.uk). Metrolink St Peter's Square, or City Centre buses, or Deansgate rail. **Open** *7pm-2am Fri; 7pm-4am Sat; other days vary.* **Map** *p54 C4* ⑥⑦

To gain entry to one of Manchester's fanciest clubs, you'll need to become a member or call up in advance to secure a place on the guest list. The programme of soulful PAs from names such as Gabrielle, Dimitri from Paris and Trevor Nelson has real appeal. A gold and chocolate colour scheme paints a sumptuous scene.

Mojo

59 Bridge Street, M3 3BQ (0845 611 8643, www.mojobar.co.uk). Metrolink St Peter's Square or Victoria, or City Centre buses, or Salford Central rail. **Open** *noon-3am Mon-Wed; noon-4am Thur-Sun.* **Map** *p54 C3* ⑥⑧

This authentic rock 'n' roll bar is ideal for those who enjoy singing along to Red Hot Chilli Peppers and Kings of Leon tunes at top volume. Customers – and staff – dance everywhere, and on everything, so grab a bourbon and a can of beer and cut loose at this favourite of the city's late-night crew. Burgers, shakes and 'frickles' (deep-fried pickles) are served until 11pm to satisfy hunger pangs.

Panacea

14 John Dalton Street, M2 6JR (833 0000, www.panaceamanchester.co.uk). Metrolink St Peter's Square, or City Centre buses, or Oxford Road rail. **Open** *8pm-3am Fri; 6pm-3am Sat; other days vary.* **Map** *p55 D4* ⑥⑨

This glitzy nightclub attracts a VIP-wannabe crowd. The decor majors on gold, copper and royal velvet, and drinks are sparkling and/or blended with visible effort. Early arrival is recommended, though don't expect to encounter any actual VIPs.

South

4A South King Street, M2 6DQ (831 7756, www.tokyoindustries.com/south).

All Star Lanes

Metrolink St Peter's Square, or City Centre buses, or Salford Central rail. **Open** 11pm-3am Mon, Tue, Thur-Sat. **Map** p54 C3 ⑨⓪

South was redesigned a few years ago by Ben Kelly of Hacienda and FAC251 fame, bringing in such additions as a bespoke Funktion One sound system but without compromising the venue's well-loved underground 'dive' feel. Clint Boon of Inspiral Carpets plays indie and rock 'n' roll tracks to a discerning crowd on Saturday nights, while Thursday's Murkage nights bring a mixture of dancehall, dubstep and hip hop.

Taps Bar & Epernay

Great Northern Tower, Watson Street, M3 4EE (819 5167, www. tapsmanchester.co.uk). Metrolink St Peter's Square, or City Centre buses, or Oxford Road rail. **Open** noon-midnight Mon-Thur, Sun; noon-2am Fri, Sat. **Map** p54 C5 ⑨①

The selling point of Taps Bar is that you can pour your own draught beer,

from standard lagers to fruit brews such as Leifmans, from a 'beer wall'. Is it a gimmick? Well, yes, and you'll be paying over the odds for the pleasure, but it does at least offer plenty of opportunity for terrible 'on the pull' gags. Upstairs is a quiet champagne and cocktail bar, Epernay, with cool views of the city by night. Food on offer includes the likes of mussels, pies and burgers.

Tiger Lounge

5 Cooper Street, M2 2FW (236 6007, www.tiger-lounge.com). Metrolink St Peter's Square, or City Centre buses, or Oxford Road rail. **Open** varies. **Map** p55 D4 ⑨②

Renamed after its eponymous Saturday nighter (the place was previously called Slice), this eternally entertaining extravaganza puts on rock 'n' roll, soul, Detroit garage and kitsch covers in swell (although sweaty), leopard-print surroundings. Somewhere to play dress-up if you're so inclined – the quirkier the outfit, the better.

Tiger Tiger

Printworks, 27 Withy Grove, M4 2BS (385 8080, www.tigertiger.co.uk). Metrolink Shudehill, or City Centre buses, or Victoria rail. **Open** noon-3am daily. **Map** p55 E2 ⓽

This big, flashy club targets itself at a youthful middle-of-the-road audience. Sprawled over multiple floors, it includes Lucky Voice karaoke pods, a grill restaurant, cocktails and proper club rooms for dancing. A destination for that hen or work do. If you like this vibe, check out the Bird Cage cabaret bar across the road.

Venue

29 Jacksons Row, M2 5WD (834 3793, www.thevenuenightclub.co.uk). Metrolink Deansgate-Castlefield, or City Centre buses, or Deansgate rail. **Open** 11pm-3am Wed; 10.30pm- 3am Fri, Sat. **Map** p55 D4 ⓬

Indie-loving students are spoilt with yet another anthem-peddling club only spitting distance from the very similar 42nd Street. As well as the usual indie weekenders, the Venue also provides a good-quality Wednesday night of classic rock 'n' roll, '60s, indie and soul tunes.

Venus

42 Maybrook House, Blackfriars, M3 2EG (834 7288, www.venusmanchester. co.uk). Metrolink Market Street, or City Centre buses, or Salford Central rail. **Open** 11pm-5am Fri; 11pm-6am Sat. Call in advance to check. **Map** p55 D3 ⓯

Venus's promoters pride themselves on providing their dressy, up-for-it crowd with a top-class club experience of Hed Kandi-esque funky, vocal house. Its extremely hot inside, so go dressed, as sensible punters do, in very little. A haven for house fans of all ages (but over 18, of course).

Arts & leisure

All Star Lanes

Great Northern Warehouse, 235 Deansgate, M3 4EN (871 3600, www.allstarlanes.co.uk). Metrolink

All hail the Albert Hall

This long-forgotten Methodist chapel is back as a gig venue.

The **Albert Hall** (p81) has quickly established itself as one of the most distinctive and atmospheric gig and club venues in the UK. It wasn't the most obvious outcome for the former Methodist Central Hall, built in 1910, which lay dusty and dormant for decades after closing in 1969. It had a short life as a nightclub until local nightlife entrepreneurs Trof took it on and rendered it fit for the purpose of live music, raving and theatre. It was a risky undertaking, but the results have paid off in spectacular fashion.

Occupying three floors, the venue opened for the 2013 Manchester International Festival, when BAFTA award-winning actress and Bolton local Maxine Peake christened the new development with a reading of Percy Shelley's *The Masque of Anarchy*. Performances since may not have remained quite so high-brow, yet the Hall's popularity has been consistent. Upcoming acts are a who's who of indie, dance and pop, be it Sam Smith, Belle & Sebastian, St Vincent or Carl Cox. And Warehouse Project (p110) have made the venue almost their second home for their mega clubs.

The main room, with its huge windows and coloured rooflights, intricate plaster and decorative metal columns, has a classic 'ballroom' design, with punters free to roam between the floor and the balcony that wraps around the space. For gigs, this offers an 'arena' feel without sacrificing intimacy or sound quality.

There's a second room in the vast complex to throw open for particularly ambitious or popular events, and plans are afoot to transform the ground floor into a new bar and restaurant. In the meantime, there are plenty of drinking spots within the building.

Deansgate-Castlefield or St Peter's Square, or City Centre buses, or Deansgate rail. **Open** 4-11pm Mon, Tue; 4pm-midnight Wed, Thur; noon-1am Fri; 11am-2am Sat; 11am-midnight Sun. **Map** p54 C5 ❾❻

The focus is on grown-up fun at this Americana-themed bowling alley. As well as a check-tiled café and bar serving shakes, gourmet burgers, fries and cocktails, there's a private party room, modelled on Elvis's personal bowling alley, and replica lanes of those under the White House. As such, it's become a destination for celebs such as Rihanna when they're in town. It's located above Manchester's now-defunct rail and water interchange, and these underground tunnels can be explored on occasional guided tours.

AMC Great Northern

Great Northern Warehouse, 235 Deansgate, M3 4EN (817 3000, www.amccinemas.co.uk). Metrolink Deansgate-Castlefield or St Peter's Square, or City Centre buses, or Deansgate rail. **Map** p54 C5 ❾❼

Screening standard movie fare in its 16 auditoria, the AMC cinema is set apart by its location: a Grade II-listed Victorian building that was once a receiving warehouse for deliveries to Central Station (now Manchester Central). The complex has expanded to include the likes of All Star Lanes bowling alley (p85), Liverpudlian Mexican chain Lucha Libre and burger joint Almost Famous (p64).

Barber Barber

Barton Arcade, 3 Deansgate, M3 2BH (832 5409, www.barberbarber.net). Metrolink Market Street, or City Centre buses, or Victoria rail. **Open** 9am-6pm Mon-Wed, Sat; 9am-7pm Thur, Fri; 11am-5.30pm Sun. **Map** p55 D3 ❾❽

This pampering parlour for gents serves wet shaves, haircuts, hot toddies and beer. The vibe is all tattoos, pomade and braces, with oversized make-up mirror lighting and vintage-style chairs to get customers in the right mood. Service is snappy.

Odeon Manchester & IMAX

Printworks, Withy Grove, M4 2BS (0333 006 7777, www.odeon.co.uk). Metrolink Shudehill, or City Centre buses, or Victoria rail. **Map** p55 E2 ❾❾

If size really does matter, the Odeon beats every other city-centre cinema hands down, with 23 screens and an IMAX theatre. Its 'gallery' also gives cinephiles the chance for a more exclusive viewing experience. Here, intimate auditoria, large leather seats and an alcohol licence mean you need to book ahead to bag your spot by the bar.

Opera House

Quay Street, M3 3HP (0844 871 3081, www.atgtickets.com). Metrolink St Peter's Square, or City Centre buses, or Oxford Road rail. **Map** p54 C4 ❿❿

Opera House is a wonderfully ornate 2,000-capacity theatre whose output of West End musicals, comedy, ballet and drama is similar to what's on at its sister venue, the Palace Theatre. True to its name, though, this house is an occasional home to regional and national opera.

Royal Exchange Theatre

St Ann's Square, M2 7DH (833 9833, www.royalexchange.co.uk). Metrolink Market Street or St Peter's Square, or City Centre buses, or Victoria rail. **Map** p55 D3 ❿❶

The Exchange, once the world's biggest commercial trading floor, has its history writ large on its interior – literally, as cotton prices are still posted high on the walls. The Victorian building was converted into a theatre in 1976, and business was, for a while, brisk – until the 1996 IRA bomb forced its closure. Reopening in 1998 with a studio space for new work, the theatre chose Stanley Houghton's play *Hindle Wakes* for its relaunch – the same work that was running when the bombing happened.

MANCHESTER BY AREA

Sienna Spa

A strong symbol of the theatre's indefatigability, it was the perfect choice for a venue that, today, continues to stage some of the city's best theatre.

Sienna Spa

Radisson Blu Edwardian, Peter Street, M2 5GP (835 8964, www.siennaspa. co.uk). Metrolink St Peter's Square, or City Centre buses, or Oxford Road rail. **Open** 6am-10pm Mon-Fri; 8am-8pm Sat, Sun. **Map** p54 C5 ⓶

This swanky day spa is located in the vaults of the former Free Trade Hall, which famously hosted gigs by Bob Dylan and the Sex Pistols, and was home to the Hallé for many years; it's now the Radisson Blu Edwardian hotel (p178). The spa has a gym, swimming pool, sauna and steam room (check out the fibre-optic lighting, designed to look like a star-studded night sky). The towels are so thick you could use them as pillows, and the lighting is forgiving. Expect top-of-the-range treatments (massages, manicures, body wraps, facials) with prices to match.

Vertical Chill

Ellis Brigham, 130 Deansgate, M3 2QS (837 6140, www.vertical-chill.com). Metrolink St Peter's Square, or City Centre buses, or Salford Central rail. **Open** 9am-6pm Tue-Sat; 11am-5pm Sun. **Map** p54 C3 ⓸

Step inside this outdoor-equipment shop and you may be surprised to see a 23ft-high wall of ice poking up between the fleeces and crampons. The -12°C monolith is perfect for practising climbing and ice-axe moves and, for those Edmund Hillary wannabes, there's an icy overhang to grapple with. Call for details of classes.

Yoga Lounge

1 The Great Northern Development, 253 Deansgate Mews, M3 4EN (834 6283, www.theyogalounge.co.uk). Metrolink Deansgate-Castlefield, or City Centre buses, or Deansgate rail. **Open** varies. **Map** p54 C5 ⓸

This hot-yoga studio and personal training gym is easily the city's most luxurious yoga space. Infrared lamps are used to heat the bodies in the room, with temperatures ranging from 36°C to 40°C, and there's a friendly atmosphere and upbeat instructors. Look out for fun candlelit sessions on Friday evenings and special events on weekends. Deals for new students offer amazing value: 20 consecutive days of yoga for £20.

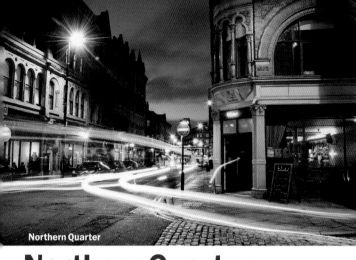
Northern Quarter

Northern Quarter

To find Manchester's self-styled 'creative quarter', follow the stream of hipsters heading up Oldham Street. The record shops, vintage boutiques and galleries exemplify the word 'independent'. Now a major cultural tourist destination, this is the place to try Manchester's famous craft beers; First Chop, Runaway and Blackjack are names to look out for. It was defiantly chain-free – and still is, to a certain extent – but where independent retailers lead, the mainstream follows; and the area is now a nightlife hotspot come Saturday night.

The action centres on Oldham Street, but explore the side lanes running west towards Shudehill and east to the Piccadilly canal, too. The friendly vibe is obvious at **Soup Kitchen**, where the close-knit creative community chows down and parties. If you're after more substantial fare, **Koffee Pot** does good-value breakfasts, or take your pick from the many curry places. Coffee is a thing too. **Fig & Sparrow** (also a shop), **North Tea Power** and **Takk** are where the locals drink, while **Teacup**, owned by DJ Mr Scruff, is more of a tourist magnet.

Part of the Northern Quarter's charm comes from its architecture: a slightly ramshackle collection of 18th- and 19th-century warehouses. Some have been beautifully restored (such as the building housing the **Buddhist Centre**), while others are, sadly, falling into a state of dilapidation. At the heart of the district is the impressive neo-Romanesque facade of the former **Smithfield Market**, which fronts on to a cobbled square. In the same block sits the **Centre for Chinese Contemporary Art** (CFCCA), while the market's sister building, now converted into the **Craft & Design Centre**, can be found on Oak Street. The centre is a hub of design and industry; products include prints, sculptures and leather goods.

Sights & museums

Centre for Chinese Contemporary Art (CFCCA)

Market Buildings, Thomas Street, M4 1EU (832 7271, www.cfcca.org.uk). Metrolink Shudehill, or City Centre buses, or Victoria rail. **Open** 10am-5pm, daily. **Admission** free. **Map** p91 B1 ❶

Established in 1986, this organisation occupies a specially designed building that was opened in 2003 and now acts as a national centre for the promotion of contemporary Chinese art. A changing programme of exhibitions and events celebrates international Chinese artists. There is also a decent shop.

Greater Manchester Police Museum

57A Newton Street, M1 1ET (856 4500, www.gmpmuseum.co.uk). Metrolink Piccadilly Gardens, or City Centre buses, or Piccadilly rail. **Open** 10.30am-3.30pm Tue; or by appt. **Admission** free. **Map** p91 C2 ❷

An easily overlooked curiosity, this converted former police station – far larger than it looks from the outside – contains early *CSI*-style case histories, the original prison cells, haunting Victorian mugshots and exhibits of grimly inventive confiscated weaponry, all overseen and explained by retired police officers.

Eating & drinking

57 Thomas Street

57 Thomas Street, M4 1NA (no phone, www.marblebeers.co.uk). Metrolink Shudehill, or City Centre buses, or Victoria rail. **Open** noon-midnight daily. **Bar**. **Map** p91 B1 ❸

This unassuming bar is the City Centre home of Manchester's best-known boutique brewery, Marble Beers. Unlike the beautiful surrounds of the Marble Arch Inn (p150), 57 Thomas Street is sparsely decorated, with just one long table stretching the length of the bar. The strength of the place can be seen in its simple combination of beer and food. Hand-pumped real ale, imported beers and an impressive ploughman's offer a satisfying, no-frills ale experience.

63 Degrees

20 Church Street, M4 1PN (832 5438, www.63degrees.co.uk). Metrolink Shudehill, or City Centre buses, or Victoria rail. **Open** noon-2.30pm, 5.30-11pm Tue-Sat. **£££**. **French**. **Map** p91 B2 ❹

This family affair is Manchester's best French restaurant. Presided over by chef Eric Moreau (the father of the *famille*), they do things by the book here. Snails, foie gras, beef fillet and roast pigeon are good choices, while the house special is chicken breast, gently poached at 63° (hence the name). A Gallic wine list and romantic lighting complete the picture. They also have a pâtisserie in the suburb of Didsbury.

Castle Hotel

66 Oldham Street, M4 1LE (237 9485, www.thecastlehotel.info). Metrolink Market Street or Piccadilly Gardens, or City Centre buses, or Piccadilly rail. **Open** noon-1am Mon-Thur, Sun; noon-2am Fri, Sat. **Pub**. **Map** p91 B2 ❺

This legendary pub, dating back to 1871, has been transformed into one of the city's finest pubs and live venues by a team that includes former *Coronation Street* actor Rupert Hill. Enjoy great ales, interesting bands – often with an acoustic bent – and spoken word events. Business is so good that the management have taken over Gullivers across the road, which offers more of the same.

Dry Bar

28-30 Oldham Street, M1 1JN (236 9840, www.drybar.co.uk). Metrolink Piccadilly Gardens, or City Centre buses, or Piccadilly rail. **Open** 11am-midnight Mon-Wed; 11am-1am Thur; 11am-4am Fri, Sat; noon-midnight Sun. **Bar**. **Map** p91 B2 ❻

A Northern Quarter mainstay long before the area's regeneration kicked in, this former Factory Records-owned venue was one of the first DJ bars in the country. A must visit for any 'Madchester' or Hacienda veterans – order a beer at Dry and you'll be perching where countless Mancunian musicians have stood. It may be a shadow of its former self, an echo of Manchester music past, but the place still holds a certain charm.

Earth Café

16-20 Turner Street, M4 1DZ (834 1996, www.earthcafe.co). Metrolink Shudehill, or City Centre buses, or Victoria rail. **Open** 11am-4pm Mon-Fri; 10am-5pm Sat. **£. Café.** **Map** p91 B1 ❼

This vegan café, in the basement of the Manchester Buddhist Centre (p104), serves food that's both fresh and, where possible, organic. The special platters are good value at round £6 for rice, a heaped plate of the daily dish (butterbean casserole, for example) and two salads. There's a range of teas and fresh juices.

Hare & Hounds

46 Shudehill, M4 4AA (832 4737). Metrolink Shudehill, or City Centre buses, or Victoria rail. **Open** 11am-11pm Mon-Sat; noon-10.30pm Sun. **Pub. Map** p91 B2 ❽

This Grade II-listed building first opened as licensed premises in 1778; looking at the wooden panels, tiling and bar-service bells, it seems that not much has changed since. It played host to the socialist debates of years past – find out more by chatting to the locals. Old-fashioned singalongs sometimes take place around open mic sessions (Wed, Thur, Sat).

Koffee Pot

84-86 Oldham Street, M4 1LF (236 8918, www.thekoffeepot.co.uk).

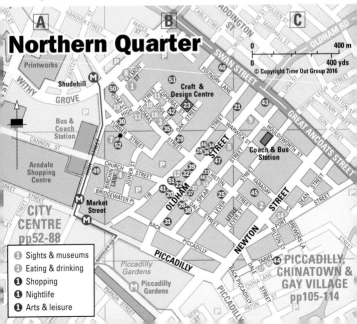

Koffee Pot p91

Metrolink Market Street, or City Centre buses, or Piccadilly rail. **Open** 7.30am-4pm Mon-Fri; 9am-4pm Sat, Sun. **£**. **Café**. **Map** p91 C1 ⑨

Home to arguably the best full english in town, the Koffee Pot has moved to a bigger location in order to accommodate even more of the city's creative types and bands in search of a post-hangover fry-up. Breakfast and a brew come in at £6.50, and once you're sat in one of the red booths, you'll find it hard to leave. The tasty, Cali-inspired daily specials are worth a go.

Luck Lust Liquor & Burn

100-102 High Street, M4 1HP (244 9425, www.lucklustliquorburn.com). Metrolink Shudehill, or City Centre buses, or Victoria Rail. **Open** noon-10pm Mon-Thur, Sun; noon-11pm Fri, Sat. **££**. **Mexican**. **Map** p91 B1 ⑩

Manchester had a serious lack of Mex until the team behind 'dirty food' sensation Almost Famous turned their hands to soft tacos, burritos and sweet potato fries. Play 'taco roulette', where one of your fish, chipotle chicken or cajun steak portions comes spice-loaded. Accompany it with tequila shots and ice-cold beer. Rather DIY inside, it's a favourite of Generation Z.

Northern Quarter Restaurant & Bar

108 High Street, M4 1HQ (832 7115, www.tnq.co.uk). Metrolink Shudehill, or City Centre buses, or Victoria rail. **Open** noon-11pm Mon-Sat; noon-7pm Sun. **£££**. **Modern European**. **Map** p91 B1 ⑪

Under the stewardship of head chef Anthony Fielden, the Northern Quarter has firmly established itself as a prime Modern British/European proposition. Lovely dishes, such as lemon thyme, salsify and walnut gnocchi, and roasted suckling pig, have made the place a reliable bet for visiting foodies.

North Tea Power

36 Tib Street, M4 1LA (833 3073, www.northteapower.co.uk). Metrolink Market Street, or City Centre buses, or Victoria rail. **Open** 8am-7pm Mon-Fri; 10am-7pm Sat; 10am-6pm Sun. **£**. **Café**. **Map** p91 B2 ⑫

Among the first cafés in Manchester to serve a flat white, NTP is one of the coolest cafés in the area, with bustling boutiques on its doorstep. Simple decor, coupled with a friendly approach and a broad selection of tea and extraordinary own-blend coffees, make it the perfect retreat. Thanks to the free Wi-Fi, it makes for an excellent mobile office too.

Café culture

Drop in, log on and soak up the caffeine vibes.

Manchester's independent cafés are great for people-watching and getting to know the comings and goings of the city. There are two key areas to aim for. The Northern Quarter is home to purist coffee house **Takk** (p95), bustling **North Tea Power** (p92), cute lifestyle store-cum-café **Fig & Sparrow** (p96) and spacious **Ezra & Gil** (20 Hilton Street, M1 1FR, www.ezraandgil.com). Meanwhile, in the city centre, places to look out for include **Pot Kettle Black** (p68), run by two professional rugby players, and the slightly snooty **Caffeine & Co** (11 St James's Square, M2 6WE, www.caffeineandco.com). Salford has Italian **Caffè Lupo** (p138).

While most coffee shops vary their blends (just as bars do with their guest beers), Takk favours London's Square Mile roasters, as well as showcasing its own Nordic-style espresso, North Projekt. North Tea Power was one of Manchester's earliest adopters of new-wave coffee culture, and they favour Has Bean roasters from Staffordshire, with whom they've collaborated to create their 'Deerhunter' blend. Unsurprisingly, Caffé Lupo serves bespoke Roman blends, hand-sourced by the Italian coffee-consultant/owner. Locally roasted Heart & Graft is another brand to watch out for.

Out in the 'burbs, Chorlton's **Barbakan** (p155) sells quality blends (ground or as beans, as well as takeaway coffee) from Clitheroe's Exchange Coffee roasters. The area is also home to **Tea Hive** (53 Manchester Road, M21 9PW, 881 0569, www.teahive.co.uk), a kid-friendly option. Tea Hive also runs the Alexandra Park café, in the old clubhouse overlooking the cricket pitch, while Longford Park, south of Chorlton, is home to another branch of Caffeine & Co.

Takk

Odd

30-32 Thomas Street, M4 1ER (833 0070, www.oddbar.co.uk). Metrolink Shudehill, or City Centre buses, or Victoria rail. **Open** *daily; times vary.*
Bar. **Map** p91 B1 ⑬

A happy haven of eclectic quirkiness, Odd is the antithesis of corporate high-street drinking dens, and welcomes a mixed crowd. Even better than the DIY decor, tasty bar snacks, cocktails and continental beers is its background music: kooky jukebox by day; sets from forward-thinking indie advocates by night. The Odd empire also includes the Blue Pig (on High Street in the Northern Quarter) and a branch in Chorlton (Oddest).

Port Street Beer House

39-41 Port Street, M1 2EQ (237 9949, www.portstreetbeerhouse.co.uk). Metrolink Piccadilly, or City Centre buses, or Piccadilly rail. **Open** *4pm-midnight Mon-Thur; 2pm-midnight Fri; noon-1am Sat; noon-midnight Sun.*
Bar. **Map** p91 C2 ⑭

This contemporary ale house doesn't shout about its role as a key player in Manchester's craft beer revolution. A huge range of perfectly kept beers rotate daily on keg and cask, and there are also bottles from the wildest brewers in Europe and the US. Nevertheless, this is an unpretentious place to drink. Many staff have gone on to work as brewers (at Cloud Water, Marble or Summer Wine, for example), making this a hands-down must for any beer fan. Their 'meet the brewer' nights are legendary. The owners also run Common bar (p102) and Chorlton's Beagle (p155).

Soup Kitchen

31-33 Spear Street, M1 1DF (236 5100, www.soup-kitchen.co.uk). Metrolink Market Street, or City Centre buses, or Piccadilly rail. **Open** *noon-11pm Mon-Wed, Sun; noon-1am Thur; noon-4am Fri, Sat.* **£**. **Café**. **Map** p91 B2 ⑮

The idea behind Soup Kitchen is simple enough: after collecting your food from the counter, you transport your grub to one of the long benches and tables and say hello to fellow diners. Select large bowls of freshly made soup (which changes daily) with hunks of fresh

bread for less than a fiver, or go for the daily hot special. There's a Berlin-inspired club downstairs, with stars of the progressive club scene playing very late (see box p100). A must for any visiting hipster, especially as the bar is a great place to meet the locals.

Takk

6 Tariff Street, M1 2FF (no phone, www.takkmcr.com). Metrolink Piccadilly Gardens, or City Centre buses, or Piccadilly rail. **Open** 8.30am-5pm Mon-Fri; 10am-6pm Sat; 11am-5pm Sun. **£**. **Café. Map** p91 C3 ⑯
Home to a legion of Mac warriors, the Takk is a minimal coffee house serving what many regard as the finest flat white in town. Their own blend is a Nordic-style espresso, and there are guest slots for trendy roasters such as Berlin's The Barn. Food includes panini, cakes and home-made baked beans. Breakfast is good value.

Tariff & Dale

2 Tariff Street, M1 2FN (710 2233, www.tariffanddale.com). Metrolink Piccadilly Gardens, or City Centre buses,

Tariff & Dale

or Piccadilly rail. **Open** 10am-midnight Mon-Wed, Sun; 10am-1am Thur; 10am-2am Fri, Sat. **££**. **Gastropub. Map** p91 C3 ⑰
Tariff & Dale is a step up from your typical NQ hangout. The former textile mill has been converted into a relaxing place in which to explore upmarket gastropub fare – the likes of pork belly with pickled beetroot – as well as fine craft beers and wines.

Teacup

53-55 Thomas Street, M4 1NA (832 3233, www.teacupandcakes.com). Metrolink Shudehill, or City Centre buses, or Victoria rail. **Open** 10am-6pm Mon, Sun; 10am-9.30pm Tue-Sat. **££**. **Café. Map** p91 B1 ⑱
Manchester DJ Mr Scruff has long been famous for his fondness for tea, setting up a tea bar at all of his Keep It Unreal club nights. It was a natural next step to launch his own café; Teacup stocks Scruff's own blends alongside a loose-leaf menu that is extremely pricey (nearly £5 a pot), but good for a treat. Hungry? Try eggs numerous ways or home-made cakes galore. This is a favourite NQ haunt for tourists. The same team owns Bonbon, a delightful artisanal chocolate shop and café on nearby John Street.

This & That

3 Soap Street, M4 1EW (832 4971). Metrolink Shudehill, or City Centre buses, or Victoria rail. Open 11.30am-4pm Mon-Thur, Sun; 11.30am-8pm Fri, Sat. **£**. **Indian. Map** p91 B1 ⑲
There's an enjoyable sense of the old-school canteen about this curry café with its plastic chairs and steaming bain-marie (across which you place your order). Asking for 'rice and three' gets you a hearty plate of boiled rice with three different curries mingling joyously together on top. Offerings vary daily, and there's usually plenty of choice, including chicken, lamb, dal and veg. For around £5, you'll get a heap of spicy wholesome food, a fresh

naan and a jug of mango lassi. The one drawback is the hard-to-find location, tucked away in the sort of alley that you might see featured on *Crimewatch* reconstructions. But think of the food that awaits, and be brave.

Shopping

The best place in the city to find independent boutiques, quirky one-off shops, vintage clothing and cutting-edge styles, the Northern Quarter attracts hip shoppers, students and fashionistas who aren't afraid to wander between curry houses, garment warehouses and graffitied walls.

Afflecks

52 Church Street, M4 1PW (839 0718, www.afflecks.com). Metrolink Market Street, or City Centre buses, or Piccadilly rail. **Open** 10.30am-6pm Mon-Fri; 10am-6pm Sat; 11am-5pm Sun. **Map** p91 B2 ⑳

This four-floor alternative shopping institution crawls with disaffected teens at the weekend – for a leisurely browse, go midweek. You'll find new designers, clubwear, vintage, fancy dress, records, homewares, cute and kitsch gifts, posters and a vast range of black T-shirts. With careful purchasing, you can emerge with gorgeous items at suitably teenage prices. The building used to be Affleck & Brown's, the city's premier department store.

Beatin' Rhythm

108 Tib Street, M4 1LR (834 7783, www.beatinrhythm.com). Metrolink Shudehill, or City Centre buses, or Victoria rail. **Open** 10am-5.30pm Mon-Sat; 11am-4pm Sun. **Map** p91 C1 ㉑

Searching for a hard-to-find soul track – or just some really good advice? Turn your ears towards this specialist Northern Soul vinyl retailer. The cosy store is tucked between the sex and hydroponics suppliers that populate the northern part of the Northern Quarter, but don't let that put you off

– choice finds in soul, rock 'n' roll, funk, doo-wop, girl group and surf rock await. Northern Soul 45s cost anything from £25 to £500 – but there's plenty for the novice collector.

Cow

61 Church Street, M4 1PD (834 4926, www.wearecow.com). Metrolink Piccadilly Gardens, or City Centre buses, or Piccadilly rail. **Open** 10am-7pm Mon-Sat; 11am-5pm Sun. **Map** p91 B2 ㉒

The Northern Quarter is Manchester's home of vintage, hence the big branch of this reworked-fashion chain (also with shops in Birmingham, Nottingham and Sheffield). Shirts and denim are a strength, and prices aren't as painful as they can be elsewhere. It's a 'pop in and pick something up' kind of place – and somewhere to meet like-minded souls while you're at it.

Craft & Design Centre

17 Oak Street, M4 5JD (832 4274, www.craftanddesign.com). Metrolink Market Street, or City Centre buses, or Piccadilly rail. **Open** 10am-5.30pm Mon-Sat; 11am-5pm Sun. **Map** p91 B1 ㉓

This long-established creative hub continues to draw the best local talent. Each floor is lined with small shops and studios, and many traders design on-site and sell their work fresh from the drawing board, sewing machine or workbench. Products include one-off bags, intricate jewellery, large-scale photographic prints, paintings, sculpture and leather goods. If you're after something special, most of artists will work to commission. The Oak Street Café in the light and airy foyer sells cakes, savoury tarts and quality coffees, and there are also changing exhibitions.

Fig & Sparrow

20 Oldham Street, M1 1JN (228 1843, www.figandsparrow.co.uk). Metrolink Market Street or Piccadilly Gardens, or City Centre buses, or Piccadilly rail. **Open** 8am-7pm Mon-Fri; 10am-6pm Sat; 11am-6pm Sun. **Map** p91 B2 ㉔

Fig & Sparrow does a fine line in local prints, greetings cards, ceramics, glassware and gifts. Everything is laid out so perfectly that it looks like an interiors magazine has just been in for a photoshoot; that's just how this independent lifestyle store rolls. The café (built from reclaimed wood) serves excellent cakes and cheese scones, soups, interesting granola and good coffee. The ideal place for a catch-up.

Fred Aldous

37 Lever Street, M1 1LW (236 4224, www.fredaldous.co.uk). Metrolink Piccadilly Gardens, or City Centre buses, or Piccadilly rail. **Open** 8.15am-5.15pm Mon-Fri; 9.15am-5.15pm Sat; 11am-5pm Sun. **Map** p91 B2 ㉖

'Supplying the creative mind since 1861' states the sign. It doesn't sell opium, but Fred Aldous does offer a huge basement packed with everything the social sketcher, dedicated designer or committed craftsperson could ever want. Aisles groan with pens, paints, glue, paper, glitter and all the little bits and pieces you need to make jewellery, cards and felt things to sell at the church fête. Staff are immensely helpful, and it's easy to believe you're a successful artist simply by sniffing the creative air.

Junk

2 Dale Street, M1 1JW (238 8517, www.junkshop.co.uk). Metrolink Piccadilly Gardens, or City Centre buses, or Piccadilly rail. **Open** 11am-6.30pm Mon-Fri; 10.30am-6.30pm Sat; noon-5pm Sun. **Map** p91 B2 ㉖

Junk sells sustainable fashion – meaning upcycled vintage items, cut for today's trends and body shapes. The shop is like a dressing-up box, with accessories galore by local designers, vintage shoes, hats, sunglasses – basically, the tools to make you look like you're made of fun. The imaginative owners also run beginners' courses in dressmaking and tailoring.

Magma

24 Oldham Street, M1 1JN (236 8777, www.magmabooks.com). Metrolink Piccadilly Gardens, or City Centre buses, or Piccadilly rail. **Open** 10am-6.30pm Mon-Sat; noon-6pm Sun. **Map** p91 B2 ㉗

Magma has three outlets in London, but retains the feel of an independent bookshop, with obscure and glossy photographic and art books. Some of the coffee-table books are the price of, er, a coffee table, but the wide range of magazines and journals offers a more affordable slice of print heaven. You can easily spend hours here, leafing through the volumes. There's also a selection of quirky postcards, T-shirts, graphic novels and gifts for those who find proper 'Art' too tiresome.

Northern Flower

58 Tib Street, M4 1LG (832 7731, www.northernflower.com). Metrolink Market Street, or City Centre buses, or Piccadilly rail. **Open** 9am-6pm Mon-Sat. **Map** p91 B2 ㉘

A flower shop with personal service and knowledgeable staff is something of a rarity these days, when the choice is often limited to wilted garage chrysanths and supermarket spider plants. At Northern Flower, you can believe that the blooms have just been picked by an elf skipping through a dew-drenched field. Find rare pot plants to liven up a dull office, ask staff for a customised romantic bouquet or just pluck a few bold blooms to cheer yourself up on the way home.

Oi Polloi

63 Thomas Street, M4 1LQ (831 7781, www.oipolloi.com). Metrolink Market Street, or City Centre buses, or Piccadilly rail. **Open** 10am-6pm Mon-Sat; noon-5pm Sun. **Map** p91 B2 ㉙

Oi Polloi seems to have the menswear market nailed thanks to a thriving online business as well as this, their flagship national store. Expect upmarket casualwear labels such as Penfield, Fjällräven, Carhartt and

Barbour, plus classic footwear from the likes of Clarks Originals, Mephisto and Converse. Accessories, covering everything from bike saddles to socks, are cool.

Oklahoma

74-76 High Street, M4 1ES (834 1136, www.oklahomacafe.co.uk). Metrolink Market Street, or City Centre buses, or Piccadilly rail. **Open** *10am-7pm Mon-Fri; 8am-7pm Sat; 10am-6pm Sun.* **Map** p91 B1 ③⓪

If a giant piñata were to explode in Manchester, the results might resemble Oklahoma. Defying categorisation, this airy, wooden-floored shop-cum-café stocks the best selection of retro and quirky cards in town, alongside bizarre and amusing cheap gifts, imported and designer homewares and a healthy dose of kitsch. If you're after Virgin Mary charm bracelets, or Magic Trees, you're in the right place. If you'd rather buy a subtitled Korean DVD and eat a bean wrap with a chai goat's-milk latte, you're also catered for. Anyone who leaves this place disappointed is a joyless soul indeed.

Oxfam

8-10 Oldham Street, M1 1JQ (228 3797, www.oxfam.org.uk). Metrolink Piccadilly Gardens, or City Centre buses, or Piccadilly rail. **Open** *10am-6pm Mon-Sat; noon-5pm Sun.* **Map** p91 B2 ③①

This huge Oxfam is not a bargain-hunter's paradise – its City Centre location is reflected in the prices. But it does specialise in collectibles, and has a vinyl section that's well worth a peek, plus several shelves of rare books. Give it a miss for clothes, though, and go to Oxfam Originals up the road (Unit 8, Smithfield Building, 839 3160), which sells the fashionistas' pick of the charity bundles, including cool bags and shoes from the 1960s to the '90s.

Piccadilly Records

53 Oldham Street, M1 1JR (839 8008, www.piccadillyrecords.com). Metrolink Piccadilly Gardens, or City Centre buses, or Piccadilly rail. **Open** *10am-6pm Mon-Sat; noon-5pm Sun.* **Map** p91 B2 ③②

A Manchester institution, Piccadilly is a much-loved, old-fashioned independent record shop. As well as a huge

Afflecks p96

Retro Rehab

91 Oldham Street, M4 1LW (839 2050, www.retro-rehab.co.uk). Metrolink Piccadilly Gardens, or City Centre buses, or Piccadilly rail. **Open** 10am-6pm Mon-Sat; noon-4pm Sun. **Map** p91 B2 ❸❹

This neat boutique stocks a good range of clothing dating from the 1950s to the '80s, alongside its own reworked vintage garments. There's a great choice of accessories, jewellery and one-off bags, but dresses are the speciality: the walls are lined with everything from mini to maxi frocks, all arranged in a handy colour-coded display.

Richard Goodall Gallery

59 Thomas Street, M4 1NA (832 3435, www.richardgoodallgallery.com). Metrolink Shudehill, or City Centre buses, or Victoria rail. **Open** 11am-6pm Tue-Fri; 11am-5pm Sat. **Admission** free. **Map** p91 B1/B2 ❸❺

This commercial gallery's window display pulls in punters with its music and vintage posters, and its so-hip-it-hurts illustrations, prints and graphic design. A second store round the corner on High Street focuses on higher-end rock photography and painting.

Rockers England

89 Oldham Street, M4 1LW (839 9202, www.rockersengland.co.uk). Metrolink Piccadilly Gardens, or City Centre buses, or Piccadilly rail. **Open** 11am-5.30pm Mon-Sat. **Map** p91 B2 ❸❻

A down to earth specialist shop that's perfect for anyone who's ever eyed up a Harley. There are racks of cool T-shirts, bags, jewellery, iron-on patches and spectacular 1950s-style dresses. Staff live the dream with quiffs, chains and hefty turn-ups, but they welcome allcomers, even if you're a lightweight who just fancies a skull-decorated lighter.

Thunder Egg

22 Oldham Street, M1 1JN (235 0606, www.thunderegg.co.uk). Metrolink Market Street, or City Centre buses,

choice of classic vinyl, it stocks the newest releases. Staff are happy to share news of forthcoming releases, or order that tricky-to-find edition – no wonder it's survived the digital revolution. We're a bit partial to Eastern Bloc Records around the corner on Stevenson Square too.

Pop

34-36 Oldham Street, M1 1JN (236 5797, www.pop-boutique.com). Metrolink Piccadilly Gardens, or City Centre buses, or Piccadilly rail. **Open** 10.30am-6.30pm Mon-Sat; 11am-5pm Sun. **Map** p91 B2 ❸❸

Pop is a student institution, selling original and recreated '60s and '70s styles upstairs, including jeans, cute tops and cotton dresses. The basement is crammed with original homewares, including Tretchikoff-style prints, tile-topped coffee tables and German lamps. Blue Daisy café is attached to the storefront, serving veggie breakfasts, salads and smoothies. For a quick, painless trip back in time, it's worth a visit – though if you're a retro purist, it may seem a bit sanitised.

Under the radar

Say hello to the city's new small clubs.

Having once been known for a cluster of smaller nights, Manchester's club scene has gone large in the past decade, with Warehouse Project (p110) leading the way for 3,000-plus-capacity events. But for those seeking a more intimate, potentially sweatier, party with a regular crowd, the city still has more than enough spots with a sense of independence and that house party vibe.

Soup Kitchen's (p94) basement is quickly gaining a reputation as one of the best small spots in the country for clubbing. Its clued-up crowd, gritty atmosphere and expertly tuned sound system have attracted the wildly popular likes of Dixon and Daniel Avery to guest behind the decks. There are also regular, reputable showcases for grime and techno, such as Swing Ting and Meandyou. With friendly, no-nonsense door staff and a no-frills set of unisex toilets, there's definitely something a bit 'Berlin' about Soup Kitchen.

Over in Salford is **Islington Mill** (p140). This was Greater Manchester's first 'fire-proof' mill, and today it's the scene of some of the city's finest parties. Björk held her Manchester International Festival after-party here, and alternative, LGBT, house and rock nights abound. The atmosphere is relaxed and drinks are affordable.

Few clubs offer a stronger sensation of a 'house party vibe' than **Antwerp Mansion** (p163) – which actually is a mansion. Situated a couple of miles out of the city centre, on the doorstep of most of Manchester's students, it attracts a young and up-for-it crowd. The Victorian building has been stripped of its former opulent furnishings, leaving two floors of vast, raw space best used for dancing hard. Mansion is now the regular home of bass-loving promoters such as Hit & Run and renowned disco-sleaze merchants HomoElectric.

Swing Ting

or Piccadilly rail. **Open** 10.30am-6pm Mon-Fri; 10am-6pm Sat; noon-5pm Sun. **Map** p91 B2 ③

This funky ladieswear store looks like the inside of a Japanese teenager's bedroom. It's packed with Hello Kitty ephemera, funny cards, cute bags and even crocheted Moomin dolls, as well as stacks of cool clothes and homewares over two floors. Party dresses and boldly patterned clothing are a speciality. It might be too visually exhausting for the over-thirties, but if you're looking for a desirable and affordable gift for your quirky mate, it's a great bet.

Travelling Man

4 Dale Street, M1 1JW (237 1877, www.travellingman.com). Metrolink Piccadilly Gardens, or City Centre buses, or Piccadilly rail. **Open** 10am-6pm Mon-Sat; 11am-5pm Sun. **Map** p91 B2 ③

Are you male? Like the odd action adventure? Love computer games? Then you'll be drawn to this shop like a moth to a lightbulb. It offers US and Japanese comics displayed on ceiling-high racks; obscure board games featuring pneumatic vixens; computer quests; figurines from the crazed imaginations of reclusive animators; and rare publications for the dedicated collector. They also host signings by graphic novelists and other nerdtacular special events. Your other half may end up dumping you due to your newly developed geekiness – but you won't notice.

Wood

55 Oldham Street, M1 1JR (832 5739, www.ashopcalledwood.com). Metrolink Piccadilly Gardens, or City Centre buses, or Piccadilly rail. **Open** 9am-5pm Mon-Sat; 10am-5pm Sun. **Map** p91 B2 ③

Menswear is on the rise in Manchester. Head to this minty green haven on Oldham Street for everything from classic labels (Wrangler, Lyle & Scott) to fashion-led Brit favourites (YMC,

Silas). Top your look off with a choice from the imaginative collection of vintage wear, as well as bags and gifts. Names to drop include Garbstore, 10 Deep, Commune, Penfield, Mishka and Call of the Wild, while their own-brand clothing label is called Cyrus Wood.

Nightlife

The **Castle Hotel** (p90) also has live music.

Band on the Wall

25 Swan Street, M4 5JZ (834 1786, www. bandonthewall.org). Metrolink Market Street, or City Centre buses, or Victoria rail. **Open** varies. **Map** p91 B1 ④

This not-for-profit venue is a one-off. It has lovingly restored 19th-century features, plus all the requisite 21st-century accoutrements – recording studio, superior acoustics, even its own interactive rooftop artwork. Expect everything from jazz and world music to new folk, spoken word and reggae. Evening classes (non-audition choirs, harmonica for beginners and so on) are great fun.

Black Dog Ballroom

Corner of Tib Street & Church Street, M4 1JG (839 0664, www.blackdog ballroom.co.uk). Metrolink Market Street, or City Centre buses, or Victoria rail. **Open** noon-4am Mon-Fri, Sun; noon-5am Sat. **Map** p91 B2 ④

With its exposed brickwork, softly lit booths and crimson-felted pool tables, this basement bar is like a little piece of New York's Lower East Side transported to the Northern Quarter. Black Dog Ballroom's real draw, though, is its generous opening times: the food menu, an appropriate mix of deli and diner, is served until 1am; while the booze flows well into the hours when decent folks should be soundly asleep.

Common

39-41 Edge Street, M4 1HW (832 9245, www.aplacecalledcommon.co.uk). Metrolink Shudehill, or City Centre buses, or Victoria rail. **Open** 11am-midnight Mon-Wed; 11am-2am Thur-Sat; noon-midnight Sun. **Map** p91 B1 ❷

A sure-fire bet for consistently friendly staff serving quality drinks in a down-to-earth and lively environment. Overhauled in 2015, the original NQ bar now offers a fresh, Scandi take on the formula. It's one of the hubs of the local scene – the city's finest DJs spin records on and off throughout the week, and upmarket bar food is served daily from lunchtime. It's part of a small group that includes Port Street Beer House (p94) and Chorlton's Beagle (p155).

Frog & Bucket

102 Oldham Street, M4 1LJ (236 9805, www.frogandbucket.com). Metrolink Market Street, or City Centre buses, or Victoria rail. **Open** 7pm-1am Mon; 7pm-2am Thur-Sat; 7pm-12.30am Sun. **Map** p91 C1 ❸

Over the years, the Frog has given an early boost to such well-known comedians as Dave Gorman, Peter Kay and the inimitable Johnny Vegas – a list the venue hopes to add to through its 'Beat the Frog' amateur stand-up sessions held every Monday. Weekends at this welcoming, old-school comedy club see more-established names in charge of entertainment, after which a cheerfully cheesy disco ensues.

Kosmonaut

10 Tariff Street, M1 2FF (no phone, www.kosmonaut.co). Metrolink Piccadilly, or City Centre buses, or Piccadilly rail. **Open** noon-midnight Mon-Wed, Sun; noon-1am Thur-Sat. **Map** p91 C3 ❹

One of the leading lights of the NQ's 'Piccadilly side' regeneration (alongside the Takk café and Port Street Beer House), Kosmonaut is a lo-fi bar with booths, cool staff and clientele, murals and a smoking area under the retro New York City-style iron fire exits. The Northern Quarter is often used as a double for NYC in films, and, with a local

beer and a pizza slice in hand, you'll be in Manhattan before you know it.

Kraak

11 Stevenson Square, M1 1DB (no phone, www.kraak.org.uk). Metrolink Market Street or Piccadilly, or City Centre buses, or Piccadilly rail. **Open** varies. **Map** p91 C2 ❺

Kraak bar is hard to find, but persevere if underground sounds are your bag. Open-hearted gay nights are a trend, as are techno parties and modern metal nights. Kraak owes much to Berlin's DIY bar scene, and is all the more special for it. A place to pop until you have to stop.

Matt & Phred's Jazz Club

64 Tib Street, M4 1LW (831 7002, www.mattandphreds.com). Metrolink Market Street, or City Centre buses, or Victoria rail. **Open** 6pm-late Mon-Thur; 4pm-late Fri; 2pm-late Sat; varies Sun. **Map** p91 B2 ❻

A much-loved Northern Quarter staple and Manchester's only live jazz club, Matt & Phred's also provides legendarily good pizza (until midnight) and cocktails. The cosy interior is the perfect setting for sounds from local and international musicians.

Mint Lounge

46-50 Oldham Street, M4 1LE (no phone, www.mintlounge.com). Metrolink Market Street, or City Centre buses, or Piccadilly rail. **Open** varies. **Map** p91 B2 ❼

This spacious club, one of the Northern Quarter's largest, opens for regular and one-off nights – but not every day. Weekends are typically home to the city's longest-running club night, Funkademia.

Night & Day Café

26 Oldham Street, M1 1JN (236 4597, www.nightnday.org). Metrolink Market Street, or City Centre buses, or Piccadilly rail. **Open** varies. **Map** p91 B2 ❽

Alfresco art

The streets are alive with art.

Manchester is a hive of creativity, with plenty to enjoy on street level, thanks largely to projects such as Out House (http://outhousemcr.thecolouringbox.co.uk), based around improving the appearance of a former public loo in the Northern Quarter's Stevenson Square and an electric substation on nearby Tib Lane. Look out for work by Tasha Whittle and other members of the One69a print studios at Salford's Islington Mill (p140). Painted shop-shutters are also a big deal in Stevenson Square, with designs by renowned graffiti artist Kelzo, among others.

Look up in this part of town and you may spot one of many tiled 'space invaders' installed by French street artist Invader in 2010. Check locations at www.space-invaders.com/world/manchester.

On Tib Street, you can walk across poetry by wordsmith Lemn Sissay. His poem, *Flags*, is pressed into the pavement in a distinctive typeface

created by artist Tim Rushton. The same font (Cypher) is used on the area's white and blue street signs; both creations were fired by local ceramicists Majolica Works.

The wall outside Afflecks (p96) features giant mosaics by Mark Kennedy. His work includes images of Morrissey, the Stone Roses, *Coronation Street* stars and a tiled quote: 'And on the sixth day, God created MANchester'.

More cult faces come courtesy of Manchester street artist Akse. His mural of *Breaking Bad*'s Walter White may have been whitewashed over, but other larger-than-life-sized paintings in his film and TV psychopaths series include characters such as the Joker, Tony Soprano and Tyrion Lannister.

If large sculptures are more your thing, marvel at George Wylie's *New Broom* (an actual, giant broom on Hilton Street), and the imposing *Big Horn* – a David Kemp artwork installed in Tib Street in 1999.

MANCHESTER BY AREA

Akse

Full of character, Night & Day is perfectly situated among Oldham Street's record shops: do some crate-digging, then head over for a relaxed beer and catch tomorrow's big act or cult faves hanging out, and – if you're lucky – playing intimate sets. Relaxed café-bar by day, world-class rock 'n' roll bar by night: no self-respecting music fan can claim a 'proper' trip to Manchester without a visit.

Ruby Lounge

28-34 High Street, M4 1QB (834 1392, www.therubylounge.org). Metrolink Market Street, or City Centre buses, or Victoria rail. **Open** varies. **Map** p91 A2 **49**

Straddling the border between the City Centre and the more bohemian Northern Quarter, Ruby Lounge has an independent streak that's more in keeping with the latter. The main attraction is the eclectic range of live acts, though the venue also hosts occasional club nights such as Revolver. The L-shaped layout can be frustrating – music fans are crammed into the scant space around the stage, while the vast bar area remains empty. It's worth it though, being a place to catch bands before they hit the big time.

Trof

8 Thomas Street, M4 1EU (833 3197, www.trofnq.co.uk). Metrolink Market Street, or City Centre buses, or Victoria rail. **Open** 10am-midnight Mon, Tue; 10am-1am Wed, Thur; 10am-3am Fri; 9am-3am Sat; 9am-midnight Sun. **Map** p91 B1 **50**

Trof is the coolest townhouse bar in Manchester. Owned by the team behind the Deaf Institute, Gorilla and the Albert Hall, this is their most straightforward 'bar', yet the quirky design that is their trademark is evident in the taxidermy, booth seating and bespoke smoking areas. Entertainment takes in gigs, DJs, quizzes and more; the breakfasts and roasts are good too – and bourbon is a thing.

Arts & leisure

Bikram Yoga Manchester

Smithfield Building, 51 Church Street, M4 1PD (834 7789, www.bikramyoga manchester.co.uk). Metrolink Market Street, or City Centre buses, or Piccadilly rail. **Open** daily; times vary. **Map** p91 B2 **51**

Not for the faint-hearted, this studio teaches Hatha yoga in a sweltering 40°C (104°F) heated room, the high temperature apparently protecting vulnerable muscles against injury. Feel the burn!

Manchester Buddhist Centre

16-20 Turner Street, M4 1DZ (834 9232, www.manchesterbuddhist centre.org.uk). Metrolink Shudehill, or City Centre buses, or Victoria rail. **Open** 10am-7pm Mon-Thur; 10am-5.30pm Fri; 10am-5pm Sat. **Map** p91 B1/B2 **52**

One of the most beautifully refurbished warehouses in the Northern Quarter houses two shrine halls (one is open throughout the day for drop-in meditation), a library (open to the public by arrangement) and a bookshop. The Bodywise centre offers everything from yoga to shiatsu massage, while the vegan Earth Café (p91) sates both body and mind.

Spa Satori

112 High Street, M4 1HQ (819 2465, www.spasatori.co.uk). Metrolink Market Street, or City Centre buses, or Piccadilly rail. **Open** 9am-8pm Mon-Fri; 9am-6pm Sat; 10am-5pm Sun. **Map** p91 B1 **53**

Satori (originally called the Inner Sanctuary Spa) is a small but perfectly formed day spa tucked away in the heart of the Northern Quarter. The range of treatments includes everything from hot stone massage to spray tans, and from Chinese acupuncture to the more usual facials, manicures and pedicures.

Chinatown

Piccadilly, Chinatown & Gay Village

Strolling down Canal Street can sometimes feel like walking on to the set of *Queer as Folk*, the late '90s TV show that propelled the area into the national consciousness. Bars, clubs and restaurants cluster around the canal, and sitting out on this traffic-free street to watch life's parade pass by is still a treat, even if the area feels a little overrun by visiting hen parties. The **Molly House** pub is a good place to start the night, while the large choice of clubs means you don't need to stop until sunrise. Canal Street is also the focal point of Manchester Pride – ten days of parades, picnics, sport, comedy, live music and partying that culminates in the Pride Parade.

Close by sits the civic centrepiece of **Piccadilly Gardens**, remodelled in 2002. Tadao Ando's concrete 'bunker' at its foot provides a barrier to the fuming buses beyond, making

for an open-air experience, although not a hugely pleasant one due to the hordes that hang out here, day and night. A fountain attracts kids (when it's working), while the bars and cafés are surprisingly good. Look out for Mexican **Barburrito** and all-British burger bar **Byron**.

A few minutes' walk away, the towering, multi-tiered **Imperial Chinese Arch** marks the start of Chinatown. Built in 1987 as a gift from the Chinese people, the arch was the first of its kind in Europe. Chinatown is lively all year round, but Chinese New Year is celebrated with particular vigour. Fireworks, food and an enormous dancing dragon top off the festivities, and institutions such as **Yang Sing** serve top-class Chinese food. The area has some excellent Asian eateries – notables include **Yuzu** (Japanese) and **Siam Smiles** (Thai).

Piccadilly Gardens

Sights & museums

Alan Turing Memorial

Sackville Park, Sackville Street, M1. Metrolink Piccadilly Gardens, or City Centre buses, or Piccadilly rail. **Map** p107 B2 ❶

Turing, a hero of the World War II Bletchley Park codebreakers, came to Manchester and helped to found one of the world's first computers (a copy of which can be seen at MOSI; p126). His story ended tragically – he committed suicide in 1954, two years after his arrest for a then-illegal homosexual relationship. His story is told in the film *The Imitation Game* (2014), starring ex-University of Manchester drama student, Benedict Cumberbatch. This statue, unveiled in 2001, sits at the heart of the city's gay village.

Imperial Chinese Arch

Faulkner Street, M1. Metrolink St Peter's Square, or City Centre buses, or Oxford Road rail. **Map** p107 A2 ❷

Manchester is home to one of Europe's largest Chinese communities, and this striking piece of architecture commemorating the fact – a gift to the city from the people of China – sits in the middle of a rather shabby square, surrounded on all sides by bustling human and vehicular traffic. A ten-minute walk away, the Centre for Chinese Contemporary Art (p90) provides a more serene appreciation of the nation's culture and art.

Mayfield Depot

Fairfield Street, M1. Metrolink Piccadilly, or City Centre buses, or Piccadilly rail. **Map** off p107 C3 ❸

The abandoned train station of Mayfield is mooted to become the new Warehouse Project nightclub. It's a fascinating historical monument to Manchester's railways; an entire 'ghost' station built in 1910 and situated a mere hop and a skip from the mainline station. Used as an overspill station until 1960, it was converted into a parcel depot for a spell in the 1970s, but has been largely deserted since 1986. Will it become a super-club? Perhaps. It was certainly an atmospheric location for Manchester International Festival performances by the likes of Massive Attack and Four Tet.

Piccadilly Gardens

Metrolink Piccadilly Gardens, or City Centre buses, or Piccadilly rail. **Map** p107 B1 ❹

Donated for public use more than two centuries ago, the land that is now Piccadilly Gardens first housed an infirmary, demolished in 1909. The present-day city council loosely interpreted the original intentions by selling off the Portland Street corner for commercial development in order to finance the 2002 overhaul of the rest of the gardens. The area now contains a walk-through fountain (mostly out of order), a thoughtful metal tree sculpture commemorating the World War II civilian dead and a controversial concrete wall courtesy of Japanese architect Tadao Ando.

Eating & drinking

BBQ Handmade Noodles King
45-47 Faulkner Street, M1 4FD (228 2882). Metrolink Piccadilly Gardens, or City Centre buses, or Piccadilly rail. **Open** varies. **££. Chinese. Map** p107 A2 ⑤

This back-to-basics Chinese restaurant is aptly named. Much loved by food bloggers, this is the place to enjoy authentic 'hand-pulled' noodles (the Tibetan braised beef is excellent) and a full-on barbecue experience.

Byron
1 Piccadilly Gardens, M1 1RG (237 3222, www.byronhamburgers.com). Metrolink Piccadilly Gardens, or City Centre buses, or Piccadilly rail. **Open** 11.30am-11pm Mon-Thur; 11.30am-11.30pm Fri; 11am-11.30pm Sat; 11am-10.30pm Sun. **£. Burgers. Map** p107 B1 ⑥

From humble beginnings in London in 2007, Byron has taken the hamburger world by storm and, at the time of writing, has nearly 60 branches across the UK. It must be something to do with its top-quality, no-messing burgers (using Scottish beef), and appealing diner-style interiors. There are also outposts in Deansgate and the Corn Exchange.

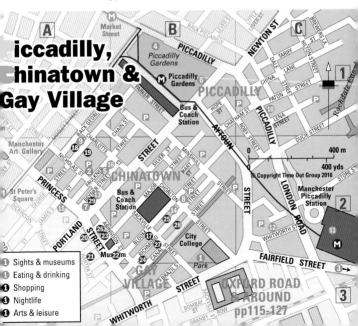

- ① Sights & museums
- ① Eating & drinking
- ① Shopping
- ① Nightlife
- ① Arts & leisure

Circus Tavern

*86 Portland Street, M1 4GX (no phone).
Metrolink St Peter's Square, or City
Centre buses, or Oxford Road rail.* **Open**
11am-11pm daily. **Pub. Map** p107 A2 ⑦
This listed boozer dates back to the
1790s, when it's said to have been the
hangout of choice for performers from
the city's then-permanent circus. One
of Tetley's heritage pubs, it's popular
with football fans – despite its diminutive size – and there's a good smattering
of United and City paraphernalia on
the walls. There's no food and no music,
but bags of atmosphere.

Habesha

*29-31 Sackville Street, M1 3LZ (228
7396, www.habesharestaurant.co.uk).
Metrolink Piccadilly Gardens, or City
Centre buses, or Piccadilly rail.* **Open**
3-11pm Mon-Fri; 1-11pm Sat; 2-11pm
Sun. **£-££. Ethiopian. Map** p107 B2 ⑧
Love sharing food? Make a beeline for
this Ethiopian canteen, which serves
sour, spongy bread (injera), dotted
with dollops of gently spiced meat and
vegetarian stews. Best enjoyed with a
cold African lager.

I Am Pho

*44 George Street, M1 4HF (236 1230,
www.facebook.com/iampho).* Metrolink
*Piccadilly Gardens, or City Centre buses,
or Piccadilly rail.* **Open** noon-11pm daily.
££. Vietnamese. Map p107 A2 ⑨
The raw beef pho here, served home-
style with the meat left to cook, slowly,
in steaming broth, is the real deal.
If you're looking for a cheap lunch,
the Vietnamese baguettes (bánh mì)
are ideal. Strip lighting and a cellar
location belie the popularity of this
Chinatown favourite.

Michael Caines
Restaurant at ABode

*107 Piccadilly, M1 2DB (247 7744,
www.abodehotels.co.uk).* Metrolink
*Piccadilly Gardens, or City Centre buses,
or Piccadilly rail.* **Open** noon-2.30pm,
6-10pm Tue-Thur; noon-2.30pm, 5-10pm
Fri, Sat. **££££. Modern European.
Map** p107 C1 ⑩

Yang Sing p111

This hotel restaurant is the spot to sample French haute cuisine overseen by Michelin star holder Michael Caines. Upmarket and locally sourced ingredients such as truffles and saddle of venison complement a stellar wine list. The basement location is the only downer.

Piccadilly Tap

Gateway House, Station Approach, M1 2GH (393 4168, www.piccadillytap.com). Metrolink Piccadilly, or City Centre buses, or Piccadilly rail. **Open** noon-varies daily. **£-££. Bar/café. Map** p107 C2 ⓫

Manchester's Piccadilly Station used to be a wasteland of chains. However, the opening of the Piccadilly Tap bar (together with coffee and lunch stop Idle Hands at no.8A, www.idlehands coffee.com), has changed things for the better. Pick up a craft beer from local stars such as Blackjack and Cloudwater or a 'train beer' to take away.

Pita Pit

3 Piccadilly Place, M1 3BN (0800 008 6490, www.pitapituk.com). Metrolink

Rainbow bright

LGBT festivals for all.

Manchester's LGBT calendar is in great shape. **Manchester Pride** (www.manchesterpride.com) is the biggie, taking place over the August Bank Holiday. The parade happens on the Saturday, after which the Village is walled off, with a wristband your only route inside. Discounted early-bird tickets are available, and a growing fringe programme means there's Pride off Canal Street too – even outlying boroughs Oldham and Bolton boast Pride events (in July and October, respectively).

To complement Pride, the **Queer Alt Manchester** collective (www.facebook.com/q.alt. manchester) hosts a plethora of alternative events, from boat parties to band nights, while in Salford, the **Peel Park Pink Picnic** (www.peelparkpinkpicnic. org.uk) is a free LGBT event in July with an emphasis on music, food and family. Also in July is **Sparkle** (www.sparkle.org.uk), the National Transgender Celebration in the Village.

Mid April welcomes **Manchester Rubber Weekend** (www.manchesterrubber.co.uk) for sexy, squeaky fun, while the end of April sees the **Great British Bear Bash** (www.man bears-manchester.co.uk). Art lovers have **Queer Contact** (www.contactmcr.com/projects/ festivals/queer-contact) every February to coincide with LGBT History Month, mixing local and international performances.

Warehouse Project

The pop-up superclub monopolises the city's after-hours scene.

If you ask anyone for Manchester's ultimate clubbing destination, the most likely answer is: the **Warehouse Project** (www.thewarehouseproject.com). WHP's phenomenal success has seen the pop-up clubbing concept move from the disused Boddingtons brewery near Strangeways prison, to a wartime air-raid shelter underneath Piccadilly Station, with various stops in between.

The party, which caters to more than 3,000 revellers a night, exists for only 12 weeks a year (September through December), culminating in an explosive New Year's Day finale. Tickets for the Friday and Saturday sessions (until around 5am) cost in the region of £30 and sell fast.

The sweaty caverns that the WHP typically employ are a far cry from the glitz and glamour of other clubs. The walls are sticky, the toilets are often Portaloos and there's little but elbow room in the smoking area. The underground, industrial feel evokes an unlicensed rave, but with a multitude of bars, sweaty dancers downing bottles of water Ibiza-style, an awesome sound and light show, and top DJs on the decks, the atmosphere is electric.

The WHP brand was launched by Sacha Lord-Marchionne and Sam Kandel, who graduated from Manchester's comparatively boutique nightclub Sankeys with a vision – which continues to grow. Interim projects have included the Masters at Work series, at Albert Hall, and festival offshoots (Kendal Calling, Park Life). Ever more famous names are involved, and the regulars are a who's who of the planet's most influential producers: Skrillex, Mark Ronson, Annie Mac and Four Tet – with a side helping of crossover acts such as Hot Chip, New Order and Public Enemy.

For an authentic taste of Manchester nightlife, Warehouse Project is, frankly, unmissable.

Piccadilly, or City Centre or Piccadilly rail.
Open 7am-6pm Mon-Fri. £. **Sandwich
bar**. **Map** p107 C2 ⑫

Enjoy healthy stuffed flatbreads at
this Canadian pitta chain. Plump
scrambled eggs, home-made falafel
and grilled chicken combine well
with flash-fried vegetables and spicy
sauce, served in a pizza-sized pitta. A
chilled vibe pervades, complete with
a mini 'vertical garden' and recycled
furnishings. There's another branch
on Deansgate.

Red Chilli

*70-72 Portland Street, M1 4GU (236
2888, www.redchillirestaurant.co.uk).
Metrolink St Peter's Square, or City
Centre buses, or Oxford Road rail.*
Open noon-11pm Mon-Thur, Sun;
noon-midnight Fri, Sat. ££. **Chinese**.
Map p107 A2 ⑬

Most Chinese restaurants focus on
Cantonese cooking, but Red Chilli dif-
ferentiates itself by offering dishes
from Sichuan and Beijing. As a result,
the menu may seem unfamiliar, listing
the likes of baked intestine with green
chilli or duck tongues with pickled
chilli, as well as an excellent deep-fried
sea bass. Both the presentation and flavours are impressive. There's a branch
opposite the University of Manchester
on Oxford Road.

Richmond Tea Rooms

*15 Richmond Street, M1 3HZ (237 9667,
www.richmondtearooms.com). Metrolink
Piccadilly Gardens, or City Centre buses,
or Piccadilly rail.* **Open** 11am-10pm Mon-
Thur; 11am-11pm Fri; 10am-11pm Sat;
10am-10pm Sun. ££. **Tearoom**. **Map**
p107 B2 ⑭

This LGBT-friendly tearoom and cocktail lounge has a self-confessed 'totally
OTT' Tim Burton-meets-*Alice in
Wonderland* theme. Lashings of velvet
and polished chandeliers are sights to
expect, alongside couples in recovery
from last night's antics. Traditional
teas feature cucumber sandwiches and
scones with cream.

Yang Sing

*34 Princess Street, M1 4JY (236 2200,
www.yang-sing.com). Metrolink St Peter's
Square, or City Centre buses, or Oxford
Road rail.* **Open** noon-11pm Mon-Thur;
noon-midnight Fri, Sat; noon-10.30pm
Sun. £££. **Chinese**. **Map** p107 A2 ⑮

Manchester's most glamorous Chinese
restaurant has enjoyed four decades of
colourful history. Through everything,
it's kept a consistency in the kitchen
that would shame many other restaurants. Don't bother with the menu: simply explain to your waiter what you like
and don't like, agree a price per head,
and a banquet will be devised for you.

Yuzu

*39 Faulkner Street, M1 4EE (236 4159,
www.yuzumanchester.co.uk). Metrolink
Piccadilly Gardens, or City Centre buses,
or Piccadilly rail.* **Open** noon-2pm, 5.30-
10pm, Tue-Sat. ££. **Japanese**. **Map**
p107 A2/B2 ⑯

Sashimi with sticky rice and miso,
agedashi tofu in fragrant broth and
perfectly formed gyoza are highlights
of this flawless Japanese experience.
Varnished wood and floral prints dec-
orate the intimate space, and service
isn't hasty – it's all about the art on
your plate. Visit at lunch and you'll pay
significantly less for the same dishes
served in the evening.

Shopping

Shopping opportunities in and
around Piccadilly are largely
limited to functional stores such
as Superdrug, M&S and Primark.
The area doesn't offer much in the
way of browsing, but there are a few
specialist stores worth seeking out.

Clone Zone

*36-38 Sackville Street, M1 3WA (236
1398, www.clonezonedirect.co.uk).
Metrolink Piccadilly Gardens, or City
Centre buses, or Piccadilly rail.* **Open**
11am-9pm Mon-Thur; 11am-10pm Fri,
Sat; noon-6pm Sun. **Map** p107 B2 ⑰

Cruz 101 p114

A Gay Village institution. CZ stocks a wide range of gay and lesbian publications – including obscure, arty and erotic magazines – and, most famously, rubber and fetish gear, and much-admired toys.

Siam Smiles Thai Supermarket & Café

48A George Street, M1 4HF (237 1555, www.facebook.com/siamsmilescafe). Metrolink Piccadilly Gardens, or City Centre buses, or Piccadilly rail. **Open** 9.30am-7.30pm Mon-Thur, Sun; 9.30am-9.30pm Fri, Sat. **Map** p107 A2 ⑱

Where better to stock up on *nam pla* (fish sauce) than this Thai supermarket, selling everything from home-made curry paste to tiny aubergines and fish balls? The café sells dishes to drive purists wild – try the banana leaf-wrapped black sticky rice pudding.

Woo Sang Chinese Supermarket

19-21 George Street, M1 4HE (236 4353, www.woosang.co.uk). Metrolink Piccadilly Gardens, or City Centre buses, or Piccadilly rail. **Open** 10.30am-7pm Mon-Fri, Sun; 10.30am-7.30pm Sat. **Map** p107 A2 ⑲

Air-dried meats, exotic vegetables, incense sticks and over 90 varieties of instant packet noodles are just some of the items available at this well-stocked Asian emporium. Fabulous packaging, fascinating ingredients.

Nightlife

Bangkok Bar

40-44 Princess Street, M1 6DD (714 0429, www.bangkokbar.co.uk). Metrolink Piccadilly Gardens, or City Centre buses, or Piccadilly rail. **Open** 5pm-late Tue-Sun. **Map** p107 A2 ⑳

This cosy, multi-faceted bar/club/Thai restaurant actively encourages good times – a bit like the much-missed queer venue Legends used to do. Look out for LGBT parties such as Club Lash and Bollox for a big night out on the tiles.

Charlie's K Bar

1 Harter Street, M1 6HY (237 9898). Metrolink Piccadilly Gardens, or City Centre buses, or Oxford Road rail. **Open** 10pm-4am Mon-Sat; 9pm-2am Sun. **Map** p107 B2 ㉑

Tatty but charming, Charlie's is a florid and ornate karaoke bar. If you've spent the day shopping for vintage garb in the Northern Quarter's quirky boutiques, this is the place in which to show off your purchases.

Club Alter Ego

105-107 Princess Street, M1 6DD (236 9266). Metrolink Piccadilly Gardens, or City Centre buses, or Oxford Road rail. **Open** 11.30pm-5am Tue, Sat; other days varies. **Map** p107 B2 ㉒

If the bland Gay Village soundscape of homogenised house turns your shimmy into a shudder, then take refuge at Club Alter Ego, home of always innovative indie shindig Poptastic. Its two weekly sessions (Tuesday and Saturday) are the venue's main draw, with a Friday-night party bringing urban sounds into the mix.

Sing it back

Karaoke has taken the Manchester mainstream by storm.

Canal Street isn't all that quiet at the best of times. However, the trend for karaoke nights in and around Chinatown and the Gay Village means that, even early in the week, there's always music (of sorts) in the air. You'll find amazingly supportive crowds at the various karaoke nights, just waiting to join in on the chorus. And, best of all, thanks to the proliferation of new venues, many offering a 'booth'-style experience, the shy and nervous can get involved too – after all, what are a few bum notes among friends?

Few places are able to better the **New Union Hotel** (111 Princess Street, M1 6JB, 228 1492, http://newunionhotel.com), one of the area's oldest gay pubs and inns, which serves up plenty of show tunes every Wednesday; while just up the road, in the heart of Chinatown, **Charlie's K Bar** (p112) dedicates almost every

night to amateur singalongs. **Orchid Lounge** (54 Portland Street, M1 4QU, 236 1388, www. siamorchidrestaurant.co.uk) is famously fun, if a little rough around the edges.

Karaoke is a mainstream affair these days, and one of the largest places to get involved is **K2** in Chinatown (52-56 George Street, M1 4HF, 238 8700, www.k2 karaoke.com). Despite mixed reviews, this collection of club spaces and private booths is a truly shiny place in which to sing your heart out with your friends – imagine being inside a giant chandelier and you get some idea of the level of sparkle involved.

Across the city centre, **Tiger Tiger** (p85) in the Printworks entertainment complex is probably the slickest experience on offer, thanks to its resident Lucky Voice pods. Booking is recommended – and, remember, no hogging that mic.

Cruz 101

101 Princess Street, M1 6DD (950 0101, www.cruz101.com). Metrolink Piccadilly Gardens, or City Centre buses, or Oxford Road rail. **Open** 11pm-5am Mon, Thur, Sun; midnight-5am Wed; 11pm-6am Fri, Sat. **Map** p107 A2 ㉓

Really two clubs in one, with a large main room and a smaller lower-level space, Cruz is Manchester's oldest gay club – but the (mostly) bright young things on its dancefloors keep its appeal fresh. The playlist includes funky house, pop, trance and R&B. Fun abounds, with such ruses as Rihanna masks distributed for free on the door, and Cha Cha Boudoir's alt-drag spectacular on the last Friday of the month. Thursday sees indie night Poptastic running the show.

G-A-Y

63 Richmond Street, M1 3WB (228 6200, www.g-a-y.co.uk). Metrolink Piccadilly Gardens, or City Centre buses, or Piccadilly rail. **Open** noon-4am daily. **Bar. Map** p107 B2 ㉔

Sister bar to the famous London club of the same name, this friendly spot has all the fun you've been seeking – and then some. Expect loads of drinks promotions and an upfront soundtrack.

Molly House

26 Richmond Street, M1 3NB (237 9329, www.themollyhouse.com). Metrolink Piccadilly Gardens, or City Centre buses, or Piccadilly rail. **Open** noon-midnight Mon, Tue; noon-1am Wed, Thur, Sun; noon-2am Fri, Sat. **Map** p107 B2 ㉕

Unlike the flashy bars that dominate the Village, this is a beautifully converted townhouse pub, with hearths, armchairs and an elevated smoking terrace complete with a garden swing. They serve craft beers, excellent G&Ts and Spanish/Latin American tapas.

Satan's Hollow

101 Princess Street, M1 6DD (236 0666, www.facebook.com/satanshollow manchester). Metrolink Piccadilly Gardens, or City Centre buses, or Oxford Road rail. **Open** 10pm-3am Tue, Fri; 10pm-4am Sat. **Map** p107 A2 ㉖

Gothic decor and rock music define this theatrical venue. However, despite its devilish architecture, fearsome lighting and, at times, oddly styled bar staff, this is one venue that never takes itself too seriously. Note that the entrance is tucked away on Silver Street.

Vanilla

39-41 Richmond Street, M1 3WB (228 2727, www.vanillagirls.co.uk). Metrolink Piccadilly Gardens, or City Centre buses, or Piccadilly rail. **Open** 7pm-late Tue-Thur; 4pm-4am Fri, Sat; 7pm-1am Sun. **Map** p107 B2 ㉗

The only bar around Canal Street with a female focus, and one of the most famous in the country. DJ nights through the week offer everything from pop to indie rock and funky house. In possession of a Y chromosome? Take a female chaperone or you won't get in.

Via

28-30 Canal Street, M1 3EZ (236 6523, www.viamanchester.co.uk). Metrolink Piccadilly Gardens, or City Centre buses, or Piccadilly rail. **Open** noon-1am Mon-Thur; noon-3am Fri, Sat; noon-1am Sun. **Map** p107 B2 ㉘

Resembling an Escher drawing, this labyrinthine venue has DJs playing party anthems at weekends, while Monday and Tuesday are karaoke nights. Simple meals are served.

Arts & leisure

Colin Jellicoe Gallery

82 Portland Street, M1 4QX (236 2716, www.colinjellicoe.co.uk). Metrolink St Peter's Square, or City Centre buses, or Oxford Road rail. **Open** noon-5pm Tue-Fri; 1-5pm Sat. **Map** p107 A2 ㉙

In business for over 40 years, this commercial art gallery is still run by Mancunian proprietor Colin Jellicoe. Primarily showcasing his own work, the gallery also puts on decent group shows.

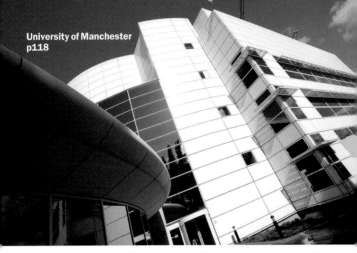

University of Manchester
p118

Oxford Road & Around

Infamous for its thundering traffic, Oxford Road nevertheless packs in so many galleries, museums and theatres that locals have christened it Manchester's 'cultural corridor'. It's also home to two universities – the **University of Manchester** and **Manchester Metropolitan** – whose 71,000 students inevitably lend a raucous flavour to the area.

At its northern end sits St Peter's Square, and **HOME**, the city's key centre for arthouse film, theatre and contemporary art; while at the other, at the start of the Curry Mile, sits historic Whitworth Park, home to the acclaimed **Whitworth Art Gallery**. Following a stunning transformation, the gallery showcases contemporary and historic art, textiles and wallpapers. It also has a fabulous, purpose-built glass café among the trees.

In between the city centre and the Whitworth Art Gallery, you'll find theatres, the **Manchester Museum**, the University of Manchester's collegiate campus (a quadrangle of Gothic buildings designed by Alfred Waterhouse – check out the atmospheric Christie Bistro), edgy music venues such as the **Deaf Institute**, **Gorilla** and **Sound Control**, and various budget eating options such as **Umami** and **Kukoos**.

Halfway along Oxford Road, **Grosvenor Park** occupies the site of a former church. In summer, this grassy retreat is dotted with sun-loving students.

Rumours of possible large-scale redevelopment may yet solve Oxford Road's traffic problems; until then, don't let the honking and spluttering jams put you off exploring this fascinating area.

Sights & museums

Manchester Museum
University of Manchester, Oxford Road, M13 9PL (275 2634, www.manchester. ac.uk/museum). Metrolink St Peter's

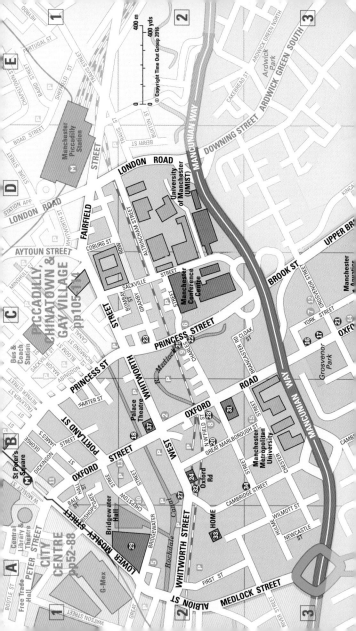

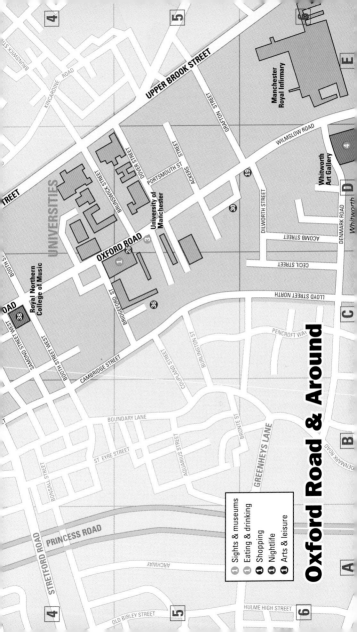

Square, or University buses, or Oxford Road rail. **Open** 10am-5pm daily. **Admission** free. **Map** p117 C5 ❶

Once a rather dusty example of a museum in the old-school mould, this building (designed in 1890 by Alfred Waterhouse, the architect of London's Natural History Museum) received a refit in 2003, allowing much-needed daylight to reach its murky corners – although its corridor layout would still confound a tomb raider. Persevere, though, for highlights that include a notable collection of Egyptian mummies, a vivarium offering refuge to critically endangered frogs and reptiles, and a full-size replica of a Tyrannosaurus skeleton (named Stan), posed in full hunting mode.

Refuge Assurance Building

Oxford Street, M60 7HA. Metrolink St Peter's Square, or City Centre buses, or Oxford Road rail. **Map** p116 B2 ❷

Also designed by Alfred Waterhouse, for the Refuge Assurance Company, this Grade II-listed building is a landmark in Manchester, thanks to its distinctive red brickwork and 217ft clock tower. It was converted to a hotel in the mid 1990s and now houses the recently renovated Palace Hotel (p178).

University of Manchester

Visitor Centre: Oxford Road, M13 9PL (306 6000, www.manchester. ac.uk). Metrolink St Peter's Square, or University buses, or Oxford Road rail. **Map** p117 D4 ❸

This sprawling academic complex is one of the country's largest educational establishments. Within the handsome collection of red-brick buildings and theatre venues (Martin Harris Centre, John Thaw Studio Theatre), performance history has been made; the golden generation of British alternative comedy (Ben Elton, Rik Mayall, Ade Edmondson) studied here, as did Benedict Cumberbatch and former BBC head of drama Ben Stephenson.

Even more impressive are the university's scientific successes. Ernest Rutherford's research led to the splitting of the atom, while 'the Baby', one of the world's first computers, was built here in 1948. Russian-born researchers Andre Geim and Kostya Novoselov won the Nobel Prize for physics for their discovery of graphene – the world's first 2D material – at the university in 2010. This led to the foundation of the £61-million National Graphene Institute with its state-of-the-art 'clean rooms' for research.

Whitworth Art Gallery

Oxford Road, M15 6ER (275 7450, www.whitworth.manchester.ac.uk). Metrolink St Peter's Square, or University buses, or Oxford Road rail. **Open** 10am-5pm Mon-Wed, Fri-Sun; 10am-9pm Thur. **Admission** free. **Map** p117 D6 ❹

Founded in 1889, the Whitworth Art Gallery reopened in 2015 after a major £15-million renovation. The Victorian frontage remains, while the rear of the building now reaches deep into Whitworth Park, with two new extensions (one redbrick, one glass and steel) that have doubled the size of the gallery. The reflective copper surfaces and tiled floors are as alluring as the collections; there's also a spectacular, light-filled new café. Historic watercolours, textiles and wallpapers by the likes of William Blake are displayed alongside the world's most exciting contemporary artists (Marina Abramovich, Cornelia Parker), all under the guiding hand of director Maria Balshaw.

Eating & drinking

Briton's Protection

50 Great Bridgewater Street, M1 5LE (236 5895, www.britons-protection.com). Metrolink Deansgate-Castlefield, or City Centre buses, or Deansgate rail. **Open** noon-midnight Mon-Thur; noon-1am Fri, Sat; noon-11.30pm Sun. **Pub**. **Map** p116 A2 ❺

Like moths to a flame, drinkers are drawn to the Briton's Protection by the red neon sign above the door. The roomy interior is pub perfection: brass fixtures and fittings, and paintings commemorating the 1819 Peterloo Massacre. (See if you can spot the two football managers who feature in the paintings.) At lunchtime, punters are mostly businesspeople; later on, Bridgewater Hall concertgoers come for a pre-show quickie. Brews from Thwaites and Robinsons are staples, but the real attractions are the 150-plus whiskies and bourbons.

EastZEast

Ibis Hotel, Princess Street, M1 7DG (244 5353, www.eastzeast.com). Metrolink St Peter's Square, or City Centre buses, or Oxford Road rail. **Open** 5-11.30pm Mon-Thur; 5pm-midnight Fri, Sat; 5-11pm Sun. **££. Indian. Map** off p116 C2 ❻

Although you might be tempted by the Curry Mile's bright lights, be warned: it's hard to find good food amid the gaudiness. Punjabi specialist EastZEast, however, is an altogether classier proposition. The family behind this hotel restaurant worked in Bradford for over 50 years, and that experience shows in the superb service, delicious karahi dishes and gargantuan naan breads. There are other branches in Whitefield (North Manchester) and Blackfriars Street in the City Centre.

Eat Goody

1 Hillcourt Street, M1 7HU (274 3000, www.eatgoody.co.uk). Metrolink St Peter's Square, or University buses, or Oxford Road rail. **Open** 11am-4pm Mon-Fri. **£. Korean. Map** p116 C3 ❼

The queue for Goody's kimchi bibimbap snakes out the door as students seek out tasty, healthy bowlfuls from this Asian hotspot. Enjoy an authentic Korean lunch a stone's throw from the Manchester Metropolitan University campus in a simple canteen setting. They don't bother with signage; just follow the crowd.

Font

7-9 New Wakefield Street, M1 5NP (236 0944, www.thefontbar.wordpress.com). Metrolink Deansgate-Castlefield, or City Centre buses, or Oxford Road rail. **Open** 11am-1am Mon-Sat; 11am-12.30am Sun. **Bar. Map** p116 B2 ❽

Another outlet of the excellent mini chain of bars, serving more than 100 craft beers.

Lass O'Gowrie

36 Charles Street, M1 7DB (273 5822). Metrolink St Peter's Square, or City Centre buses, or Oxford Road rail. **Open** 4.30-11pm Mon, Tue; noon-midnight Wed-Sat; noon-11pm Sun. **£. Gastropub. Map** p116 C2 ❾

The Lass is a Manchester institution; its stated aim has been to create the perfect village inn. The simple food ably assists that aim with brilliant own-made pies and artisanal sausages. There are six ales on tap, which sometimes make an appearance on the food menu too, as in the steak and Black Sheep Ale pie.

Peveril of the Peak

127 Great Bridgewater Street, M1 5JQ (236 6364). Metrolink Deansgate-Castlefield, or City Centre buses, or Deansgate rail. **Open** noon-11pm Mon-Thur; noon-midnight Fri, Sat; noon-10.30pm Sun. **Pub. Map** p116 B2 ❿

This Grade II-listed building, which was named after a stagecoach that was renowned for the speed at which it made its trips from Derbyshire, is arguably Manchester's most distinctive pub. Once you're past the green-tiled exterior, you'll find all sorts of people inside, at all times – though it gets particularly packed on Fridays and Saturdays, and Man United fans are in abundance on match days. The pub is also said to have its own ghost. The brews vary, but favourites include ales from Ossett, Black Sheep and Copper Dragon. There's a pool table in the cramped back room, and darts and table-football in the front.

MANCHESTER BY AREA

San Carlo Fumo

*1 St Peter's Square, Oxford Road, M1 5AN
(236 7344, www.sancarlofumo.co.uk).
Metrolink St Peter's Square, or City
Centre buses, or Oxford Road rail.* **Open**
noon-11pm Mon-Thur, Sun; noon-1am
Fri, Sat. **£££. Italian. Map** p116 B1 ⑪
Adored by Manchester United players
and visiting celebs such as Rihanna,
the San Carlo restaurant chain, owned
by the Distefano family, is a supremely
glamorous UK-wide operation. For
the move into the cocktail market
with Fumo, they brought in expert
mixologist Jamie Jones. House-infused
vermouths (endorsed by Martini
itself), a negroni made with Fernet-
Branca, and sumptuous lavender
vodka served with a fragranced pur-
ple ribbon wrapped around the stem,
are highlights. Food is inspired by
Venetian small plates. Other outlets in
Manchester include San Carlo and San
Carlo Cicchetti (for both, p70), both in
the city centre.

Sandbar

*120 Grosvenor Street, M1 7HL (273
1552, www.sandbarmanchester.co.uk).
Metrolink St Peter's Square, or Oxford
Road buses, or Oxford Road rail.* **Open**
noon-midnight Mon-Wed, Sun; noon-
1am Thur; noon-2am Fri, Sat. **Bar.
Map** p116 C3 ⑫
Sandbar could be the smallest labyrinthine bar in the city – just when you
think you've found your preferred spot,
you'll find more pews in another section. The elongated bar counter offers
an astounding selection of cask ales
and imported lagers, including a range
of Belgian delights. There are pizzas
and other Italian-slanted fare to eat,
while the entertainment is broad, span-
ning poetry readings to art exhibitions,
live music to free comedy.

Temple

*100 Great Bridgewater Street, M1 5JW
(278 1610). Metrolink St Peter's Square,
or City Centre buses, or Oxford Road
rail.* **Open** noon-midnight Mon-Thur;

noon-1am Fri, Sat; noon-11pm Sun.
Bar. Map p116 B2 ⑬
As you'll realise as soon as you see it,
this subterranean venue (full name:
the Temple of Convenience) was once
a public lavatory. Now it's one of
Manchester's most alternative and dec-
adent (albeit cramped) boozers. Home
to one of the finest jukeboxes in town
and occasional haunt of local rock roy-
alty (in the form of Elbow frontman
Guy Garvey), it's the place to head if
you prefer your beer to be strong, continental and bottled. See also sister bar
Big Hands (p122).

Umami

*147-153 Oxford Road, M1 7EE (273
2300, www.umami.cc). Metrolink St
Peter's Square, or University buses, or
Oxford Road rail.* **Open** noon-11pm Mon-
Sat; noon-10pm Sun. **££. Japanese.
Map** p116 C3 ⑭
This aptly named noodle and sushi
bar serves a set lunch for less than £5,
which may feature soup noodles, rice,
curry, and/or gyoza and salad. Other
bargains include sushi, ramen, spicy
rendang, and salt and pepper tofu. The
only drawback is the cellar location.
Wooden banqueting tables and a good
range of Asian lagers save the day.

Zouk Tea Bar & Grill/
Kukoos

*The Quadrangle, M1 5QS (233 1090,
www.zoukteabar.co.uk). Metrolink St
Peter's Square, or City Centre buses, or
Oxford Road rail.* **Open** noon-midnight
daily. **££. Pakistani. Map** p116 B3 ⑮
Zouk cost a cool million to fit out, and
it shows – inside, it's all luxurious
seating and glittering chandeliers. But
it's the open-plan kitchen that forms
the restaurant's centrepiece, neatly
illustrating that great cooking is at the
heart of the Zouk experience. Try the
delicately spiced king prawn karahi.
The restaurant has an upmarket takeaway, Kukoos, around the corner on
Oxford Road, where bestsellers include
falafel wraps and mango lassis.

Shopping

Studenty Oxford Road offers many charms (including the **8th Day** vegan megastore), but visitors should also be sure to head south on one of the 40-odd bus routes to Rusholme and the Curry Mile, where the numerous eateries are punctuated by Asian stores selling exotic groceries, saris, books, music and gold jewellery.

8th Day

111 Oxford Road, M1 7DU (273 4878, www.8thday.coop). Metrolink St Peter's Square, or City Centre buses, or Oxford Road rail. **Open** *9am-7pm Mon-Fri; 10am-5pm Sat.* **Map** *p116 C3* **16**
Vegans and vegetarians congregate at this Oxford Road lifestyle store, which sells all manner of 'free from' foods, organic vegetables, freshly baked breads and hundreds of takes on houmous and tofu. The deli counter offers hunky chocolate flapjacks and burritos; natural cosmetics made

by companies such as Dr Hauschka and Weleda are another draw. The simple café in the basement is a calming place for a restorative salad with tahini dressing, or stew of the day. Be prepared to pay for soothing your conscience, though.

Johnny Roadhouse

123 Oxford Road, M1 7DU (273 1111, www.johnnyroadhouse.co.uk). Metrolink St Peter's Square, or University buses, or Oxford Road rail. **Open** *9.30am-5.30pm Mon-Sat.* **Map** *p116 C3* **17**
Trading from the same premises for more than 50 years, Johnny Roadhouse is a rite of passage for every Manc musician and wannabe. Johnny himself passed away in 2009, with tributes from many famous patrons flooding in, but his much-loved music superstore lives on, offering three floors of brass, string and percussion instruments and effects. The Smiths were regulars here, and the shop also featured in the LS Lowry-style video for Oasis's 'The Masterplan'.

Black Dog NWS p122

Venus

St James' Building, 95 Oxford Street,
M1 6ET (228 7000, www.venusin
manchester.co.uk). Metrolink St Peter's
Square, or City Centre buses, or Oxford
Road rail. **Open** 8am-6pm Mon-Fri;
9am-4pm Sat. **Map** p116 B2 ⓲

One of the first designer flower shops in
the city, Venus continues its modern floral revolution. Don't expect to find any
feeble carnations or daffs here: instead,
there are lush, verdant bursts of tropical colour; spiky, graphic shapes; and
imaginative arrangements.

Nightlife

Big Hands

296 Oxford Road, M13 9NS (272
7309). Metrolink St Peter's Square, or
University buses, or Oxford Road rail.
Open 10am-2am Mon-Fri; noon-3am
Sat; 6pm-1am Sun. **Map** p117 D6 ⓳

The musical smarts of Big Hands'
defiantly independent crowd – com-
pounded by regular after-gig visits
from touring musicians – have made
this bar an essential indie hangout. Stop
off here for a pre-Academy pint, and
warm your ears up with an eclectic variety of tunes. The music policy ranges
from reggae to rock and Northern soul.
Several smoking terraces, including a
large one upstairs, offer the chance for
a breath of fresh air.

Black Dog NWS/Xolo

11-13 New Wakefield Street, M1 5NP
(236 4899, www.blackdogballroom.
co.uk). Metrolink St Peter's Square, or
City Centre buses, or Oxford Road rail.
Open *Black Dog* noon-4am daily. *Xolo*
11pm-4am Fri, Sat. **Map** p116 B2 ⓴

These two bars from the city's Black
Dog crew (see p101 for their original bar
in the Northern Quarter) dish up late-
night fun. Day of the Dead-themed Xolo
is all about club sounds, hosting DJs
and indie acts at weekends, whereas
Black Dog NWS is a straight-up late
bar, with pool tables and drinks deals.
Both are popular with students.

Deaf Institute

135 Grosvenor Street, M1 7HE (276
9350, www.thedeafinstitute.co.uk).
Metrolink St Peter's Square, or
University buses, or Oxford Road rail.
Open 4pm-3am daily. **Map** p116 C3 ㉑

The Deaf Institute is part of the Trof
empire, which includes Gorilla (p123)
and the Albert Hall (p81). The Grade
II-listed building (built as, yes, an institute for deaf and dumb people in 1878)
has been converted into a cavernous
café-bar and music hall, with original
lecture-hall seating dating from the
early 1900s. Weekend club nights take
in everything from 1990s hits to gang-
sta rap, while the live venue is the city's
finest for new indie sounds.

FAC251: The Factory

112 118 Princess Street, M1 7EN (272
7251, www.factorymanchester.com).
Metrolink St Peter's Square, or City
Centre buses, or Oxford Road rail.
Open varies. **Map** p116 C2 ㉒

FAC251 opened a few years back in
the former head office of Factory
Communications, which has been
credited with the birth of that whole
'Madchester' thing. Co-owned by Peter
Hook of New Order and in a building
proclaimed to be both the labour of love
and bête noir of 'Mr Manchester', Tony
Wilson, the club is steeped in die-hard
Factory folklore. However, far from
being a rehashing of Factory-branded
offerings, FAC251's musical menu is
refreshingly varied. Three floors rever-
berate with Motown, tropical, hip hop,
indie, experimental, disco and more –
see the website for weekly listings.

Fifth

121 Princess Street, M1 7AG (236
2754, www.fifthmanchester.com).
Metrolink St Peter's Square, or City
Centre buses, or Oxford Road rail. **Open**
11pm-3am Mon; 10.30pm-3am Wed,
Fri; 10.30pm-3.30am Thur; 10pm-3am
Sat. **Map** p116 C2 ㉓

This popular, student-friendly club
offers the usual raft of cheap drinks,

Gorilla

and draws dancers to the floor with its revamped sound and light systems. Indie tunes make up the soundtrack most nights of the week.

Gorilla

54-56 Whitworth Street West, M1 5WW (407 0301, www.thisisgorilla. com). Metrolink St Peter's Square, or City Centre buses, or Oxford Road rail. **Open** 11.30am-midnight Mon-Fri; 9am-midnight Sat, Sun. Opening times extended on event nights. **Map** p116 B2 **24**
Gorilla is probably Manchester's coolest live venue, restaurant and bar. Housed in a railway arch, it's been tastefully decked out in reclaimed speakers and old school-gym flooring by the team behind the Deaf Institute (p122) and the Albert Hall (p81). The club space is less refined than the main bar, but does its job just fine with DJs such as Jon Hopkins, Mike Skinner and DJ Harvey, and the occasional live show. A mezzanine overlooking the dancefloor has nooks and crannies to chill out in, while cocktails are a draw in the gin bar. Food includes a top-rate roast dinner. In short, it ticks all the right boxes.

Joshua Brooks

106 Princess Street, M1 6NG (273 7336, www.joshuabrooks.co.uk). Metrolink St Peter's Square, or City Centre buses, or Oxford Road rail. **Open** 11am-3am Mon-Wed; 11am-4am Thur, Fri; noon-4am Sat; noon-3am Sun. **Map** p116 C2 **25**
This low-key student hangout manages to keep everyone happy, with match screenings, a lively early-evening drinking atmosphere, and a basement space after dark for clubbers. Independently promoted events rotate monthly. It's one of the city's best options for progressive electronic music, alongside Gorilla (left) and Soup Kitchen (p94).

Manchester Academy 1/2/3 & Club Academy

University of Manchester Students' Union, Oxford Road, M13 9PR (275 2930, www.manchesteracademy. net). Metrolink St Peter's Square, or University buses, or Oxford Road rail. **Open** varies. **Map** p117 D5 **26**

Four spaces on the university campus accommodate acts across all genres, from unsigned to well established. The Academy includes Club Academy, home to a range of student-oriented evenings. However, several more atmospheric venues have opened in recent years (Deaf Institute, Albert Hall, the Ritz), and the Academy's live-music stronghold has suffered as a result.

Ritz

100 Whitworth Street West, M1 5NQ (236 3234, www.theritzmanchester.com). Metrolink St Peter's Square, or City Centre buses, or Oxford Road rail. **Open** varies. **Map** p116 B2 ❷

This ex-ballroom's sprung dancefloor has been graced by generations of Mancunians who have revelled until the early hours under ornate coving dating from 1928. Saturday serves up a big, Euro-dance disco. Even better are the gigs, by acts such as Everything Everything and Elbow, which show off the club's unique atmosphere.

Sound Control

1 New Wakefield Street, M1 5NP (236 0340, www.soundcontrolmanchester.co.uk). Metrolink St Peter's Square, or City Centre buses, or Oxford Road rail. **Open** varies. **Map** p116 B2 ❷

Steeped in pop history, this live venue and club lies in the heart of student territory. Head here for new producers and indie bands on the rise. Today, the interior is all exposed pipes and ducts, but in 1984 it was a musical instrument shop where Alan 'Reni' Wren read an advertisement that lead to the formation of one of Manchester's finest bands, the Stone Roses.

Arts & leisure

Bridgewater Hall

Lower Mosley Street, M2 3WS (907 9000, www.bridgewater-hall.co.uk). Metrolink Deansgate-Castlefield, or City Centre buses, or Deansgate rail. **Map** p116 A2 ❷

HOME

With such impressive musical accoutrements as a 5,500-pipe organ, and a menu of 300-plus events every year, there's no better place to tune into classical, jazz, pop and world music. The concert hall is also the performing home of the Hallé and the BBC Philharmonic orchestras.

Contact Theatre

Devas Street, off Oxford Road, M15 6JA (274 0600, www.contactmcr.com). Rusholme buses, or Oxford Road rail. **Map** p117 D5 ③⓪

With its castles-in-the-air façade, artistic director Matt Fenton at the helm and regular showcases of new theatre, spoken word, dance and music events, Contact has the advantage when it comes to attracting a younger crowd.

Dancehouse

10 Oxford Road, M1 5QA (237 9753, www.thedancehouse.co.uk). Metrolink St Peter's Square, or City Centre buses, or Oxford Road rail. **Map** p116 B2 ③①

Although best known for its comedy nights, this art deco former cinema puts on dance, drama and music gigs, and is also the home of the Northern Ballet School.

Dog Bowl

Whitworth Street West, M1 5WW (228 2888, www.blackdogballroom.co.uk). Metrolink St Peter's Square, or City Centre buses, or Oxford Road rail. **Open** noon-1am Mon-Thur, Sun; noon-3am Fri, Sat. **Map** p116 B2 ③②

Owned by the team behind late-night bars such as Black Dog Ballroom (p101), Dog Bowl is a back-to-basics bowling alley that serves great burgers. Additional treats include free bowling for kids on Mondays, £5 lunch deals and a weekday happy hour from 4pm. Good for no-frills fun.

HOME

2 Tony Wilson Place, First Street, M15 4FN (200 1500, www.homemcr.org). Metrolink St Peter's Square, or City Centre buses, or Oxford Road rail. **Open** *Building* 10am-11pm Mon-Sat; 11am-11pm Sun. **Map** p116 A2 ③③

Manchester's newest cultural hub opened in 2015. Combining the old Cornerhouse art galleries, cinemas and café, and the former Library Theatre Company, this purpose-built centre forms part of a new public plaza that incorporates green spaces and picnic areas, and the four-star Innside by Melia hotel (p180). The two theatres present newly commissioned work, while five cinema screens focus on new, European and/or independent releases, and the art galleries present the best in contemporary art. You're sure to find something of interest.

International Anthony Burgess Foundation

Chorlton Mill, Cambridge Street, M1 5BY (235 0776, www.anthonyburgess. org). Metrolink Deansgate-Castlefield, or City Centre buses, or Oxford Road rail. **Open** *Café* 10am-3pm Mon-Fri. **Map** p116 B3 ③④

The Foundation opened in 2010 as a repository for a vast collection of Burgess ephemera, from the author's musical instruments and typewriters to his manuscripts and library. The city's most famous author is perhaps also its most infamous – a love-hate relationship evident on both sides. 'As a piece of civic planning, or rather unplanning, I think it's terrible,' he once said of Manchester – and yet Burgess remained proud of his northern roots. The Foundation also hosts regular cultural events, and has a decent café.

Manchester Aquatics Centre

2 Booth Street East, M13 9SS (275 9450, www.better.org.uk). Oxford Road buses, or Oxford Road rail. **Open** 6.30am-10pm Mon-Fri; 7am-6pm Sat; 7am-10pm Sun. **Map** p116 C3 ③⑤

Built to host the 2002 Commonwealth Games, and central Manchester's only public swimming pool, the Manchester

Aquatics Centre is home to two 50m pools, as well as fitness studios.

Martin Harris Centre for Music & Drama

University of Manchester, Bridgeford Street, M13 9PL (275 8951, www.martinharriscentre.manchester.ac.uk). Oxford Road buses, or Oxford Road rail. **Map** p117 C5 ③⑥

This venue quietly hosts some of the city's best literary events. Its concert hall is home to the Quatuor Danel string quartet (look out for free lunchtime concerts), while the John Thaw Studio Theatre holds a reading series that has featured such luminaries as Will Self, John Banville and Jeanette Winterson.

Palace Theatre

Oxford Street, M1 6FT (0844 871 7615, www.atgtickets.com). Metrolink St Peter's Square, or City Centre buses, or Oxford Road rail. **Map** p116 B2 ③⑦

Massive musical productions, big-name comedians and celebrity-stuffed Christmas pantos regularly play to a packed house here. The theatre also stages dance productions by the English National Ballet, among others, as well as new works such as *wonder.land* as part of the Manchester International Festival.

Royal Northern College of Music

124 Oxford Road, M13 9RD (907 5200, www.rncm.ac.uk). Metrolink St Peter's Square, or Oxford Road buses, or Oxford Road rail. **Map** p117 C4 ③⑧

One of the UK's leading conservatoires, the RNCM balances a fierce reputation for teaching against an internationally acclaimed performance programme. If mention of student musicians conjures up images of amateurs, think again. Only the very gifted study here. It also pulls in international players for its annual celebrations of brass, the Manchester Jazz Festival, and progressive-culture showcase Future Everything.

Manchester Aquatics Centre p125

Literary lifestyles

The written word plays a big role on the city's cultural scene.

Hassan Blasim

Where once Manchester was known solely for its music (and, perhaps, its football), the city has in recent years forged a reputation in the wider cultural arena. And while the big-name performances of the **Manchester International Festival** (p35) tend to dominate the headlines, the city today is as much a hotbed of literary activity as it is of artistic endeavour.

The **Manchester Literature Festival** (p36) features literary luminaries – enticing the likes of Margaret Atwood to the city for a rare public appearance – often in atmospheric places such as Manchester Cathedral. It also supports publishers such as Manchester's Comma Press,

whose authors include David Constantine and Hassan Blasim, whose book *The Iraqi Christ* won the Independent Foreign Fiction prize in 2014.

The presence in the city of two international writing schools supports the scene: alumni of the University of Manchester's Centre for New Writing (led by Martin Amis, Colm Tóibín and, most recently, Jeanette Winterson) include Betty Trask Award-winner Jenn Ashworth.

Manchester Metropolitan University's Writing School is buoyed by its creative director and Poet Laureate, Carol Ann Duffy, who also hosts a number of public events. Graduates include Emma Jane Unsworth. The school also runs the annual £10,000 Manchester Writing Competition with fiction and poetry strands, as well as the Manchester Children's Book Festival every summer.

Theatre plays its part as well, thanks to the Bruntwood Prize for Playwriting, Britain's largest such contest, which gives writers the chance to see their work performed at the Royal Exchange Theatre. Previous winners include Alistair McDowall, whose work has since been performed at London's Royal Court and National theatres. Meanwhile, **Contact Theatre** (p125) hosts the city's most dynamic spoken-word events, although offbeat venues such as **Gullivers** (www.facebook.com/GulliversNQ), the **Castle Hotel** (p90) and the **Briton's Protection** (p118) also stage edgy reading and open-mic nights.

Deansgate Locks

Castlefield & Deansgate Locks

MANCHESTER BY AREA

With its atmospheric railway arches, cleaned-up canals and seemingly endless supply of tiered locks and cobblestones, Castlefield remains one of the city's best outdoor spots. Even the nearby 47-storey **Beetham Tower** doesn't detract from the 150-year-old (and some) industrial architecture. Though it can be quiet on weekdays, Castlefield offers something that the rest of the city is often missing: peace and tranquillity.

Overlooked by a vast Victorian viaduct, the main attraction in the neighbourhood is the sprawling **MOSI (Museum of Science & Industry)**. Nearby are the remains of a Roman fort (Mamucium) and gardens, and the outdoor Castlefield Arena, which has played host to everything from Björk (during the Manchester International Festival) to the world's largest salad bowl. For many, the highlight is simply sitting outside **Dukes 92** pub, tucking into man-size slabs of cheese and bread. Frequent outdoor events, from screenings of football matches to music festivals, bring Castlefield to life during the summer.

Closer to the centre of town, Deansgate Locks has a series of bars frequented by the tanned and brash, as well as the excellent **Comedy Store** – each venue tucked inside a railway arch and facing on to the canal. Just behind the red-brick entrance to Deansgate station is one of the city's better contemporary art spaces, **Castlefield Gallery**.

Sights & museums

Beetham Tower

301-303 Deansgate, M3 4LQ. Metrolink Deansgate-Castlefield, or City Centre buses, or Deansgate rail. **Map** p129 C2 ❶
Beetham Tower's fame rests chiefly on its height – the 47-storey tower soars

561ft (171m), making it by far the tallest building in the city, and, at the time it opened in 2006, the tallest in the UK outside London. Split as it is between residential apartments (the Olympian penthouse is occupied by the building's architect, Ian Simpson), offices and the Hilton hotel (p176), there's little here for the casual tourist except the pricey Cloud 23 (p130) – a 'sky bar' with outstanding views across the city and the surrounding countryside.

Castlefield Gallery

2 Hewitt Street, M15 4GB (832 8034, www.castlefieldgallery.co.uk). Metrolink Deansgate-Castlefield, or City Centre buses, or Deansgate rail. **Open** 1-6pm Wed-Sun. **Admission** free. **Map** p129 C2 ❷

An artist-run gallery specialising in the conceptual end of the creative scale, Castlefield showcases emerging practitioners and new media. Note that the twin-level building's location is somewhat hidden.

MOSI (Museum of Science & Industry)

Liverpool Road, M3 4FP (832 2244, www.mosi.org.uk). Metrolink Deansgate-Castlefield, or City Centre buses, or Deansgate rail. **Open** 10am-5pm daily. **Admission** free. **Map** p129 B1 ❸

This family-friendly playground of vintage technology is set among the converted remains of the world's oldest surviving passenger railway station. Following a £9 million refurb, MOSI's highlights include an interactive gallery – Experiment! – aimed at inspiring children; the huge Power Hall of thrusting, steaming turbines that resembles something from the feverish dreams of Brunel; and the Air & Space Hall with its display of airborne greats, including a colossal Shackleton bomber. And all this comes for free – and even more exhibition space will open up by 2018. See box p133.

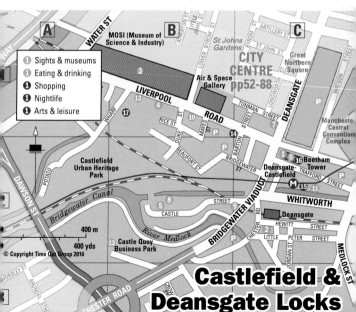

Castlefield & Deansgate Locks

Eating & drinking

Akbar's

73-83 Liverpool Road, M3 4NQ (834 7222, www.akbars.co.uk). Metrolink Deansgate-Castlefield, or City Centre buses, or Deansgate rail. **Open** *5-11pm Mon-Thur; 5-11.30pm Fri, Sat; 4-11pm Sun.* **££. Indian. Map** p129 B1

This curry chain from Bradford provides one of the slickest experiences in town. Nihari (from the Lahori menu – slow-cooked lamb, in an unctuous sauce) and chicken-liver tikka are two treats, while the favourites (balti, korma) come with family-sized naans. There's also a curried offal selection.

Albert's Shed

20 Castle Street, M3 4LZ (839 9818, www.albertsshed.com). Metrolink Deansgate-Castlefield, or City Centre buses, or Deansgate rail. **Open** *noon-10pm Mon-Thur; noon-10.30pm Fri;*
10.30am-11pm Sat; 10.30am-9.30pm Sun. **£££. International. Map** p129 B2

Lobster thermidor croquettes, rabbit gnocchi, roast loin of venison, Lancashire cheese and onion pie – the most complicated thing about the menu at this converted quayside toolshed is that you'll have a hard time deciding what to eat. There are solid – if less architecturally interesting – branches in West Didsbury (Barlow Moor Road) and upmarket Worsley.

Cloud 23

Hilton Manchester Deansgate, 303 Deansgate, M3 4LQ (870 1670, www. cloud23bar.com). Metrolink Deansgate-Castlefield, or City Centre buses, or Deansgate rail. **Open** *11am-1am Mon-Thur, Sun; 11am-2am Fri, Sat.* **Bar. Map** p129 C2

Set on the 23rd floor of the Hilton Deansgate (p176), this luxe 'sky bar' is one of the most talked-about venues

Cloud 23

in the city. Offering incredible panoramic views from its floor-to-ceiling windows, it's also the highest point in Manchester in which you can order a cosmopolitan – that's got to be worth drinking to. Afternoon teas are available too. Book a table or a slot on the guest list to avoid disappointment.

Dimitri's

Campfield Arcade, Tonman Street, M3 4FN (839 3319, www.dimitris.co.uk). Metrolink Deansgate-Castlefield, or City Centre buses, or Deansgate rail. **Open** 11am-midnight Mon-Thur, Sun; 11am-2am Fri, Sat. **££. Greek. Map** p129 C1 ❼

No prizes for guessing the Greek heritage of this lively, long-established restaurant. The menu is packed with tasty meze dishes, great for soaking up the ouzo. If you can tolerate the crime against language, order the Kalamata Plata, a feast of sharing nibbles. There's also a branch (Olive & Vine) on Wilmslow Road, next to Parsonage Gardens in Didsbury.

Dukes 92

18-25 Castle Street, M3 4LZ (839 3522, www.dukes92.com). Metrolink Deansgate-Castlefield, or City Centre buses, or Deansgate rail. **Open** 11.30am-11pm Mon-Wed; 11.30am-midnight Thur; 11.30am-1am Fri, Sat; noon-10.30pm Sun. **Pub. Map** p129 B2 ❽

The capacious canalside patio of the enduringly popular Dukes 92 is one of the best outdoor spots in the city. Come here to enjoy a summer pint and share a cheese and pâté plate; they stock a range of artisanal cheeses, mostly from the British Isles.

Knott

374 Deansgate, M3 4LY (839 9229, www.knottbar.co.uk). Metrolink Deansgate-Castlefield, or City Centre buses, or Deansgate rail. **Open** noon-11.30pm Mon-Wed, Sun; noon-midnight Thur; noon-12.30am Fri, Sat. **Bar. Map** p129 C2 ❾

The Knott has been squeezed in beneath railway arches and shakes violently whenever a loco rumbles overhead (slightly unnerving the first time it happens). An excellent food menu complements the range of fine bottled beers and craft-brewery cask ales. It's a regular winner of CAMRA's best local pub award.

Oxnoble

71 Liverpool Road, M3 4NQ (839 7760, www.theox.co.uk). Metrolink Deansgate-Castlefield, or City Centre buses, or Deansgate rail. **Open** 11.30am-midnight Mon-Thur, Sun, 11.30am-1am Fri, Sat. **££. Gastropub. Map** p129 B1 ❿

Proper pub food – braised ox cheek with mash, ham hock terrine, steak and ale pie – is served alongside a raft of well-kept real ales. The smart interior is moodily dark, with lots of glossy wood and tartan upholstered chairs. For those who can't face the journey home – or afford the Hilton, opposite – there are ten guest rooms (p180).

Revolution

Arch 7, Whitworth Street West, M1 5LH (839 7558, www.revolution-bars. co.uk/deansgate). Metrolink Deansgate-Castlefield, or City Centre buses, or Deansgate rail. **Open** noon-2am Mon-Thur; noon-3am Fri, Sat; 11am-2am Sun. **Bar. Map** p129 C2 ⓫

Revolution's exposed brick walls and leather seating draw a young urbane crowd for after-work drinks and (in the basement club) late-night dancing. It's also popular for food; though upscale pub grub might not be particularly adventurous, it's the pick of the bunch on Deansgate Locks. There's 50% off food on Mondays.

Sapporo Teppanyaki

91 Liverpool Road, M3 4JN (831 9888, www.sapporo.co.uk). Metrolink Deansgate-Castlefield, or City Centre buses, or Deansgate rail. **Open** noon-11pm Mon-Sat; noon-10.30pm Sun. **££. Japanese. Map** p129 B1 ⓬

Comedy Store

Sapporo Teppanyaki offers a spectacle as well as a Japanese dining experience that's particularly popular with families. Order a meal and watch as the 'show chef' dices, tosses and grills ingredients before your eyes. Best for group outings – the theatrics may prove too much during intimate meals.

Wharf

6 Slate Wharf, M15 4ST (220 2960, www.brunningandprice.co.uk/thewharf). Metrolink Castlefield-Deansgate, or City Centre buses, or Deansgate rail. **Open** 11am-11pm Mon-Thur; 11am-midnight Fri, Sat; 11am-10.30pm Sun. **Pub.** **Map** p129 B2

Set in Castlefield's canal basin, the Wharf has an impressive terrace from which to admire the boats in summer. While the interior is less thrilling (bog-standard modern pub), ales from the likes of Macclesfield's Redwillow brewery are a draw. The food, from sandwiches to Sunday roasts, is up to Brunning & Price's usual high standards.

Nightlife

Cask

29 Liverpool Road, M3 4NQ (819 2527). Metrolink Deansgate-Castlefield, or City Centre buses, or Deansgate rail. **Open** noon-11pm Mon-Sat; noon-10.30pm Sun. **Map** p129 C1

Blink and you'll miss Cask's eggshell-blue frontage. Apart from an impressive selection of over 150 beers in a cosy environment, what might catch your attention is the sign that says 'Bring your own food'. With limited space on the premises – and one of the best chip shops in Manchester next door (the Fish Hut) – this is not as strange as it seems.

Comedy Store

Arches 3 & 4, Whitworth Street West, M1 5LH (839 9595, www.thecomedy store.co.uk/manchester). Metrolink Deansgate-Castlefield, or City Centre buses, or Deansgate rail. **Open** Shows from 8pm. **Map** p129 C2

Scientific endeavour

The ever-popular MOSI keeps changing for the better.

At the heart of the Industrial Revolution and a key player in the development of the computer, nuclear physics and graphene, Manchester has a long and distinguished history of scientific and technological endeavour. The museum dedicated to showcasing these achievements, **MOSI** (Museum of Science & Industry, p129), is a family-tastic – and free – place that's built on and around the site of the world's oldest surviving passenger railway station.

The sprawling museum and its unrivalled collection of early steam trains and vintage planes pulls in 700,000 visitors each year. Part of the Science Museum Group (which also includes London's Science Musem and York's National Railway Museum), it has enjoyed extensive refurbishments in recent years. The latest additions include the entrance hall, interactive galleries and cafés – which are a particular treat for pizza fans.

There's an excellent gift shop too, and don't forget to take a selfie on the way in. The main entrance features a gargantuan, 50-screen 'media wall', packed with images of gurning visitors and happy kids. There are digital displays, exciting games and an intriguing collection of historic items to check out before making your way around the five listed buildings, 16 galleries and working steam train (which runs along a short stretch of track dating from 1830).

As is evident by the groups of squealing children, the interactive Experiment! gallery is among the most popular. And why not,

when a child can lift an entire Mini using only a crank, discover how many of Manchester's homes could be lit if rubbish were used as a power source, and race giant bubbles of air through oil and water.

Temporary exhibitions cover subjects as diverse as how brains work or particles accelerate, while displays on the history of cotton production in Manchester are less dry than they sound. The Power Hall is home to one of the world's largest collections of working steam mill engines, and the new entrance hall is an atmospheric location for occasional late openings and wine tastings.

From 2018, three buildings dating from 1830 (including the first ever railway warehouse) will become a more adult-focused exhibition area. As befits a museum dedicated to discoveries in science and industry, MOSI is always evolving.

This venue, the northern outpost of the long-running London laughter-factory, is at the heart of Manchester's current comedy renaissance, with big names from the stand-up circuit appearing in its theatre-style auditorium. Propping up one end of the bustling Deansgate Locks cluster, it's a good option for drinks and a show.

Arts & leisure

LivingWell

Hilton Manchester Deansgate, 303 Deansgate, M3 4LQ (870 1786, www. livingwell.com). Metrolink Deansgate-Castlefield, or City Centre buses, or Deansgate rail. **Open** 6am-10pm daily. **Map** p129 C2 ⑯

Compact size aside, this gym and health club inside the Hilton hotel has plenty to offer, not least a luxurious 20m pool with views over Deansgate that's magical at sunset. Among its unique features are panes of glass in the floor of the pool, through which swimmers can spy on guests in the hotel lobby below. Day passes for non-members cost only £10, which

includes use of the steam room, sauna and gym if you so desire. Chances are, though, you'll not make it further than the giant hot tub.

Y Club

Liverpool Road, M3 4JR (837 3535, www.yclub.org.uk). Metrolink Castlefield-Deansgate, or City Centre buses, or Deansgate rail. **Open** 6am-10pm Mon-Fri; 8am-7pm Sat; 8am-6pm Sun. **Map** p129 B1 ⑰

Part of the Castlefield Hotel, the Y Club has a different feeling to other local health clubs thanks to a welcoming policy and lack of pretension among its members. Classes include circuits, yoga and Zumba (you can do a class for £5 without being a member, or sign up for a £10 day pass), while facilities include exercise studios, trampolines and a retro sports hall complete with running track elevated to near the ceiling. Martial arts and wrestling are strengths, and the YMCA Harriers running club (who are based here) command respect in competitions nationwide. There's also a pool, steam rooms and a women-only sauna.

LivingWell

Millennium footbridge p141

Salford & Salford Quays

Salford

Let's get one thing straight: Salford isn't in Manchester. There's nothing that will rile the locals more than mistaking the two – on both sides of the divide. Manchester and Salford are two separate cities that just happen to share a border. Salfordians are proud of their industrial heritage and tight-knit communities, and the Smiths' *The Queen is Dead* album cover (shot at **Salford Lads Club**) put Salford on the musical map.

In recent times, the cultural focus has shifted to blossoming Salford Quays, and its MediaCity complex, complete with the BBC's northern HQ. Chapel Street is another hotspot, thanks to nearby **Islington Mill**. This converted warehouse hosts the Sounds From the Other City music festival (www.soundsfromtheother city.com) – which sprawls out from the Mill to take over pubs and even churches along Chapel Street – and includes a gig space, B&B, café and studios for creatives: it's a cool place to hang out.

You'll find plenty of traditional pubs in Salford. The **Eagle Inn** and **New Oxford** are the real deal, while **MaltDog** is leading the craft beer revolution up in Monton. Head to the five-star **Lowry Hotel** for afternoon tea, **Puccini's** for pasta with Manchester United players, and, if you can find it, bar **Under New Management** for great cocktails.

Visitors should bear in mind that, aside from Salford Quays, Salford is largely a city where people live and work rather than a tourist destination. There's plenty to explore in this part of Greater Manchester, but do keep your wits about you. If you do take the car, don't leave anything of value on display.

Sights & museums

Buile Hill Park

Eccles Old Road, M6 8GL (www.salford. gov.uk/builehill.htm). Metrolink Weaste, or Salford buses, or Salford Crescent rail. Many of Salford's parks have a hidden-gem quality to them, and the largest park in the city, Buile Hill, comes with surprising historical and cultural cache, too. It was a key defence site in both world wars. Artist LS Lowry was a regular visitor in the early 1900s, and author Frances Hodgson Burnett is said to have written her much-loved children's book *The Secret Garden* at Buile Hill Mansion; this stately home, dating from 1827, lies abandoned at the park's centre. Park facilities include tennis courts, playgrounds, outdoor gym equipment and fun tree trails.

Ordsall Hall

322 Ordsall Lane, M5 3AN (872 0251, www.salfordcommunityleisure.co.uk). Metrolink Exchange Quay, or bus 84, 250, 251, 255, 256, 263. **Open** 10am-4pm Mon-Thur; 1-4pm Sun. **Admission** free. **Map** p137 B3 ①
Ordsall, around a mile and a half from Salford Central station, is an unlikely setting for this splendid Grade I-listed house. Dating from the 14th century, the building contains medieval, Tudor, Stuart and Victorian elements; a £6.5-million revamp has restored many of its original features, including chandeliers, oak timbers and wall sconces in the Great Hall, and the aptly named 16th-century Italian Plaster Ceiling Room.

The manicured lawns and orchards stocked with historic varieties of apples, pears and berries offer little comfort to the building's ghosts. Look out for a lady wearing white in the Great Hall, and a young girl who's often been seen on the stairs. The ghosts are so famous, in fact, that they have their own social-media account (@TheOrdsallGhost on Twitter) and live video webfeed; the hall even hosts sleepovers for fans hoping to meet the aforementioned spooks.

St Philip's with St Stephen

St Philip's Place, M3 6FJ (834 2041, www.salfordchurch.org). Metrolink Victoria, or Salford buses, or Salford Central rail. **Open** *Services* Holy Communion 9.45am Sun. *General visiting* 10am-4pm Wed. **Map** p137 A3 ②
St Philip's, a 1820s neoclassical Anglican church, is one of a handful of 19th-century buildings to survive the neglect suffered by many of its Chapel Street neighbours. Built by Robert Smirke (who also designed the British Museum in London), the church is distinctive thanks to a colonnaded entrance topped by a Perpendicular bell tower. Under the stewardship of the Reverend Andy Salmon, this is one forward-thinking place of worship. As at nearby Sacred Trinity church, regular concerts are held here, featuring the likes of Florence and the Machine and the BBC Philharmonic Orchestra. The latter have an on-off residency at the University of Salford's Peel Hall, a little further down Chapel Street.

Salford Lads Club

St Ignatius Walk, M5 3RX (872 3767, www.salfordladsclub.org.uk). Bus 33. **Open** *Smiths Room* 11.30am-1.30pm Sat. **Admission** free.
Featured on the inside cover of the Smiths' album *The Queen is Dead*, this registered charity, established in 1903, still fulfils its original function as a sports club and community centre, although it's now open to both boys and girls. The spot is a magnet for Smiths devotees, and the surrounding streets host regular pilgrimages of often rather worried-looking fans. The club has a specific room devoted to the band, where you'll find all sorts of memorabilia, as well as a collection of images that fans have sent in of themselves in the classic cover pose, plus a large mosaic by local artist Mark Kennedy. If you'd like to visit the room other than on a Saturday, email info@salford ladsclub.org.uk to arrange it.

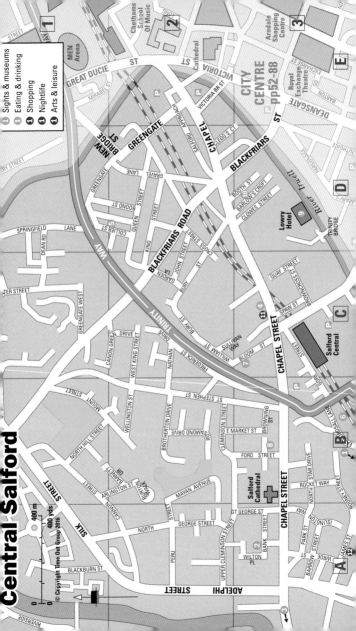

Central Salford

© Copyright Time Out Group 2016

0 400 m
0 400 yds

Sights & museums
Eating & drinking
Shopping
Nightlife
Arts & leisure

CITY CENTRE pp52-88

MEN Arena

Chetham's School Of Music

Arndale Shopping Centre

Royal Exchange Theatre

Lowry Hotel

Salford Cathedral

Salford Central

River Irwell

TRINITY BRIDGE

1 2 3

A B C D E

Salford Museum & Art Gallery

Peel Park, The Crescent, M5 4WU (778 0800, www.salfordcommunityleisure. co.uk). Salford buses, or Salford Crescent rail. **Open** 10am-4.45pm Mon-Fri; noon-4pm Sat, Sun. **Admission** free. **Map** p137 A3 ❸

Inevitably overshadowed by its more prestigious neighbours both up and down the road (its Lowry collection has been transferred to the Lowry; p145), this gallery nevertheless has a good selection of Victorian art, including JC Dollman's striking painting *Famine*, and examples of late Pre-Raphaelite work by Sir Edward Burne-Jones. Take a stroll along Lark Hill Place – an atmospheric re-creation of a typical northern street in Victorian times – which is crammed with vivid period sights and sounds.

Eating & drinking

Caffè Lupo

142 Chapel Street, M3 6AF (no phone, www.lupocaffe.co.uk). Metrolink Victoria, or Salford buses, or Salford Central rail. **Open** 8am-5pm Mon-Fri; 9am-5pm Sat. **Café. Map** p137 C3 ❹

Sample coffee topped with freshly whipped cream, single-estate hot chocolate, lasagne and tiramisu at this simple Italian café. Mismatched chairs and just-polished wood lend a boho vibe; freshly cut flowers add charm. Contemporary art gallery, the International 3 (p140), is next door.

Eagle Inn

19 Collier Street, M3 7DW (819 5002, www.joseph-holt.com). Metrolink Victoria, or bus 135, or Salford Central rail. **Open** 12.30pm-1am Mon-Thur, Sun; 12.30pm-2am Fri, Sat. **Pub. Map** p137 D2 ❺

The Eagle Inn is a relic, dating from 1848, now lovingly brought back to life and infused with youthful exuberance by the team behind the Northern Quarter's Castle Hotel (p90). The tiled floors and snugs are joined by a modern performance space that plays host to indie stars on the rise, and includes a lofty viewing gallery. Beers focus on the Joseph Holt stable.

First Chop Brewing Arm

Unit 3, Trinity Row, Trinity Way, M3 5EN (07970 241398, www. firstchopbrewingarm.com). City Centre buses, or Salford Central rail. **Open** varies. **Brewery. Map** p137 B3 ❻

First Chop is both a brewery and well-established brew tap located just over the Manchester/Salford border. From a railway arch HQ – which doubles as a venue for party-focused DJs and live acts such as Jesca Hoop – the brewery produces an appealing range of craft beers, including six gluten-free ones. Handmade by brewer-patron, Richard Garner, the SYL (a black IPA) has won several best-in-show awards. Check the website for opening hours.

Kings Arms

11 Bloom Street, M3 6AN (832 3605, www.kingsarmssalford.com). Metrolink Victoria, or City Centre buses, or Salford Central rail. **Open** noon-midnight daily. **Pub. Map** p137 C3 ❼

This is a real gem, an alcopop-free zone sitting pretty in the no-man's-land between Manchester and Salford (it's an easy stroll from the city centre). Owner Paul Heaton (one-time lead singer in British pop acts the Housemartins and the Beautiful South) chooses the beers (often from local breweries) and there's often hearty food to enjoy. There's plenty going on too: the fantastic vaulted room upstairs, a listed dancehall dating from 1883, hosts gigs, theatre and comedy nights; or you can join the Knitting Club in the snug. All told, it's hard to fault this pub – even the jukebox has won awards.

MaltDog

169 Monton Road, Monton, M30 9GS (07541 553646, www.maltdog.com). Metrolink Ecdes, or bus 33, or Ecdes rail.

Open 5-11pm Mon, Tue; 4-11pm Wed, Thur; 1-11pm Fri, Sat; 1-10pm Sun. **Bar**.

MaltDog's pedigree as an independent beer shop and bar stands out even in the rapidly gentrifying suburb of Monton. Sample from a rotating array of craft beers (many from local brewers, and from the US), fine wines and farmhouse ciders at this neighbourhood favourite. Decor is laid-back: think comfortable seats and simple wooden tables.

New Oxford

11 Bexley Square, M3 6DB (832 7082, www.thenewoxford.com). Metrolink Victoria, or Salford buses, or Salford Central rail. **Open** noon-midnight daily. **Pub. Map** p137 B3 ⑧

This Salford institution stands on Bexley Square, the scene of a long-forgotten 'battle' between police and protesters over unemployment in the crisis-hit 1930s. Today, it's all about booze: there's an ever-rotating choice of up to 18 cask ales, plus a bottled selection that embraces Belgium, Holland and Germany. The fruit beer and lambic range is welcome, and the place was awarded Cider Pub of the Year in 2014 by North Manchester CAMRA. The Fall's Mark E Smith is a sometime patron.

Puccini's

171-175 Chorley Road, Swinton, M27 4AE (794 1847, www.puccinirestaurant. co.uk). Bus 12, 25, 36, 38, or Swinton rail. **Open** noon-2.30pm, 5.45-10pm Tue-Sat; 2-9pm Sun. **££. Italian**.

A 1980s-style Italian restaurant for those who love both pasta and Manchester United. Many dishes were created for specific football players, some of whom are still regulars; penne alla Giggs, for example, is Ryan Giggs' favourite, with minced steak, cream and chilli. The walls are decked with Man U memorabilia, including signed T-shirts and players' photos, to the extent that little of the original architecture (which lies within the walls of a brutalist-era concrete shopping mall) is visible. The atmosphere is welcoming and prices are reasonable.

Salford Museum & Art Gallery

River Bar & Grill

Lowry Hotel, 50 Dearmans Place, M3 5LH (827 4041, www.the lowryhotel. com). Metrolink Market Street, or Salford buses, or Salford Central rail. **Open** 7-10.30am, noon-2pm, 2.15-4pm, 6-10.30pm Mon-Fri; 7.30-11am, 11.30am-2pm, 2.15-4pm, 6-10.30pm Sat; 7.30-11am, 12.30-3pm, 3.15-5pm, 7-10pm Sun. **£££. Bar/grill. Map** p137 D3 **9**

You can come to the upmarket Lowry Hotel (p181) for breakfast all the way through to dinner. A rather disappointing grill-style restaurant complements the bar, which remains a favourite of pop stars such as Rihanna, and famous football managers (Sven Goran-Eriksson was a regular). As well as offering a good-value lunch menu, this is a great spot for afternoon tea: ask if you can sit outside on the raised riverside balcony with views of the Irwell.

Under New Management

Barlow's Croft, M3 5DY (832 6699, www.unm-bar.co.uk). Metrolink Victoria, or Salford buses, or Salford Central rail. **Open** 5pm-1am Mon-Wed; 5pm-2am Thur; 5pm-4am Fri; 7pm-4am Sat; 7pm-1am Sun. **Bar. Map** p137 D3 **10**

Despite its obscure back-alley location and a wilful lack of external signage, UNM is arguably Salford's finest gin-mill. Inside, low lights, leather booths and spartan decor leave plenty of room to admire the main event: an expertly put-together cocktail list that has, quite rightly, won several industry awards both in this incarnation and when the bar was called Corridor. They stock only the finest (often British) boutique spirits, cordials and mixers, so you're on to a winner if you order 'off' menu too. Choose your tipple, then relax and enjoy the laid-back feel that makes this after-hours drinking den worth seeking out.

Arts & leisure

International 3

142 Chapel Street, M3 6AF (07960 038063, www.international3.com).

Metrolink Victoria, or Salford buses, or Salford Central rail. **Open** (during exhibitions) noon-5pm Wed-Fri. **Admission** free. **Map** p137 C3 **11**

This independent artist-run concern presents a changing programme of high-quality contemporary art in its tiny, one-room gallery. Shows are reliably interesting. A visit is ideally combined with tiramisu and an espresso at Caffè Lupo (p138) next door.

Islington Mill

James Street, M3 5HW (07947 649896, www.islingtonmill.com). Salford buses, or Salford Central rail. **Open** varies. **Map** p137 A3 **12**

This converted cotton warehouse has led something of a cultural revolution in Salford over the past decade. The building, just a short walk from the centre of Manchester, contains 50 studios that are mainly occupied by creatives, a recording studio, gig space, B&B and more besides. It also has close links with Chapel Street, a mile-long stretch of Victorian pubs, university buildings and churches just a stone's throw away. A recent refurb means the Mill is now soundproofed; thanks to a no-holds-barred booking policy, it's now one of the city's most exciting bets for live and DJ-based metal, techno and indie music. And while Chapel Street and its surroundings are still a very long way from the scrubbed-up glamour of Manchester, Islington Mill offers the kind of edgy underground entertainment you'd kick yourself if you missed.

Salford Quays

Salford may have taken longer to redevelop than Manchester, but its trump card is **MediaCity** (or MediaCityUK, to be true to the branding gurus – www.mediacity uk.co.uk), which has been drawing crowds to Salford Quays' spectacular waterfront since 2011. The regeneration of these former

MediaCity

industrial docks began in earnest well over a decade ago – see www.thequays.org.uk for details.

A 15-minute tram ride west of Manchester city centre, and with its own hotels, apartments, waterside park and shops, this £650-million media island is the new home of ITV, numerous BBC departments and the BBC Philharmonic Orchestra, as well as scores of digital, TV and film companies, studios, and freelance and small business spaces such as the Landing.

Outside the BBC headquarters is a central plaza with a capacity of more than 5,000. Enormous digital screens brighten the space, which is fringed by an open-water swimming centre (**Uswim**) and family-friendly pubs such as the **Dockyard**. Weekends and evenings are often punctuated by live music and film screenings, as well as some truly captivating public arts events, including interactive light sculptures (visit www.quaysculture.com for more information about what's on).

The **Lowry** arts centre sits close by, surrounded by made-for-footballer apartments and the **Lowry Outlet** shopping mall, while a number of funky footbridges span the Manchester Ship Canal connecting MediaCity to **Imperial War Museum North** on the southern shore. Strictly speaking, the museum isn't in Salford: it's in the borough of Trafford. We just thought we'd better set the record straight before you start asking for directions.

Sights & museums

BBC Tours
MediaCityUK, M50 2EQ (www.bbc.co.uk/showsandtours/tours/media_city). Metrolink MediaCityUK, or bus X50. **Tours** 10.30am, 12.30pm, 3pm Mon-Wed; times vary Sat, Sun. **Admission** £10.75; £7-£9.75 reductions; £31.50 family. **Map** p143 A2 ⑬
While the BBC is not strictly open to the public, visitors can pop into the building's fun-packed foyer during working

Imperial War Museum North

hours and at weekends. It's well worth a look, thanks to changing displays of television faves, such as Daleks from the *Doctor Who* sci-fi series or life-sized characters from *The Furchester Hotel*. For a proper look around, book tickets (online only) for an official 90-minute tour of the building and its most famous shows and sets. These take in everything from exploring the studios where huge shows such as *Match of the Day*, *Mastermind* and *Blue Peter* are made, to having a go at presenting the news. There are also tours aimed specifically at children (aged six to 11). Book as far in advance as possible, as all the tours are very popular.

Imperial War Museum North

The Quays, Trafford Wharf Road, Stretford, M17 1TZ (836 4000, www. iwm.org.uk). Metrolink MediaCityUK, or bus X50. **Open** 10am-5pm daily. **Admission** free. **Map** p143 A2 ⓮

Surely Manchester's most striking building, the IWM North's brain-boggling design is star architect Daniel Libeskind's concept of a shattered globe (representing the world divided by conflict). Inside, floors and walls gently slope and disorient visitors. More a museum of peace than a museum of war, the place works hard at being an entertaining and educational multimedia-led venue. Its permanent displays, which include artillery, audio-visual shows and hands-on exhibits, are supplemented by temporary shows, often aimed at children, which draw on franchises such as the BBC's *Horrible Histories* series. The 100ft high AirShard tower (£1.20) offers an impressive, if vertiginous, view and there's a space-age-style café where pizza is a speciality.

Eating & drinking

Convenience and a choice of reputable chain restaurants are the prevailing themes of the Salford Quays drinking and dining experience. But change is afoot following the opening of a **Booths** supermarket and café, and local independent restaurant **Damson** and the **Dockyard** pub. The last two are both owned by restaurateur Steve Pilling, who first made his name at the assorted Chop Houses in Manchester's city centre.

While the Quays is not yet a foodie destination, things seem to be moving in the right direction. The Lowry Outlet's 'plaza restaurants' include some reliable family favourites – Nando's and Pizza Express among them – while its food court hosts takeaway options such as Harry Ramsden's. Close to the MediaCityUK Metrolink station, you'll find branches of Prezzo and Wagamama. The cafés at the Lowry and Imperial War Museum North are also good bets.

Booths

The Garage, Red Building, MediaCityUK, M50 2BS (713 3750, www.booths.co.uk/ store/media-city-uk). Metrolink MediaCityUK, or bus X50. **Open** *Supermarket* 7am-10pm Mon-Sat; 11am-5pm Sun. *Café* 8.30am-5.30pm Mon-Sat; 10.30am-4pm Sun. **£. Café. Map** p143 A1 ⓯

The only Greater Manchester outlet of multi-award-winning supermarket Booths. Famous across the north of England (and beyond) for its splendid range of meat, bread, wine, beer and cheese – often sourced from local artisan suppliers – Booths has a cult following with good reason. This particular branch has a reasonable café too.

Damson MediaCity

Orange Building, MediaCityUK, M50 2HF (751 7020, www.damson restaurant.co.uk). Metrolink MediaCityUK, or bus X50. **Open** noon-2.45pm, 5-9.30pm Mon-Sat; noon-5.30pm Sun. **£££. Modern European. Map** p143 B2 ⓰

The well-established Heaton Moor Damson (p167) has spawned a bigger sibling at MediaCity. The smart decor in greys and mauves, and views of the area's imposing ship canals from a first-floor terrace, complement the excellent cooking. Ham hock and

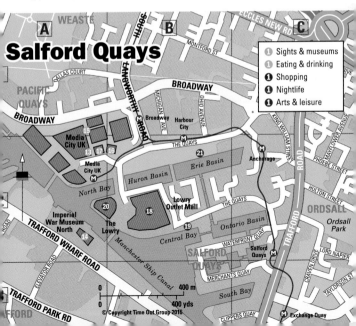

Lowry

smoked bone marrow raviolo (starter) and seared duck breast with spice-roasted pineapple (main) are typical choices, and the tasting menu (dinner only) includes a vegetarian version. The wine list is a serious concern. Fancy food aside, this branch is family-friendly and wheelchair accessible.

Dockyard

Dockhouse, MediaCityUK, M50 2EQ, (359 3848, www.dockyard. pub). Metrolink MediaCityUK, or bus X50. **Open** *9am-11pm daily.* **Pub**. **Map** p143 A2 ⑰

Your search for great beer and gourmet burgers ends here, in this spacious, warehouse-style pub in the heart of MediaCity's central plaza. A convivial atmosphere that's particularly suited to families is another bonus – it's the ideal place to while away a Sunday. There's a branch in Spinningfields too.

Shopping

Lowry Outlet

The Quays, M50 3AH (848 1850, www.lowryoutlet.co.uk). Metrolink MediaCityUK, or bus X50. **Open** 10am-6pm Mon-Wed, Fri; 10am-8pm Thur; 10am-7pm Sat; 11am-5pm Sun. **Map** p143 B2 ⑱

This factory outlet mall offers clothes, books, gifts and homewares at discounts of between 25% and 70%. What you'll get depends largely on how happy you are to devote hours to rummaging. The selection of shops is patchy, although the Flannels, M&S and Molton Brown outlets usually make a trip worthwhile. Cinemas and various chain eateries, including Pizza Express, enable you to make a day of it. At weekends, look out for food markets in the Plaza between the Outlet and the Lowry arts centre.

Arts & leisure

Helly Hansen Watersports Centre

15 The Quays, M50 3SQ (877 7252, www.salfordcommunityleisure.co.uk/ watersports-centre). Metrolink Harbour City, or bus X50. **Open** *Summer* 8.30am-8.30pm Mon-Fri; 9.30am-5.30pm Sat, Sun. *Winter* 8.30am-4.30pm Mon-Fri; varies Sat, Sun. **Admission** from £5. **Map** p143 B2 ⑲

Salford Quays' former ship canal seems like an unlikely spot for outdoor fun – but that's precisely what you'll find at what was previously known as Salford Watersports Centre. The complex is set on Ontario Basin, just a

few minutes' walk from the Metrolink station. Many activities are open to complete novices, such as open-water swimming, kayaking, canoeing and wakeboarding, while people with previous experience of sailing and windsurfing can join in regular sessions. There are numerous courses too.

Lowry

Pier 8, The Quays, M50 3AZ (0843 208 6000, www.thelowry.com). Metrolink MediaCityUK, or bus X50. **Open** *Galleries* 11am-5pm Mon-Fri, Sun; 10am-5pm Sat. **Admission** *Galleries* free. **Map** p143 A2/B2 ⑳

A long way from the grimly functional mill buildings so often captured by its namesake artist (and raison d'être), this waterside building marked a tipping point for the previously isolated Salford Quays development when it opened in 2000. The Lowry houses the world's largest collection of LS Lowry's art, and regularly presents themed exhibitions of the 'matchstick' man's work.

Lowry is only half of the story, however, as the centre brings together a marvellous mix of visual and performing arts projects under one roof. As well as contemporary art (everything from photography to conceptual art shows),

the steel-clad wonder has hosted more award-winning theatre productions than any other regional venue. Blockbuster musicals, dance, opera, comedy, ballet, children's shows, jazz, folk and popular music acts, and West End productions – they all come here.

The restaurant and terrace bar, situated on the south side of the building, offer great views along with sustenance. Handy for the IWMN too.

Uswim

Dock 9, The Quays, M50 3AZ (no phone, www.uswimopenwater.com). Metrolink MediaCityUK, or bus X50. **Open** *Apr-Oct* 5.30-8pm Wed; 8-11am Sat. **Admission** £8; £4-£6 reductions. **Map** p143 B2 ㉑

The Quays' former ship canal has become a world-class destination for watersports, and in particular for open-water swimming. There are two key providers: Uswim, which has a 750m circuit; and the Helly Hansen Watersports Centre's 500m course (p144). Both places use contemporary aeration systems and microbiological monitoring, meaning a healthy experience is guaranteed. Keep an eye on the website for changes to the schedule and current water temperatures. Wetsuit hire is available.

Etihad Stadium p150

North Manchester

Sometimes overlooked in favour of South Manchester's more affluent suburbs, the north races ahead of its southern sister when it comes to international sporting facilities. Two miles from the centre, the **Etihad Campus** (formerly known as Sportcity) is a sprawling complex that houses the National Squash Centre, a 6,000-seat athletics arena, the Regional Tennis Centre and the Manchester Velodrome, home of the National Cycling Centre, with seven and a half miles of exhilarating mountain bike trails at the adjacent Clayton Vale park.

The Etihad Campus is part of the legacy of the 2002 Commonwealth Games, an event that did much to reverse economic decline in north-east Manchester. The city tackled the huge event with gusto, pulling off a 'best ever' Games and in the process creating some of the best sporting facilities in the country. Today, it's the largest conglomeration

of sporting facilities in Europe. The Etihad Campus continues to host national and international fixtures, from badminton, cycling and squash championships to niche events such as the National Taekwondo Championships and even toddler balance bike racing.

No tour of the area would be complete without a visit to Manchester City's football ground – the **Etihad Stadium**. The 55,000-capacity arena is a match for United's 'theatre of dreams' at Old Trafford (p165), and arguably draws a more loyal and local crowd. The stadium is connected to the city centre by the Metrolink tramline.

Further north, **Heaton Park** continues the sporting theme. As well as 600 acres of parkland, an 18th-century house and farm centre, it has four championship-standard bowling greens as well as an excellent café run by the team behind the Eagle & Child gastropub (p172) in Ramsbottom.

It's not all sport in this part of town, though: the philanthropic legacy of the Industrial Revolution is clearly evident in the ambitious architecture and artworks scattered across North Manchester, from Ancoats' **Halle St Peter's** to the impressive Edwardian **Bury Art Museum & Sculpture Centre** and the imposing grandeur of **Bolton Town Hall**.

Sights & museums

1 Angel Square & NOMA

Miller Street, M4 4PR (834 1212, www. co-operative.coop/corporate/aboutus/ one-angel-square). Metrolink Shudehill, or City Centre buses, or Victoria rail.
The headquarters of the Co-operative Bank, aka 1 Angel Square, has been compared to a sliced egg, thanks to its spiral-tiered design. Conceived by architect Mike Hitchmough, it was said to be the greenest building on earth when it opened in 2013. Innovations include rainwater and heat recycling systems, and acres of duvet-like exposed concrete that acts as a 'thermal sponge'. It's also the first completed piece in Manchester's 20-acre, £800-million NOMA development, which includes renovating the Grade II-listed modernist New Century Hall (where Jimmy Hendrix once played) and investing in new public squares, offices and hotels.

Bolton Town Hall

Victoria Square, Bolton, BL1 1RU (01204 333333, www.boltonsmayors. org.uk). Bus 36, 37, or Bolton rail. **Open** *Tours* (from 2016); phone the mayor's office on 01204 331090. **Admission** *Tours* free.
Bolton has never been content to sit in Manchester's shadow. Its Town Hall, completed in 1873 and dominating the town centre, easily has enough grandeur to rival its Manchester counterpart. The neoclassical design, featuring a grand Corinthian portico, imposing clock tower and sweeping staircase,

reveals how important Bolton was during the 'Cottonopolis' era – it was once one of the world's most productive centres of cotton-spinning. Today, as then, culture plays a part in daily life, with the curving sweep of the 1930s Le Mans Crescent at the rear of the building providing a home not only for the Town Hall (and its recently refurbished theatre venue, the Albert Halls, which is set to reopen in 2017), but also for a museum, art gallery, aquarium, library and restaurant.

Bury Art Museum & Sculpture Centre

Moss Street, Bury, BL9 0DR (253 5878, www.buryartmuseum.co.uk). Metrolink Bury, or bus 135. **Open** 10am-5pm Tue-Fri; 10am-4.30pm Sat. **Admission** free.
A grand Edwardian building, the Bury Art Museum is worth a visit to see founder Thomas Wrigley's collection of 200 or so artworks, including paintings by Constable, Turner and Landseer. The museum also stages exhibitions of contemporary art, and is keen on kids: a table in the middle of the main gallery encourages reading, role playing and colouring-in.
Round out a Bury cultural day-trip by also visiting the working steam trains of East Lancashire Railway (www.eastlancsrailway.org.uk), and the military Fusilier Museum (www.fusiliermuseum.com), whose collection dates from Napoleon's time.

Hallé St Peter's

40 Blossom Street, Ancoats, M4 6BF (237 7000, www.halle.co.uk). Metrolink Market Street, or City Centre buses, or Piccadilly rail. **Open** varies.
Built in 1859, this Grade II-listed deconsecrated church (now beautifully renovated) is a rehearsal and recording space for the Hallé Orchestra, Choir and other ensembles. Located in the conservation area of Ancoats, a hub of activity during the Industrial Revolution that consists of massive, red-brick spinning mills and close-knit

housing, it's occasionally open to the public (see website for details). The church was the location of Kenneth Branagh's *Macbeth* performances for Manchester International Festival 2013. The adjacent public square is a good spot to catch some rays, although it's best avoided after dark.

Heaton Park

Off Middleton Road, Prestwich, M25 2SW (773 1085, www.heatonpark.org. uk). Metrolink Heaton Park, or bus 59. **Open** 8am-dusk daily. **Admission** free. Nestled in the foothills of the Pennines, Heaton Park is one of Europe's largest municipal parks. It contains eight English Heritage-listed buildings, a lake (with rowing boats for hire), four championship-standard bowling greens, a golf course, a herd of Highland cattle and a petting farm. The park hosts numerous concerts throughout the year. At its heart is Heaton Hall, an elegant Palladian country house designed by James Wyatt in the late 18th century, and the former home of the Earls of Wilton. Although partially restored, the house is currently closed to the public.

The café next to the petting farm serves delicious, seasonal British food.

Heaton Park Tramway

Heaton Park, Prestwich, M25 2SW (740 1919, www.heatonparktramway.org.uk). Metrolink Heaton Park, or bus 59. **Open** *Museum* Easter-Oct noon-5pm Sun. *Trams* Summer 1-5pm Sat; noon-5pm Sun. Winter noon-4pm Sun. **Admission** *Museum* free. *Tram fare* £1.50 return. Run by volunteers, this small and lovely museum is housed in an old tram shelter, from which restored vehicles run for much of the year (see the website for a schedule). The original system fell into disuse in the 1930s, and the park's tramlines were released from beneath a layer of tarmac only in the late 1970s. The building includes transport memorabilia, demonstration models, a shop and a maintenance pit where you can see the trams being restored.

HMP Manchester/ Strangeways

1 Southall Street, M60 9AH (817 5600). Metrolink Victoria, or bus 134, 135, or Victoria rail.

Manchester Jewish Museum

The intriguingly named Strangeways is now known officially as HM Prison Manchester. In part, it owes its fame to the Smiths' 1987 album *Strangeways, Here We Come* and to the 1990 riot that led to its extensive rebuilding. It was designed by Manchester Town Hall architect Alfred Waterhouse in the 1860s; only the most disastrous of tourist excursions will end up within its walls, but its panopticon design and prominent ventilation tower, 234ft high, makes it a very distinctive landmark on the edge of the city centre.

Manchester Jewish Museum

190 Cheetham Hill Road, M8 8LW (834 9879, www.manchesterjewishmuseum. com). Metrolink Victoria, or bus 42, 135, or Victoria rail. **Open** 10am-4pm Mon-Thur, Sun; 10am-1pm Fri. Closed Jewish holidays. **Admission** £4.50; £3.50 reductions.

Just outside the city centre in Cheetham Hill lies the Jewish Museum, in an old synagogue founded in 1874. Downstairs is the fully restored former place of worship; upstairs, the ladies' gallery houses a permanent display cataloguing the history of the still-prominent local Jewish community. Helpful guides explain various ritual and historical facts. Another exhibition space typically shows contemporary work by artists of Jewish heritage, while the events programme includes theatre, comedy, film screenings, and book readings.

Museum of Transport

Boyle Street, M8 8UW (205 2122, www. gmts.co.uk). Metrolink Queens Road or Victoria, or bus 42, 135, or Victoria rail. **Open** *Sept-July* 10am-4.30pm Wed, Sat, Sun; *Aug* 10am-4.30pm daily. **Admission** £4; free-£2 reductions.

Two halls house over a century's worth of lovingly restored public transport vehicles; the collection is one of the largest of its kind. The timeline starts with a 19th-century horse-drawn carriage

and concludes with a Metrolink tram. An atmospheric, 1950s-style tearoom rounds off a visit with panache.

Eating & drinking

Baum

33-37 Toad Lane, Rochdale, OL12 0NU (01706 352186, www.thebaum.co.uk). Metrolink Rochdale, or bus 17, 24, or Rochdale rail. **Open** 11.30am-11.30pm Mon-Thur; 11.30-1am Fri, Sat; 11.30am-11pm Sun. **Pub.**

Nothing special to look at, the Baum is all about great food and drink. Choose from seven real ales on handpump, one guest cider and more than 30 continental draught and bottled beers. The hearty food includes the likes of dry-cured bacon chops, roasts and a more-ish 'beef rag pie'. A deserving winner of CAMRA's National Pub of the Year award in 2015.

Clarence

2 Silver Street, Bury, BL9 0EX (464 7404, www.thedarence.co.uk). Metrolink Bury, or bus 135, 163. **Open** 11am-11pm Mon-Sat; noon-11pm Sun. **Pub.**

This new pub/restaurant is located in a grandiose Edwardian building dating from 1905. Recently refurbished to please the pickiest hipster, it has a state-of-the-art brewery in the basement (Silver Street Brewing Co) and adventurous pub grub. Start, perhaps, with Bury black pudding and leek croquettes, followed by maple-cured Old Spot pork chop or a burger with skinny fries. The same team also runs Bury's popular Automatic café. For more upmarket pub food, check out Chorlton's Parlour (p159) and the Marble Arch (p150).

Lamb Hotel

33 Regent Street, Eccles, M30 0BP (07827 850252, www.joseph-holt.com). Metrolink Eccles, or bus 33, or Eccles rail. **Open** 11.30am-11pm Mon-Thur; 11.30am-11.30pm Fri, Sat; noon-11pm Sun. **Pub.**

Octagon Theatre

As good as it gets when it comes to original pub decor. Built in 1906, this is a largely unspoilt Grade II-listed Holt pub, with a superb wood-panelled billiards room complete with full-size table. Other features include exquisite glazed tiles, a clutch of high-ceilinged rooms and a huge mahogany bar, enclosed by thick etched glass.

Marble Arch

73 Rochdale Road, M4 4HY (832 5914, www.marblebeers.com/marble-arch). Metrolink Victoria, or North Manchester buses, or Victoria rail. **Open** *noon-11pm Mon-Thur, Sun; noon-midnight Fri, Sat.* **Pub**.

Victorian tiling and a sloping floor give this place a historic feel. It was the first pub in the Marble Beers family, though the brewery itself outgrew the pub's back room several years ago. It still serves Marble standards such as Ginger, Lagonda IPA and the award-winning Earl Grey IPA, alongside guest beers from the country's finest brewers. Exemplary pub food includes hard-to-find British and European cheeses. There's a decent jukebox too.

Slattery

197 Bury New Road, Whitefield, M45 6GE (767 7761, www.slattery.co.uk). Metrolink Whitefield, or bus 135, or Whitefield rail. **Open** *Dining room 9am-4pm Mon-Fri; 9am-3.30pm Sat. Shop 9am-5.30pm Mon-Fri; 9am-5pm Sat.* **££. Tearoom**.

The Slattery family have been baking since 1967, and crafting chocolates since 1991. They now operate a dining room that serves breakfasts and lunches, as well as a range of chocolate-based goodies – the beautiful Swiss hot chocolate is simply orgasmic. They'll even teach you the arts of chocolate-making.

Arts & leisure

Manchester City Football Club

Etihad Campus, M11 3FF (444 1894, www.mcfc.co.uk). Metrolink Etihad Campus, or bus 216, 217, 231. **Open** *Tours 10.30am-3.30pm Mon-Thur, Sat; 10.30am-3.30pm, 5pm Fri; varies Sun.*

The 55,000-capacity Etihad Stadium hosted the 2002 Commonwealth Games before being converted to become the home ground of Manchester City FC. On site, you'll find a club shop, a canteen (with food by Jamie Oliver's Fabulous Feasts), an athletics track and squash courts, and a museum (call to book tours; £16, £10 reductions). In addition to City home games, the stadium occasionally hosts big-name concerts and other events.

Manchester Climbing Centre

Bennett Street, West Gorton, M12 5ND (230 7006, www.manchesterclimbing centre.com). Bus 201, 203, 205, 206, or Ardwick rail. **Open** *10am-10pm Mon-Fri; 10am-6pm Sat, Sun.*

Practise your belaying and leading in this Grade II-listed church, which now houses one of the largest indoor climbing walls in Europe. Hang around under the huge stained-glass windows on the 75 tied routes and two bouldering walls, or brush up on your rope skills with specialist courses. All levels are catered for here, from complete beginners (including children) to experienced climbers. The café (good cakes, Wi-Fi access) has a viewing gallery from which to watch the action. Visitors can book a taster session in advance (£30 for one person, £15 for each additional person), while competent climbers can pay per session (£9 non-members).

Manchester Velodrome

Stuart Street, Philips Park, M11 4DQ (223 2244, www.nationalcyclingcentre. com). Metrolink Velopark, or bus 216, 217, 231. **Open** 8am-10pm daily.

As the home of the British Cycling Team, the Velodrome's track is one of the best in the world, but the place still welcomes all levels of ability. If riding a fixed-gear bike appeals, hour-long taster sessions (from £12.40) provide full kit and advice on riding the steep banking – and how to stop a bike without brakes. There's also a BMX track, and a mountain bike course at Clayton Vale Park, right next to the Velodrome. Basketball, netball, spinning classes (branded 'Wattbike') and badminton are also on offer – check the website for more information.

If you want to see big-name cyclists in action, come to one of the Revolution Series races, held in the winter season, which regularly pull in crowds of 3,000.

Octagon Theatre

Howell Croft South, Bolton, BL1 1SB (01204 520661, www.octagonbolton. co.uk). Bus 36, 37, or Bolton rail.

This perennially popular theatre takes its name from its octagonal auditorium. This isn't the result of architectural whimsy: clever design means directors can choose from theatre-in-the-round, traditional end-on or 'thrust', depending on the production, and audiences are guaranteed excellent sightlines.

Fancy pants

Dress for success with Manchester's fancy dress shops.

Manchester's Gay Village promises a lively party for everyone, and a diverse bunch they are: on any night, the pavements and clubs are teeming with every kind of partygoer. Unsurprisingly, they are catered for by some rather fabulous costumiers, many with a fetish bent. But it's not just the Village revellers that want to look fabulous: with some 75,000 students, and hen parties seemingly around every corner, this is a city that's big on fancy dress. On any night out, you're likely to bump into a gaggle of inexplicably dressed Smurfs or bell-bottomed '70s stars meandering along Oxford Road, through the Northern Quarter and down Canal Street.

To hire or buy affordable gear, head to Strangeways – not for a prison outfit, but for something special from **All Things Fancy Dress** (149 Great Ducie Street, M3 1FB, 832 3918, www.all thingsfancydress.co.uk). Or try the legendary **Attic Fancy Dress** shop (Afflecks Palace, 52 Church Street, M4 1PW, 832 3839, www.atticfancydress.co.uk); it's run by an amiable father and son who truly know their stuff and will take the time to kit you out properly. **Luvyababes** (819 5395, www.luvyababes.co.uk), in the Arndale Centre (p52), also has costumes for kids, and the kind of ready-made outfits (superheroes, nurses) that don't require much preparation.

Manchester United
Football Club p165

South Manchester & Stockport

South Manchester

Manchester's wealthier communities are concentrated in its southern reaches, where suburban boutiques, eateries and gardens make the short trip out of the centre worth the effort. Alhough other Mancunians tend to roll their eyes at mention of the organic-buying media types who populate Didsbury and Chorlton (rumour has it that one newsagent in Chorlton sells more *Guardian* newspapers than anywhere else in the UK), there's much to recommend these suburbs.

While the city centre isn't particularly rich in open space, the southern suburbs have enough of the green stuff to make up for it. From **Fletcher Moss** in Didsbury to **Tatton Park** further out of town, there's plenty of parkland to get you pink-cheeked after over-indulging in the city's more urban pursuits.

Heading south along the Oxford Road takes you towards Rusholme's Curry Mile, a riotous strip of neon lights, booming bhangra, swishing saris and curry houses so tightly packed that it'd be rude not to stop off and sample a bhuna or balti (the curries aren't always great, but the experience is). Traffic here can be horrendous in early evening.

Fallowfield is primarily a student stomping ground. For more cultural delights, head over to Gorton in the south-east to visit the **Manchester Monastery**, or down to Withington, West Didsbury and Didsbury Village. West Didsbury's Burton Road has become an eating destination for urbanites, with cool bars such as **Volta** and **Solita** offering excellent cocktails and food. Across the road, **Greens** (co-owned by celebrity chef Simon Rimmer) serves veggie dishes capable of sating even the most hardened of carnivores.

The **Rose Garden** is another superb restaurant, delivering English dishes and local produce.

Further north, along Princess Road, the dramatic **Hulme Arch Bridge** straddles the carriageway, a symbol of the area's impressive regeneration. Once a concrete jungle of dank flats and gloomy walkways, the Hulme of the 1960s was rebuilt in the '90s; regeneration has continued apace with the arrival of the **HOME** arts centre and cinema (p125), and huge investment from the likes of Manchester Metropolitan University in student facilities.

Comfortable boozers abound in the south, and it's easy to lose a Sunday afternoon browsing the papers and downing pints of locally brewed craft beer. Chorlton's **Marble Beer House**, **Font** and the **Beagle** are a fine trio, while Withington's **Red Lion**, complete with beer garden and bowling green, is the perfect place to relax if the sun shines.

Those seeking retail therapy will be delighted by the quirky boutiques and independent record stores that clutter the streets in West Didsbury and Chorlton. Burton Road is again the place to head for in the former, while Chorlton's equivalent is Beech Road, where boutiques and boozers vie for space between delis and restaurants. Beech Road's charms remain unaffected by new shops and bars opening around Wilbraham and Barlow Moor Road – among them **Palate** cheese and ale bar.

As with the north, this slice of Greater Manchester is awash with sports venues. Old Trafford is home to **Manchester United**'s 'theatre of dreams', as well as to **Lancashire County Cricket Club**'s ground.

Sights & museums

Elizabeth Gaskell's House
84 Plymouth Grove, Ardwick, M13 9LW (273 2215, www.elizabethgaskellhouse.
co.uk). Bus 197. **Open** 11am-4.30pm, Wed, Thur, Sun. **Admission** £4.95; £3.95 reductions.

After years of neglect, the home of Elizabeth Gaskell has been immaculately restored. One of Manchester's most esteemed novelists, Gaskell wrote in the 19th-century 'industrial' genre; Charles Dickens was a visitor to the house, and Charlotte Brontë was a close friend. The Regency-style villa has been restored to its original glory, complete with newly commissioned period wallpapers, carpets and upholstery – plus a fully functional kitchen garden and café. A unique and atmospheric afternoon awaits. See box p168.

Fletcher Moss
Wilmslow Road, Didsbury, M20 2SW (998 2117, www.manchester.gov.uk). Metrolink Didsbury Village or East Didsbury, or Oxford Road buses, or East Didsbury rail. **Open** dawn-dusk daily. **Admission** free.

Donated to the public by Alderman Moss in 1914, these lovely gardens – stretching across some 21 acres – are notable for their rare plant species. A nature trail winds through woods before opening on to the River Mersey, but the real draw is the tiered rock garden overlooking the tennis courts. A tiny teahouse (noon-5pm Tue-Sun) offers tea, cake and ice-cream.

Gallery of Costume
Platt Hall, Rusholme, M14 5LL (245 7245, www.manchesterartgallery.org/ visit/gallery-of-costume). Oxford Road buses. **Open** 1-5pm Mon-Fri; 10am-5pm Sat, Sun. **Admission** free.

Housed in an 18th-century textile merchant's home, this collection is the largest of its type in Britain (though only a fraction of the 20,000-plus items are on display at any one time). High fashion from the 17th century to the present is represented, while the contrasting selection of working attire from the neighbouring South Asian community is also interesting.

Barbakan

Manchester Monastery

Gorton Lane, Gorton, M12 5WF (223 3211, www.themonastery.co.uk). Bus 205, 206, or Ashburys rail. **Open** noon-4pm Sun. **Admission** free. *Tours* from £7.50.

Designed by Edward Pugin and built 1863-67, this spectacular piece of ecclesiastical architecture – originally the Monastery of St Francis – served as a focus for the local community for over a century. Falling attendances (and declining numbers of monks) meant it was abandoned by the Franciscan order in 1989, and thereafter stripped of its contents by successive property developers, vandals and art thieves. A decade later, it was on the World Monuments Fund list of the globe's 100 most endangered sites. Much of the pilfered statuary has since been recovered, and a £6.5-million renovation in 2007 saw the building restored to its former glory. It now houses concerts, weddings and conferences, and runs regular tours.

Pankhurst Centre

60-62 Nelson Street, Chorlton-on-Medlock, M13 9WP (273 5673, www. thepankhurstcentre.org.uk). Oxford Road buses. **Open** 10am-4pm Thur. **Admission** free.

Saved from demolition in 1979, this Georgian house is where the remarkable Emmeline Pankhurst brought up her daughters Sylvia, Christabel and Adela, all active Suffragettes. She founded the militant Women's Social & Political Union (WSPU) here in 1903. Today, the Pankhurst Centre functions in two ways: as a women-only space for workshops and projects; and as a bookshop and exhibition room (men admitted) recreating Pankhurst's parlour.

Tatton Park

Knutsford, Cheshire (01625 374400, www.tattonpark.org.uk). Knutsford rail. **Open** *Park* Late Mar-late Oct 10am-7pm daily. Late Oct-late Mar 11am-5pm Tue-Sun. *Mansion, garden, farm, Old Hall* varies. **Admission** *Park* (per car) £5. *Mansion, garden, farm* £6; £4 reductions; £16 family. *Combined ticket* £11; £5.50 reductions; £27.50 family.

Get lost in the Cheshire countryside in this 1,000-acre park with its freely roaming deer, lakes, and excellent working farm with rare-breed pigs and birds. A walled garden has fruit trees and fig houses; you can sample some of this fresh produce in the on-site restaurant or buy to take home in the garden shop. The 200-year-old Mansion features unchanged state rooms, but the real attractions are outside – the RHS-endorsed gardens include an 1850s fernery and Japanese landscaping. Keep an eye out for garden-based artwork in 2016, when the Tatton Park Biennial returns. Bikes and trailers for kids can be hired.

Victoria Baths

Hathersage Road, Chorlton-on-Medlock, M13 0FE (224 2020, www.victoria baths.org.uk). Bus 191, 197, or Ardwick rail. **Open** *May-Nov* 11am-4pm 1st Sun of mth. **Tour** *Apr-Nov* 2pm Wed. **Admission** varies. *Tours* from £4.

The winner of BBC's *Restoration* in 2003, this former municipal baths (opened in 1906) has had £4.5 million worth of development: walls, roof, windows and floors have all been restored – though you can't yet go swimming again. Regular vintage fairs, and art and music events, including immersive theatre productions, are held here, as well as tours of the building.

Wythenshawe Park & Hall

Northenden, M23 0AB (998 2117, www.manchester.gov.uk). Metrolink Wythenshawe Park, or bus 41. **Open** *Park* dawn-dusk daily. *Hall* varies; see www.wythenshawehall.com.

Many of Wythenshawe Hall's original Tudor timbers – it was built in 1540 – survived a Parliamentarian assault when it held out as a Royalist stronghold during the Civil War (hence the listed Oliver Cromwell statue opposite). The hall stands in 250-acre Wythenshawe Park, whose mix of meadows, formal gardens and woodlands is supplemented by a petting farm, pitch and putt, horse-riding facilities and a horticultural centre.

Eating & drinking

Art of Tea

47 Barlow Moor Road, Didsbury, M20 6TW (448 9323, www.theartoftea. co.uk). Metrolink Didsbury Village, or *Didsbury buses, or East Didsbury rail.* **Open** 9am-11pm Mon-Sat; 10am-10pm Sun. **£-££**. **Café**.

What could be more British than tea and cakes in a kooky vintage café, complete with groaning bookshop and a picture framer out the back? This place gets the simple things in life just right. As well as brunch and brekkie stuff, they do a great bottle of wine, pizzas and occasional gigs.

Barbakan

67-71 Manchester Road, Chorlton, M21 9PW (881 7053, www.barbakan-deli. co.uk). Metrolink Chorlton, or Chorlton buses. **Open** 8am-5.30pm Mon-Fri; 8.30am-5pm Sat. **£**. **Café**.

Chorlton is famous for it's café culture, and you'll find few spots more authentic than this European specialist bakery and deli. Enjoy a chocolate croissant and house-blend coffee on the no-frills decking. Cheeses from across Europe are available, as well as Italian, Middle Eastern and Polish goods, but the real strength is the 50-plus breads. The Norlander rye and Chorlton sourdough are musts.

Beagle

458 Barlow Moor Road, Chorlton, M21 0BQ (881 8596, www.beagles about.com). Metrolink Chorlton, or Chorlton buses. **Open** 4pm-midnight Tue-Thur; 2pm-1am Fri; 10am-1am Sat; 10am-midnight Sun. **Pub**.

This family-friendly pub is run by the team behind the Independent Manchester Beer Convention, so look out for choices from London's Kernel brewery and Holmfirth's Summer Wine, as well as regional highlights. The owners also run Common Bar and Port Street Beer House, but a Cali-Mex menu brings something fresh to the table. There's a large conservatory and retro bird paintings.

Coriander

485 Barlow Moor Road, Chorlton, M21 8AG (881 0340, www.coriander

restaurant.co.uk). Metrolink Chorlton, or Chorlton buses. **Open** 5-11pm Mon-Fri; 4-11.30pm Sat, Sun. **££. Indian.**
Coriander has expanded to two outlets in Chorlton. Freshly cooked traditional curries are a draw, but it's the specials, such as chicken urban-style (with chickpeas, peppers and onion) or home-style (with okra), vegan dishes and great fish that make this the one that people save up for. The central Chorlton branch is bright and breezy, with lashings of chrome; the other outlet is at 279 Barlow Moor Road.

Fallow
2A Landcross Road, Fallowfield, M14 6NA (224 0467, www.fallowcafe.com). Fallowfield buses. **Open** 10am-midnight Mon-Wed, Sun; 10am-2.30am Thur-Sat. **££. Café-bar.**
This friendly place is a stone's throw from Fallowfield's many boozers, so most of the customers will be students eating off a hangover with a hearty breakfast, or, more likely, a falafel or cajun chicken burger. The upstairs space hosts open-mic nights, film screenings, quizzes and more.

Font
115-117 Manchester Road, Chorlton, M21 9PG (871 2022, www.thefontbar. wordpress.com). Metrolink Chorlton, or Chorlton buses. **Open** 11am-12.30am Mon-Thur, Sun; 11am-1am Fri, Sat. **Pub.**
People who love beer love Font, because this unpretentious bar has more than 20 perfectly kept cask ales and kegged beers to choose from, alongside 160 bottles and a fistful of traditional ciders. Beers from the world's finest craft brewers appear here before other places. Local names of note include Shindigger, Cloudwater and First Chop. There are branches off Oxford Road in the city centre and in Fallowfield too.

Greens
43 Lapwing Lane, Didsbury, M20 2NT (434 4259, www.greensdidsbury.co.uk).

Metrolink Burton Road, or Didsbury buses, or East Didsbury rail. **Open** 5.30-10.30pm Mon; noon-2pm, 5.30-10.30pm Tue-Fri; noon-2.30pm, 5.30-10.30pm Sat; 12.30-9.30pm Sun. **££. Vegetarian.**
After a visit to Greens, it's more or less compulsory for carnivores to declare: 'I loved it, and I'm not even vegetarian.' The set menu (two courses for £12, lunch & 5.30-6.30pm Mon-Thur) provides brilliant value, but if you're out on a Saturday night, we recommend the pumpkin wontons with kimchi, homemade gnocchi, and house Lancashire cheese and basil bangers. Oh, and be sure to save a little room for the peanut-butter jelly parfait. Co-owner is TV chef Simon Rimmer.

Horse & Jockey
9 The Green, Chorlton, M21 9HS (860 7794, www.horseandjockeychorlton. com). Metrolink Chorlton, or Chorlton buses. **Open** noon-11pm Mon-Thur; noon-midnight Fri; 9am-midnight Sat; 9am-11pm Sun. **££. Gastropub.**
Beloved of Chorlton natives, the recently overhauled Horse & Jockey is a pub with great food, genuine heart and a mind-blowing rotation of guest cask ales, as well as its own brews from the in-house Bootleg brewery. If you'd rather not indulge in an alcoholic beverage, it also has a coffee machine the size of the Death Star. Look out for weekend events such as fireworks, food festivals and Easter-egg hunts on the Green outside. It's a great spot for a sunny day.

Jai Kathmandu
45 Palatine Road, Northenden, M22 4FY (946 0501). Bus 41, 43. **Open** noon-2.30pm, 6-11.30pm Mon-Thur; noon-2.30pm, 6pm-midnight Fri, Sat; 6-11pm Sun. **££. Nepalese.**
Although this restaurant (unconnected to West Didsbury's Great Kathmandu) may not appear to be much from the outside, the Nepalese-centred cooking is a cut above most curry-house fare.

Spicy kidney kebabs and a rich bhuna gosht stand out on the menu.

Jem & I

1C School Lane, Didsbury, M20 6RD (445 3996, www.jemandirestaurant. co.uk). Metrolink Didsbury Village, or Didsbury buses, or East Didsbury rail. **Open** noon-2pm, 5.30-10pm Tue-Thur; noon-2pm, 6-10.30pm Fri, Sat; noon-4pm Sun. **££. Modern British**.

This popular Didsbury restaurant is run by the gifted Jem O'Sullivan (previously chef at the Lime Tree). Enjoy competitively priced dishes such as seared scallops with brown shrimp risotto or slow-cooked lamb belly with celeriac rösti.

Kyotoya

28 Copson Street, Withington, M20 3HB (445 2555). Metrolink Withington, or Withington buses. **Open** noon-3am Tue-Sat; 2-10pm Sun. **££. Japanese**.

Japanese restaurants aren't a Mancunian forte – which makes this enclave of sushi in the student badlands a real treat. Amid woody surrounds, order fresh fish and associated creations, with a flask of saké on the side. Surprisingly for a sushi restaurant, it's an affordable treat. Good take-out too.

Lime Tree

8 Lapwing Lane, West Didsbury, M20 2WS (445 1217, www.thelimetree restaurant.co.uk). Metrolink Burton Road, or Didsbury buses, or East Didsbury rail. **Open** 5.30-10pm Mon, Sat; noon-2.30pm, 5.30-10pm Tue-Fri; noon-8pm Sun. **£££. Modern French**.

Chef-patron Patrick Hannity's refined operation has loyal customers who can border on the fanatical in their evangelising, but their fervour is well placed. The Lime Tree wears its French influences lightly, so dishes of crisp, confit Goosnargh duck leg are accompanied by local black pudding and seasonal leaves. Hannity produces much of the rare-breed meat on his own Macclesfield Forest farm.

Marble Beer House

57 Manchester Road, Chorlton, M21 9PW (881 9206, www.marblebeers.com). Metrolink Chorlton, or Chorlton buses. **Open** noon-11pm Mon-Wed; noon-midnight Thur-Sun. **Pub**.

This small, intimate pub has a nice line in reclaimed furniture and seven hand-pulls serving their famous own-brews and guest ales. Ginger Marble and the award-winning Earl Grey IPA are worth the trip alone. There are some mighty strong bottled Belgian beers too. The coffee is also good. There's a sister pub in the Northern Quarter – 57 Thomas Street (p90) – plus the Marble Arch (p150) in North Manchester.

Metropolitan

2 Lapwing Lane, West Didsbury, M20 2WS (374 9559, www.the-metropolitan. co.uk). Metrolink Burton Road, or Didsbury buses, or East Didsbury rail. **Open** 10am-11pm Mon, Tue, Sun; 10am-11.30pm Wed, Thur; 10am-midnight Fri, Sat. **££. Pub**.

This sprawling, loveable pub is a prime venue in which to enjoy a traditional roast dinner – but booking is advisable. With its assortment of large tables and ramshackle bookshelves, the Met is a great venue for a lost Sunday. Evening dishes tend towards high-quality pub fare (cumberland wellington, chicken kiev).

Palate

516 Wilbraham Road, Chorlton, M21 9AW (882 0286, http:// palatechorlton.co.uk). Metrolink Chorlton, or Chorlton buses. **Open** noon-11pm daily. **££. Bar**.

Solid wood tables and floors make for a rustic look at this new addition to Chorlton's food and drink scene. Sharing platters of British charcuterie and cheeses are joined by small plates (brown lentil and mushroom pâté with sourdough), creative salads and robust mains such as lamb rump with Greek salad. There's prosecco on tap and a well-thought-out wine list too.

Suburban delis

For foodie treats, look beyond the city centre.

Lovers of fine foodstuffs should make a beeline for Chorlton and West Didsbury, both established outposts on the deli frontier. Local names such as **Barbakan** (p155) and **Unicorn Grocery** (p163) are fast gaining national recognition for their breads and ethical produce, respectively. Also in Chorlton, **Hickson & Black's** (559 Barlow Moor Road, 881 2001, M21 8AN, www.hicksonandblacks.co.uk) sells cured meats and farmhouse cheeses, while French-leaning **Épicerie Ludo** (p160) is well known for its bread, wine and macarons.

A Taste of Honey (138 Burton Road, M20 1JQ, 434 5217, www. atasteofhoney.co.uk; *pictured*) is a labour of love selling olives, antipasti, harissa with rose petals and more. They also work with two local roasters, Ancoats Coffee and Passion Fruit Coffee Roasters, to offer whole and ground beans.

Didsbury Village dwellers will claim the **Cheese Hamlet** (706 Wilmslow Road, M20 2DW, 434 4781, www.cheesehamlet.co.uk) and **Axons Butchers** (5 Barlow Moor Road, M20 6TN, 445 1795) were there long before the trendies moved in down the road. A relative newcomer is **Bisous Bisous** (663 Wilmslow Road, M20 6RA, 222 4480, www.bisousbisous.co.uk), sister pâtisserie to the Northern Quarter's much-loved French restaurant 63 Degrees (p90).

The up-and-coming suburb of Levenshulme boasts **Trove** (p160), which serves a cracking organic breakfast in its café, typically accompanied by its award-winning sourdough. There's also a branch

of ethnic food hall **Manchester Superstore** (536-538 Stockport Road, M12 4JJ, 224 3441), which is ideal for tracking down hard-to-find spices and fresh herbs. Further south will bring you to **Cheshire Smokehouse** (Vost Farm, SK9 5NU, 01625 548499, www.cheshiresmokehouse.co.uk), just outside Wilmslow.

Fine foods and decent delis are not just available to the residents of South Manchester. Tuck into the Sunday special (six bagels, a packet of smoked salmon and sides for £5) at **Let's Fress** (70 Bury Old Road, M45 6TL, 798 0343) in North Manchester's Jewish enclave of Prestwich, while **JA Hyman** (also known as Titanics – 123 Waterloo Road, M8 8BT, 792 1888) stocks a range of deli delights, kosher and otherwise.

Parlour

60 Beech Road, Chorlton, M21 9EG (881 4871, www.theparlour.info). Metrolink Chorlton, or Chorlton buses. **Open** noon-late daily. **££. Pub.**

Everyone can cook a roast dinner – but few bars and pubs in Manchester have won national awards for theirs. By serving the best meat from local butchers, with gargantuan yorkshire puds, a nut roast to rival the most unctuous pork belly, and fine cheeses, it's no surprise the Parlour is always packed. Enjoy local real ales and punchy reds in boho-pub surrounds.

Petra Restaurant

267 Upper Brook Street, M13 0HR (274 4441, www.petra2eat.co.uk). Bus 50, 54, 113, 130, 147. **Open** 11.30am-2.30pm, 5-11pm Mon-Fri; 5-11pm Sat, Sun. **££.**
Middle Eastern.

This unlicensed restaurant off a busy main road has a tasty take on Middle Eastern cuisine, from the delightful baba ganoush – aubergine and garlic dip sweetened with pomegranate – to a range of delicately spiced kebabs. For a small corkage fee, you can bring your own beer or wine.

POD

30 Albert Road, Levenshulme, M19 2FP (248 7990, www.postofficedeli. wordpress.com). Levenshulme buses, or Levenshulme rail. **Open** 10am-5pm Mon-Wed; 10am-11pm Thur; 10am-midnight Fri, Sat; 10am-4pm Sun. **£. Café.**

A cool alternative to the fast-food restaurants that dominate the Levenshulme culinary landscape, POD (an acronym of Post Office Deli rather than a reference to capsule-like dimensions) serves great coffee and burgers, plus inventive sandwiches and breakfast dishes including 'The Full Levy' with own-made potato and shallot cakes.

Red Lion

532 Wilmslow Road, Withington, M20 4BT (434 2441, www.redlionpub manchester.co.uk). Metrolink Withington,

or Withington buses, or Burnage rail. **Open** 11am-11pm Mon-Wed; 11am-11.30pm Thur; 11am-12.30am Fri, Sat; noon-11.30pm Sun. **Pub.**

Marston's is the beer of choice at this cavernous pub with a whitewashed 200-year-old façade. It's one of the most popular boozers in the area, especially in summer, with bonuses being the long-running Monday-night quiz and a tremendous chippy (Andy's) opposite, to satisfy those post-pub munchies.

Rose Garden

218 Burton Road, West Didsbury, M20 2LW (478 0747, www.therosegarden didsbury.com). Metrolink Burton Road or West Didsbury, or Didsbury buses. **Open** 6-10.30pm Mon-Fri; 6-11pm Sat; 12.45-7.30pm Sun. **£££. Modern British.**

Modern British cuisine is hard to get right – but this family affair comes close. Pan-Asian aspects creep into dishes such as pork belly with squid and pineapple salsa, or rhubarb panna cotta with ginger sorbet. In fact, head chef and co-owner William Mills is seldom short of ideas. Wines include English varietals, and the interior, designed by Mills' architect dad, is a talking point: Japanese love hotel meets English country garden.

Royal Oak

729 Wilmslow Road, Didsbury, M20 6WF (434 4788). Metrolink Didsbury Village, or Disbury buses, or Burnage rail. **Open** noon-11pm Mon-Thur, Sun; noon-12.30am Fri, Sat. **Pub.**

Among the glitz and neon of the numerous chains that have taken over South Manchester's most affluent suburb, this place is a haven for traditionalists, being one of the few remaining places where you can quaff a pint of dark mild. Drama buffs will love the theatrical posters and memorabilia.

Seoul Kimchi

275 Upper Brook Street, M13 0HR (273 5556, www.facebook.com/ seoulkimchimanchester). Bus 147.

MANCHESTER BY AREA

Open 11.30am-3.30pm, 5-9.30pm daily. **£-££. Korean**.

This simple, unassuming diner behind Manchester Royal Infirmary is the place for *bulgogi* (barbecued meat), prawn bibimbap, kimchi pancakes (*jeon*) and plum ice-cream. You'll probably be sharing a table with Korean expats. What better way to meet the locals? The location makes this something of a destination diner.

Solita

School Lane, Didsbury, M20 6RD (434 4884, www.solita.co.uk). Metrolink Didsbury Village, or Didsbury buses. **Open** noon-10pm Mon-Thur; 11am-11pm Fri, Sat; 11am-10pm Sun. **££**. **American**.

Solita has a branch in the Northern Quarter, but it's their rapid expansion into the suburbs of Prestwich and Didsbury that illustrates the high standards of this US-inspired 'dirty food' purveyor. Cocktails, such as the Twelve Dollar Shake, are excellent, but most people are lured in by such creations as the Big Manc burger and the pulled pork sundae with half butter, half mash. Steaks are good too.

Trove

1032 Stockport Road, Levenshulme, M19 3WX (224 8588, www.trovefoods. co.uk). Bus 171, 192, or Levenshulme rail. **Open** 8am-5pm Mon-Fri; 9am-10pm Sat; 10am-5pm Sun. **££**. **Café**.

Like a fine sourdough, the gentrification of the suburb of Levenshulme is happening at its own pace. As yet, there are few places to draw custom from the city centre, except for the Trove bakery-cum-café. Own-made breads and a lifestyle-store vibe (flowers, must-have salt and pepper shakers, cute kids) are paired with excellent eggs, coffee and popular supper clubs.

Volta

167 Burton Road, West Didsbury, M20 2LN (448 8887, www.voltafoodand drink.co.uk). Metrolink Burton Road

or West Didsbury, or Didsbury buses. **Open** noon-midnight Tue-Thur, Sun; noon-1am Fri; 11am-1am Sat. **Bar**.

A decadent-feeling bar-restaurant, all reclaimed wood and vintage finds. Food and booze are worth the trip, with padrón peppers, rare-breed steak-frites and the negroni all choices of note. It's a step up from sister bar Electrik (p163) in Chorlton, owned by the DJ duo Justin Crawford and Luke Cowdrey.

Wine & Wallop

97 Lapwing Lane, Didsbury, M20 6UR (446 2464, www.wineandwallop.co.uk). Metrolink West Didsbury, or Didsbury buses. **Open** noon-11pm Mon-Thur; noon-midnight Fri, Sat; noon-10.30pm Sun. **Wine bar**.

Both floors of this townhouse bar are devoted to wine, yet the beer offering ('wallop' is an old English term for mild ale) is competitive. A total of 13 beer pumps run the length of the bar, with sustenance provided by sharing plates of cheese or charcuterie. If only all neighbourhood bars had such a great drinks list.

Shopping

Belly Button

240 Burton Road, West Didsbury, M20 2LW (434 4236, www.bellybutton designs.com). Metrolink Burton Road or West Didsbury, or Didsbury buses. **Open** 10.30am-6pm Mon-Sat; noon-4pm Sun.

This Manchester-based company sells its unique greetings cards all over the world, but don't expect naff floral designs or lengthy poems. Instead, it has simple, quirky designs printed on high-quality paper, as well as a good range of blank cards, wrapping paper, notebooks and gifts.

Épicerie Ludo

46 Beech Road, Chorlton, M21 9EG (861 0861, www.epicerieludo.co.uk). Metrolink Chorlton, or Chorlton buses. **Open** 9am-10pm daily.

A night at the Plaza

Stockport's art deco cinema is a treat for the eyes and ears.

Elegance isn't a word that's often associated with a night at the flicks, but patrons at the **Stockport Plaza** (p167) expect to step into another era, and to do so with a bit of class. From usherettes with doily headdresses to Pathé newsreels played before the main feature, the Plaza delights in its position as a 1930s Super Cinema, a Grade II-listed building and much-loved anachronism in the heart of Stockport.

Built in 1932, at the height of the Depression and during the switchover from silent movies to 'talkies', the Plaza served as an escape for people used to the hard life of a northern industrial town. From 1967 to 1999, the building was a Mecca bingo hall, but was converted back to a cinema by a charitable trust in 2000, and fully restored, to the tune of £3.2 million, in 2009.

Featuring a single screen with an impressive 1,314 seats, the Plaza certainly knows its clientele: several recent screenings could have sold out three times over. And then there's the Compton organ, which is kept in pristine condition so that the likes of Radio 2 organist Nigel Ogden can accompany the occasional silent movie double bills. Organ music also precedes regular classic movie screenings. When it's not showing films, the venue operates as a variety theatre: everything from edgy comedy with Jimmy Carr to pantos, classic plays and folk music.

MANCHESTER BY AREA

In Chorlton's beating, bustling heart, you'll find this fabulous French deli selling baguettes, fine sausages, cheese and wine. Artisan-made macarons are a speciality. Be warned: it gets very busy on the weekends, when everyone hits Beech Road for brunch.

Kingbee Records

519 Wilbraham Road, Chorlton, M21 0UF (860 4762, www.kingbeerecords. co.uk). Metrolink Chorlton, or Chorlton buses. **Open** 10am-5.30pm Mon-Sat.
Record shops are ten a penny in Manchester – but some still achieve legendary status. Despite sitting on an anonymous suburban drag, Kingbee is the worst-kept secret in town. DJs, obsessives and musicians (both famous and aspiring) make regular visits here to stock their collections with rare, deleted and obscure 45s, and albums from the annals of ska, soul, rock and psychobilly.

Levenshulme Antiques Village

Old Town Hall, 965 Stockport Road, Levenshulme, M19 3NP (225 7025, www.theantiquesvillage.com). Bus 192, 197, or Levenshulme rail. **Open** 10am-5pm Mon-Sat; 11am-4pm Sun.
Levenshulme's Victorian Town Hall is home to antiques and vintage finds from the 1960s and further back in time. Pick up G Plan furniture, toby jugs, vintage costume jewellery and French-polished dressers. There are toy collectors too, and a café that sells a good-value breakfast and cakes.

Levenshulme Market

See box p74.

McQueen

54 Beech Road, Chorlton, M21 9EG (881 4718, www.mcqueenchorlton.wordpress. com). Metrolink Chorlton, or Chorlton buses. **Open** 10.30am-6pm Mon-Fri; 10am-6pm Sat; 11.30am-5.30pm Sun.
Not to be confused with the late fashion designer, McQueen is a small, independent boutique with hand-picked stock that includes up-and-coming labels, established designers and quirky one-offs for men and women. Shoes and bags add to the offerings, and while the shop can sometimes resemble a Primrose Hill-set jumble sale (with the prices to match), it is delightfully British.

Moth

154 Burton Road, West Didsbury, M20 1LH (445 9847, www.mothstyle. bigcartel.com). Metrolink Burton Road or West Didsbury, or Didsbury buses. **Open** 10.30am-6pm Tue-Sat; noon-5pm Sun.
Find your inner Scandinavian in this whitewashed lifestyle store, where everything speaks of a calmer life. Cashmere throws are woven in stone hues, while ceramics, lampshades, jewellery and bags are hopelessly desirable. Local stylist and interior designer Hazel Marchant is the talented owner-curator.

Sifters

177 Fog Lane, Burnage, M20 6FJ (445 8697, www.sifters-records-manchester. co.uk). Metrolink East Didsbury, or Didsbury buses, or Burnage rail. **Open** 9.30am-5.30pm Mon, Tue, Thur-Sat.
Enjoying the timeless publicity of a mention in an Oasis song (Mr Sifter in 'Shakermaker'), this small second-hand record shop must emit a high-pitched whistling noise that only obsessive collectors (generally young men in studenty jackets) are able to hear. Not that 'normal' people won't find anything – Sifters has everything from Loretta Lynn to Les Négresses Vertes – it's just that they'll need some sharp elbows to snatch up that rare Nirvana import.

Steranko

172 Burton Road, West Didsbury, M20 1LH (448 0108, www.steranko.co.uk). Metrolink Burton Road, or Didsbury buses. **Open** 10.30am-6pm Mon-Sat; 11.30am-4.30pm Sun.

Steranko sells minimal designs for men and women, along the lines of the city centre's Oi Polloi. Think Toast for women, Oliver Spencer for men, and you're on the right track. Steranko's accessories and footwear are particularly strong: keep an eye out for hand-finished Filson bags, Timex watches and Saltwater sandals.

Trafford Centre

M60 junctions 9 & 10, M17 8AA (746 7777, www.intu.co.uk/traffordcentre). Metrolink Stretford, or bus X50, 250. **Open** *Shops* 10am-10pm Mon-Fri; 10am-9pm Sat; noon-6pm Sun.

This huge, shiny mall caters for every whim and is therefore generally bursting at the seams with bag-laden shoppers. All the major fashion names are here, as well as branches of John Lewis and Selfridges, while Barton Arcade hosts homewares stores such as Next and Laura Ashley. In between are smaller chains, gift stores, endless cafés and a vast food court, topped with a multi-screen cinema. The decor has an incongruous neoclassical theme, with marble halls, frolicking nymph murals and Romanesque busts surveying the retail frenzy. The complex includes a Sea Life Centre aquarium, indoor crazy golf, Legoland Discovery Centre and a mooted new IKEA.

Unicorn Grocery

89 Albany Road, Chorlton, M21 0BN (861 0010, www.unicorn-grocery.co.uk). Metrolink Chorlton, or Chorlton buses. **Open** 9.30am-7pm Tue-Fri; 9am-6pm Sat; 11am-5pm Sun.

This large wholefood grocery store, co-operatively run, sells everything the environmentally conscious shopper could wish for. The produce is locally sourced, organic and/or GM-free, and all household products can be guaranteed not to kill fish or turn squirrels radioactive. There's also a wide range of dairy-free, gluten-free and sugar-free items.

Nightlife

Antwerp Mansion

Rusholme Grove, Wilmslow Road, M14 5AG (www.antwerpmansion.com). Fallowfield buses. **Open** varies.

Set in its own grounds, this faded Victorian mansion was once home to the Belgian consulate. Today, however, it's best known for providing a unique, rough-around-the-edges setting for some of the wildest legal parties in Manchester. Underground promoters such as Hit & Run host nights dedicated to drum and bass, breaks and sound system culture as part of a programme that includes craft fairs, comedy nights and experimental theatre.

Electrik

559A Wilbraham Road, Chorlton, M21 0AE (881 3315, www.electrikbar. co.uk). Metrolink Chorlton, or Chorlton buses. **Open** 1pm-12.30am Mon; noon-12.30am Tue-Thur; noon-1.30am Fri; 11am-1.30am Sat; 11am-12.30am Sun.

Before Electrik, Chorlton's bar life was obstinately focused on the salubrious but secluded Beech Road area. Electrik heralded a shift back to the arterial centre, and a lively crowd packed up against its patio doors is now a prominent feature of the Chorlton weekend. Opened by the collective behind Manchester's Electric Chair club, Electrik hosts occasional DJ nights and has a sister venue, Volta (p160), in Didsbury. An intimate, lively setting, it also has decent daytime coffee and food – including hearty roasts.

Fuel Café Bar

448 Wilmslow Road, Withington, M20 3BW (448 9702, http://fuelcafebar. tumblr.com). Metrolink Withington, or Didsbury buses. **Open** 11am-midnight Mon-Thur; 11am-2am Fri; 10am-2am Sat; 10am midnight Sun.

A relaxed vegetarian café-bar by day, by night Fuel hosts a diverse programme of events by independent promoters. Listen out for acts from

Take it to the limit

Ski, snowboard, climb, bounce, play – and more.

The £31-million **Chill Factore** (0843 596 2233, www.chillfactore.com), the country's longest real-snow indoor ski slope, is located at Trafford Quays Leisure Village, near the Trafford Centre. The main slope is 180 metres long, plus there's a 40-metre nursery slope. There's a separate area for families and non-skiers, with sledging lanes, a 60-metre luge slide and tubing lanes. There's even a section for under-4s, with a maze, tunnels, mini slides, toys and a playhouse.

The Chill Factore complex also has a 12-metre indoor climbing wall – but that's by no means the peak of the activities on offer in the Leisure Village and surrounds. The **Air Kix** indoor skydiving centre at Trafford Way (0845 331 6549, www.airkix.com) is a surprisingly affordable blast. You need to be four or older to give it a go – which is not the case at **Play Factore** indoor play centre (0844 824 6030, www.playfactore.com), located underneath the Chill Factore, which welcomes everyone, including babies. As well as acres of soft play, admission includes access to the laser arena, giant slide and go-karts.

Wait, there's still more action! **Jump Nation** (0845 609 0799, www.jumpnation.com), located around the corner at Textilose Road in Trafford Park, is Europe's largest trampoline park. Given Manchester's famously inclement weather, advance booking is essential for all facilities.

local labels such as Red Deer Club. There's also a friendly and eclectic open-mic night, occasional readings and film-screening nights.

Koh Tao

310 Wilmslow Road, Fallowfield, M16 6XQ (www.facebook.com/kohtao fallowfield). Fallowfield buses. **Open** 6pm-1.30am Mon-Wed, Sun; 6pm-2.30am Thur-Sat.

Manchester's students are spoilt for choice thanks to their vast numbers and spending power. One of the most fun options is this Thai beach-bar-themed joint that offers pre-rave parties, and its own deep house, techno, disco and funk nights. Drinks continue the theme, with the likes of SangSom buckets and Chang beer. Pop-up barbecues complete the picture.

Manchester Apollo

Stockport Road, Ardwick Green, M12 6AP (0844 477 7677, www.o2apollo manchester.co.uk). Bus 192, or Ardwick rail. **Open** varies.

A staple of the Manchester gig circuit, and not far from Piccadilly, this historic theatre turned midsized concert venue is packed nightly by music fans seeking hip hop, dance, rock or cheesy pop. Pay more for a civilised seat on the balcony, or grab a piece of the action on the dancefloor. It's also known as the O2 Apollo.

Strange Brew

370 Barlow Moor Road, Chorlton, M21 8AZ. (no phone, www.strange brewbar.co.uk). Metrolink Chorlton, or Chorlton buses. **Open** 4-11pm Mon-Thur; 4pm-midnight Fri; 2pm-midnight Sat; 2-11pm Sun.

This boho haven specialises in good beer and fun times. Something of a local favourite (in an earlier incarnation it was run by Lee Gorton, former front man of local band Alfie), it's a place to kick back and relax. There's a programme of live shows, DJs and open-mic nights; the simple, woody interior and changing array of draught beers makes for a chilled vibe.

Arts & leisure

Belle Vue Greyhound Stadium

Kirkmanshulme Lane, Gorton, M18 7BA (0870 720 3456, www.lovethedogs.co.uk/ bellevue). Bus 201, 203, 204, or Belle Vue rail. **Open** from 2.15pm Wed; 6pm Fri, Sat; 11am Sun.

Four race meetings a week, every week, featuring one of the world's fastest animals – the greyhound. Choose from trackside bellowing and fast food or the more refined option of three courses and polite cheering in the Grandstand restaurant.

Lancashire County Cricket Club

Talbot Road, Old Trafford, M16 0PX (282 4000, tickets 0844 499 9666, www. lccc.co.uk). Metrolink Old Trafford, or bus 15, 255, 256, 263. **Open** Sept-Mar 9am-10pm daily. *Apr-Aug* times vary.

The home of the LCCC for 150 years, the pavilion at Old Trafford is now looking a little tatty. On the cards is a controversial £70-million modernisation programme, which will include expansion, although at time of writing the future of the scheme was uncertain. The Lodge, a 68-room hotel overlooking the pitch, provides a place to stay for die-hard fans, while a small museum (only open on 1st XI and International match days) displays 200 years' worth of cricketing memorabilia.

Manchester United Football Club

Sir Matt Busby Way, Old Trafford, M16 0RA (868 8000, www.manutd.com). Metrolink Old Trafford, or bus X50, 250, 251, 255, 256, 263. **Open** (except match days) *Museum* 9.30am-5pm daily. *Tours* 9.40am-4.30pm daily. **Admission** *Museum* £11; £8.50 reductions; £36 family. *Museum & tour* £18; £12 reductions; £54 family.

The stadium of the world's most famous football team may not be in the most glamorous of locations, but it nevertheless has one of the Premier League's largest capacities (76,000). If you can't get your mitts on a match-day ticket (they're extremely hard to get hold of without a season ticket), console yourself with United's impressive museum. Trot down the players' tunnel as part of the popular behind-the-scenes tour (book online).

Sale Sharks & Salford Red Devils

AJ Bell Stadium, 1 Stadium Way, Ecdes, M30 7EY (286 8926, www.salesharks. com, www.thereddevils.net). Bus 67, 100. Sale Sharks, one of the oldest and most successful rugby union clubs in England, has recently moved to a state-of-the-art stadium, which they share with the Salford Red Devils, a rugby league team that doesn't have quite the same feted status.

Stockport

Stockport may be seen as a plainer, less fashionable sister to Manchester, but it still manages to hold its own. The vast borough is made up of eight districts and reaches from Manchester to the Peak District. Visitors can head out to Mellor and Marple for pubs and walks, Bramhall and Lyme Park (p170) for their historic houses, and into Heaton Moor for drinks and dinner. Stockport town centre itself is a mix of high-street shops and cobbled streets, with a splendid 15th-century marketplace and Victorian covered hall. It's also home to the landmark brick viaduct, as painted by Lowry, and the UK's first (and only) hat museum.

Sights & museums

Hat Works Museum

Wellington Mill, Wellington Road South, SK3 0EU (474 2399, www.stockport. gov.uk). Bus 42, 192, 197, 203, or Stockport rail. **Open** 10am-5pm Tue-Sat; 11am-5pm Sun. **Admission** free. *Tours £4.75; free-£3.50 reductions.* Proudly describing itself as 'the UK's only museum devoted solely to the hatting industry', Hat Works is a quaint experience, displaying machinery and memorabilia from local hatting factories (once the town's prime trade, hence Stockport County FC's nickname of the Hatters). A second floor is crammed with headwear donated by everyone from Vivienne Westwood to Fred Dibnah, plus there's an extensive family area where kids can play dress-up.

Staircase House

30-31 Market Place, SK1 1ES (474 4444, www.stockport.gov.uk). Bus 42, 192, 197, 203, or Stockport rail. **Open** 1-5pm Tue-Fri; 10am-5pm Sat; 11am-5pm Sun. **Admission** £4.75; free-£3.50 reductions. Located behind the tourist information office, Staircase House offers a modern presentation of the city's architectural history told through the surviving layers of this impressive building. Dating from the 15th century, and continuously occupied until shortly after World War II, its rooms are filled with replica period furnishings and artefacts, most of which can be handled. The Jacobean staircase (from which the museum takes its name) is of particular note, and there's a little café too.

Stockport Air Raid Shelters

61 Chestergate, SK1 1NE (474 1940, www.stockport.gov.uk). Bus 42, 192, 197, 203, or Stockport rail. **Open** 1-5pm Tue-Fri; 10am-5pm Sat; 11am-5pm Sun. **Admission** £4.75; free-£3.50 reductions. Dating from 1939, this spacious wartime shelter is carved out of Stockport's natural sandstone cliffs and protected 6,500 citizens from German bombs. Today, you can explore the network of tunnels with a guide, including the sleeping, eating and first-aid areas below the city streets. There was even a room for nursing mothers.

Stockport Art Gallery & War Memorial

Wellington Road South, SK3 8AB (474 4453, www.stockport.gov.uk). Bus 42, 192, 197, 203, or Stockport rail. **Open** 1-5pm Tue-Fri; 10am-5pm Sat; 11am-5pm Sun. **Admission** free.

In contrast to the grand colonnaded entrance, the gallery space that hosts a changing programme of art exhibitions consists of just a pair of drab, functional rooms. Beyond is the more impressive Memorial Hall, featuring a statue of Britannia with a kneeling warrior, beneath a beautiful glass-domed ceiling, and surrounded by engraved lists of the fallen.

Eating & drinking

Bakers Vaults

Bakers Vaults Market Place, SK1 1EU (480 9448, www.bakersvaults. robinsonsbrewery.com). Bus 42, 173, 192, 197, 203, or Stockport rail. **Open** noon-1am daily. **Pub.**

Owned by the team behind Chorlton's Parlour (p159) and Manchester's Castle Hotel, Bakers Vaults is a cool alternative to the other, more traditional pubs in this area, although it remains under the auspices of Robinson's brewery. It has plenty of drinking history under its belt as a turn-of-the-20th-century gin palace. In fact, parts of the building date from 1775, and it stands on the foundations of Stockport Castle. They have regular live music and Northern soul nights, as well as hearty food.

Damson

113 Heaton Moor Road, SK4 4HY (432 4666, www.damsonrestaurant. co.uk). Bus 42A, 84, 197, or Stockport rail. **Open** 5.30-9.30pm Mon-Thur; noon-2.30pm, 5.30-9.30pm Fri; 5-10pm Sat; noon-7.30pm Sun. **£££. Modern British**.

This established restaurant in South Manchester has spawned a bigger sibling (p143) in Salford's MediaCity. The team behind Sam's Chop House (p69)

run the show, so expect the same great quality, albeit with significantly subtler flavours. Grilled fillet of plaice with sea aster, cockles, mussels and wild garlic pesto, and roasted rump of lamp with pea and mint mousseline, are typical of the menu's delights.

Swan with Two Necks

36 Princes Street, SK1 1RY (480 2341, www.swanwithtwonecks.robinsons brewery.com). Bus 42, 173, 192, 197, 203, or Stockport rail. **Open** noon-7pm Mon-Thur; noon-11pm Fri, Sat; noon-6pm Sun. **Pub.**

Built in 1926, this is a long, narrow Robinson's pub, and one of several in Stockport town centre that have made it into CAMRA's Inventory of Historic Pub Interiors (the nearby Queen's Head is another). There's a snug, a vault and a comforting amount of wood and glass. The food is traditional pub grub, with huge portions followed by a small bill.

Nightlife

Blue Cat Café

17 Shaw Road, Heaton Moor, SK4 4AG (432 2117, www.bluecatcafe.co.uk). Bus 84, or Heaton Chapel rail. **Open** 7pm-midnight Mon, Thur-Sun.

The Blue Cat is a little enclave of city bohemia picked up and transplanted to the 'burbs. It proudly showcases the best new bands, both local and touring, operating a policy of original music only, with no tribute or cover bands allowed. Past highlights include Johnny Marr and Viva Stereo. The venue stages a famous open-mic night on a Monday.

Arts & leisure

Stockport Plaza

The Plaza, Mersey Square, SK1 1SP (477 7779, www.stockportplaza. co.uk). Bus 42, 173, 192, 197, 203, or Stockport rail. See box p161.

Novel encounter

Discover some home truths at Elizabeth Gaskell's house.

If a Victorian novelist's home sounds like a dry affair, this near-perfect villa and garden (p153) just south of Manchester's city centre will come as a pleasant surprise. The writer in question is Elizabeth Gaskell, who wrote a letter to a friend in 1850: 'We have a house,' adding that, 'it certainly is a beauty… I must try and make the house give as much pleasure to others as I can.' Following a £2.5-million renovation, which included the commissioning of bespoke fabrics and exacting replicas of joinery and ironwork, as well as the planting of species noted in Gaskell's books, the house and gardens continue to give pleasure to guests in the 21st century.

The elegant, Regency-style villa was completed in 1841; Gaskell lived there with her family from 1850 until her death in 1865. She found fame during her lifetime with the novels she wrote in the house, including *Cranford* and *North and South*. Visitors can explore her study, before moving into the other rooms where guests such as Charlotte Brontë, Charles Dickens, John Ruskin and Harriet Beecher Stowe were welcomed on a regular basis. Her daughters took music lessons in the drawing room with conductor Charles Hallé.

The house and garden is a superb example of the villas of this period – and one of very few to survive in Manchester. As such, it is a relic of social history, showcasing how local people lived in the 1800s, what plants they grew and how they ate and worked together as a family.

Alderley Edge

Days Out

The listings in this guidebook cover only central Greater Manchester. In this chapter, you'll find highlights of the wider urban area, along with trips that dip into the beautiful countryside that surrounds the city.

Alderley Edge

About 15 miles south of Manchester, into the footballer belt, the plush little town of Alderley Edge is something of a magnet for the Cheshire set. The town centre is full of boutiques, bijou restaurants and amusingly expensive charity shops; aim for the junction of London Road and Stevens Street for the most browsable.

You can pass a happy hour indulging in material pursuits here, but what distinguishes Alderley Edge from other wealthy satellite towns is the primeval geological feature that gives the town its name. Just over a mile away via the B5087 (Macclesfield Road), the edge itself is a red sandstone escarpment some 600 feet high, thought to be the result of a cataclysmic prehistoric flood. On a clear day, you can see for miles across the Cheshire plain.

The land is owned by the National Trust and, on certain days (call 01625 584412 or check www.nationaltrust. org.uk/alderley-edge), you can turn up for a guided walk that will point out the geological history as well as a wealth of intriguing features, including the site of a beacon (part of a system of beacons ready to alert the country to the arrival of the Spanish Armada), a hermit's refuge, and the face of a wizard carved into the rock. The walk points to the folklore that formed the basis for Alan Garner's brilliant Edge-set 1960 children's novel *The Weirdstone of Brisingamen*.

Take a refreshment break at the Wizard tearoom (Fri-Sun), next to the car park. Then, if you're driving, head for Nether Alderley Mill (Congleton Road, Nether Alderley, SK10 4TW, 01625 527468, www.nationaltrust. uk/nether-alderley-mill; open 1-3.30pm

Lyme Park

Thur, Sat, Sun), but plan ahead: it's open only as part of a 30-minute tour (£6, £3 reductions). A gem of an Elizabethan cornmill, complete with working water-wheel, it's a mile south on the A34.

Getting there Take the train from Manchester Piccadilly to Alderley Edge. By car, take the A34 from the city centre.

Lyme Park & around

Disley, Stockport, Cheshire SK12 2NX (01663 762023, www.nationaltrust.org. uk/lyme-park). **Open & admission** varies; check website for details.

This attractive country house on the threshold of the Peak District has much to recommend it, and is the setting for Colin Firth's memorable appearance from the lake in the 1995 BBC adaptation of *Pride and Prejudice*. As well as that happy memory, visitors will be treated to roaming herds of red and fallow deer on the numerous country walks. If you're on foot, note that the park entrance is more than a mile from the hall and buildings; a shuttle bus operates when the house is open – check the website for details.

Lyme Hall dates from Tudor times, and Tudor elements survive, although most of the present-day building dates from extravagant 18th-century renovations. It's surrounded by an elegant series of Victorian conservatories and gardens. All the usual National Trust facilities – knowledgeable guides, a café and shop – are present and correct, and there's also Crow Wood, a large adventure playground complete with a giant slide, badger den and rope walks. Runners can also take in clearly marked routes (1.5-4 miles) around the estate or join an organised fun run.

For a taste of the Peak District proper, nip across the Derbyshire border five miles away to the rambler-friendly village of Hayfield. It's one of the best access points to the rugged moorland and mountain of Kinder Scout, the historic site of the 1932 mass trespass that ultimately led to today's right to roam. Should Kinder prove a little too ambitious, then the village of Little Hayfield is a mile away on paths and minor roads, or you could follow one of the paths on the Sett Valley Trail (follow

One of the industrial jewels in the National Trust's crown, Quarry Bank Mill is an impressively preserved 18th-century mill building, the centre of a working community established by Samuel Greg that was both socially and technologically revolutionary for its time. Set in a wooded country estate, it's a living portal to the past, as well as being a pretty setting for rambles and picnics.

Approached down a hill, the vast red-brick building stands next to the river (the first mill was powered by a waterwheel, a stunning example of which is still active). The damp local climate was ideal for cotton processing – too dry, and the cotton wouldn't stretch – and the mill is a reminder of what made the region the industrial powerhouse it was.

At the start of the walk-through tour, museum interpreters in period dress show you early spinning techniques before taking you into halls of still-operative machinery – the deafening clatter of the demonstration is an experience in itself. In the neighbouring Apprentice House you can see where a significant number of orphaned children lived and worked. A decent café provides refreshments and meals, setting you up for a walk around the Styal Country Estate on a route past the man-made lakes and tributaries that powered the mill.

Ten minutes' walk away is Styal village. Once an insignificant hamlet, it developed into a workers' colony when Greg established the mill, and today it remains mostly unaltered from the mid 19th century – the shop, school, chapel and cottages are all remnants of this sprawling monument to the Industrial Revolution. It may look familiar – Styal has featured in period dramas such as the BBC's *Peaky Blinders*. It's also worth making a detour to the charming community-run café, store and art gallery, Earlams (Altrincham Road, Styal, SK9 4JE, 01625 404713, www.earlams.co.uk).

signs from Hayfield station car park or call into the information centre on Station Road; 01663 746222). For a light bite, try Rosie's US-style toasties and cupcakes (41 Kinder Road, SK22 2HS, 01663 745597, www.rosiesinhayfield.com). The Red Lion (112 Buxton Road, High Lane, Stockport, SK6 8ED, 01663 765227, www.redlionhighlane.co.uk) is hard to beat for gastropub grub on the drive back. It's owned by the team behind Damson MediaCity (p143) and serves excellent beer, wine and roasts.

Getting there Lyme Park is on the A6, 12 miles south of Manchester. To reach Hayfield, continue on the A6, then turn left on the A6015 after Disley. Disley train station is half a mile from the park gates; the line (or a bus, or a mile's walk) also connects to New Mills, from where you can get a bus to Hayfield.

Quarry Bank Mill

Quarry Bank Road, Styal, Wilmslow, Cheshire SK9 4LA (01625 527468, www.nationaltrust.org.uk/quarry-bank). **Open** 10.30am-5pm daily. **Admission** £5 per car. *Attractions varies.*

Getting there By car, take the B5167 out of the city centre, then the B5166 to Quarry Bank Mill, a journey of about ten miles. There are regular buses (bus 200) from Manchester Airport and Wilmslow train stations.

Ramsbottom

This agreeable Victorian mill town in the moorlands of north Manchester was established during the early 19th century by Daniel and William Grant – who live on in fiction as Dickens' Cheeryble brothers in *Nicholas Nickleby*. The town nestles in the Irwell Valley below looming Holcombe Hill and it's a real draw for foodies, thanks to the award-winning Chocolate Café (2 Bolton Street, BL0 9HX, 01706 822828, www.chocolate-cafe.co.uk), the Levanter Spanish café (10 Square Street, BL0 9BF, 01706 551530, www.levanterfinefoods.co.uk), and the Irwell Works Brewery Tap (Irwell Street, BL0 9YQ, 01706 825019, www.irwellworksbrewery.co.uk), not forgetting the farmers' market on the second Sunday of every month. It also makes a good base for other activities. A good way to get there is on the East Lancs Steam Railway (0161 764 7790, www.eastlancsrailway.org.uk), which chugs its way between Heywood, Bury and Rawtenstall at weekends.

Following Bridge Street up the hill brings you to Edward Allington's *Tilted Vase* sculpture in the marketplace, part of the 40-mile Irwell Sculpture Trail (www.irwellsculpture-trail.co.uk). A less ambitious hike is Holcombe Hill itself. Follow Carr Street and head uphill bearing to the left, past the Shoulder of Mutton pub (tempting as it might be, the Hearth of the Ram or the Eagle & Child are the gourmets' favourite pubs in the area), and take the path of your choice. Once you've ascended – a straightforward hour's walk for all levels (or there's a road for cheats with cars) – you'll see the Peel Tower, a landmark for miles around. Built in 1852 in tribute to Sir Robert Peel, the 19th-century prime minister

(born in nearby Bury) and founder of the modern police force, the tower is sometimes open at weekends (you'll know because the flag is raised; or you can call 0161 253 5899). Climb the tower's 148 steps to get an even more striking view than from its base.

Getting there By car, take the M66 then the A676. By public transport, take the Metrolink to Bury, then bus 472, 474, 477 or 484.

Ashton-under-Lyne

Ashton is one of the less glamorous satellites orbiting the M60 ring road (to the east); but despite its lack of pzazz, it contains a pair of undersung but excellent museums that should ensure a gently memorable day out. In the town centre, the Museum of the Manchester Regiment (Ashton Town Hall, OL6 6DL, www.tameside.gov.uk) commemorates the experiences and sacrifices of the Manchester Regiment, which was established in 1881 and associated with the town for many years. The Regiment is best known for the World War I poets who served with it, including Wilfred Owen. Among the regimental memorabilia, a recreation of a trench is a sobering experience. The museum is closed for refurbishment until summer 2016.

A mile away across the town centre – following Stamford Street and then, after the roundabout, Park Parade – the Portland Basin Museum (Portland Place, OL7 0QA, 0161 343 2878, www.tameside.gov.uk, closed Mon) nudges up alongside the Ashton Canal, from where occasional barge trips run (call the Tameside Canalboat Trust on 07482 188026 for details). The old warehouse is crammed full of artefacts from a century or so ago, and also has a lovingly recreated 1920s street. A stop at Lily's (75-83 Oldham Road, OL6 7DF, 0161 339 4774), an authentic south Indian veggie café, is an absolute must.

Getting there Take bus 216, 217, 219 or 231 from Manchester city centre, or drive there on the A635. There's an excellent tram service too.

Essentials

ABode

Hotels

Manchester's hotel scene has undergone a radical overhaul in recent years. High-spec and budget hotels have multiplied, while the city's older establishments have been treated to makeovers. The **Hilton**, which opened in 2006, is located in the lower half of the 47-storey Beetham Tower (p128). As one of the country's tallest buildings, it continues to dominate the skyline.

The spa at the Grade II-listed **Midland Hotel** enjoyed a major revamp in 2015, and this historic hotel is on exceptional form in other ways too – acclaimed chef Simon Rogan now runs the famous French restaurant and its more casual sister restaurant, Mr Cooper's House & Garden. The **Palace Hotel** has undergone a £22-million overhaul to restore its turn-of-the-20th-century glory days (and compete with the emerging talent), while the **Radisson Blu Edwardian**

at the historic Free Trade Hall remains a VIP favourite.

The Eclectic Hotel Collection, a leading boutique brand, has added a fourth site to its portfolio – **King Street Townhouse** offers a second city centre option alongside **Great John Street Hotel** and its south Manchester hotels, **Didsbury House** and **Eleven Didsbury Park**.

Ex-United stars have also entered the market, with Ryan Giggs and Gary Neville opening **Hotel Football** in the shadow of Old Trafford to offer a slick, football-themed stay for travelling footie fans and tourists.

Business and budget chains have smartened up their looks (and their acts), meaning that standards across the city are generally high. Latest offerings include the slick new **Innside** by Spanish brand Melia, next to the HOME arts complex just

ESSENTIALS

south of the city centre. With room availability doubling in the last six years, there's never been a better choice of places to stay.

City Centre

ABode

107 Piccadilly, M1 2DB (247 7744, www.abodehotels.co.uk). Metrolink Piccadilly Gardens, or City Centre buses, or Piccadilly rail. **£££**.

The ABode chain has successfully made its modern mark on this Grade II-listed warehouse while retaining many original features, including the walnut and wrought-iron staircase. The 61 rooms (rated from 'comfortable' to 'fabulous') all feature luxury toiletries, monsoon showers and flatscreen TVs. The basement restaurant serves Michael Caines' creations. There's an in-house bar, but there's fun to be had at Malmaison's Malbar across the road.

Arora Hotel

18-24 Princess Street, M1 4LY (236 8999, www.arorahotels.com). Metrolink St Peter's Square, or City Centre buses, or Piccadilly rail. **£££**.

Formerly co-owned by Cliff Richard, the Arora is a vision of early noughties cool, with sleek, modern rooms and funky furniture. The refurbished 24 Bar & Grill, with private dining facilities, is a good spot for a steak. The business-oriented Arora is a favourite stop-off for airline crews.

Britannia Manchester

35 Portland Street, M1 3LA (228 2288, www.britanniahotels.com). Metrolink Piccadilly Gardens, or City Centre buses, or Piccadilly rail. **££**.

The Britannia's main selling points are its location – on Piccadilly Gardens – and very reasonable rates. The ostentatious decor won't be to everyone's taste, but it's perfect for those who like a bit of faded grandeur, with a sweeping gold staircase and huge chandeliers.

SHORTLIST

Best new
- Hotel Football (p180)
- King Street Townhouse (p176)

Best for hipsters
- Great John Street Hotel (p176)
- Hatters (p179)
- Islington Mill (p181)

Hotels with heritage
- Midland Hotel (p177)
- Palace Hotel (p178)
- Radisson Blu Edwardian (p178)

On a budget
- Hatters (p179)
- New Union Hotel (p179)
- Oxnoble (p180)

Best breakfast
- Great John Street Hotel (p176)
- Whitehouse Manor (p182)

Stellar restaurants
- King Street Townhouse (p176)
- Midland Hotel (p177)

Best suites
- Didsbury House Hotel (p182)
- Light Aparthotel (p183)
- Radisson Blu Edwardian (p178)

Best spa
- Midland Hotel (p177)
- Radisson Blu (p181)

Location, location, location
- ABode (left)
- Innside by Melia (p180)

Best traditional
- Abbey Lodge (p181)
- Etrop Grange (p181)

ESSENTIALS

Great John Street Hotel

Great John Street, M3 4FD (831 3211, www.eclectichotels.co.uk). Metrolink Deansgate-Castlefield, or City Centre buses, or Salford Central rail. **££££**.

Great John Street, one of four Eclectic Hotels in the city, pulls out all the stops to deliver a luxurious boutique experience. Housed in an old Victorian schoolhouse, it offers individually designed duplex suites with hand-carved furniture, roll-top baths and super-sexy fabrics. The hotel doesn't have guest parking or a restaurant (though there's informal dining in the lounge, with some of the city's best afternoon teas), but the chichi bar and rooftop hot tub make up for it.

Hilton

303 Deansgate, M3 4LQ (870 1600, www.hilton.co.uk) Metrolink Deansgate-Castlefield, or City Centre buses, or Deansgate rail. **£££**.

There may be a set of swanky apartments above, but for 23 impressive floors the Beetham Tower belongs to the Hilton – as witnessed by the unmissable branding. Rooms are equipped with the latest technology (ergonomic work stations, laptop access). The Cloud 23 bar (p130), halfway up the tower, is straight out of *Lost in Translation* and does a mean afternoon tea (booking essential). The ground-floor Podium restaurant-bar delivers decent regional dishes. International football players are a common sight at the Hilton.

Jurys Inn

56 Great Bridgewater Street, M1 5LE (953 8888, www.jurysinn.com). Metrolink Deansgate-Castlefield, or City Centre buses, or Deansgate rail. **££**.

Well placed for the Bridgewater Hall (opposite), Manchester Central and Deansgate Locks, this purpose-built Jurys Inn offers decent, fairly priced accommodation. Bedrooms and communal areas have all been refurbished according to the inoffensive Jurys Inn brand spec.

King Street Townhouse

10 Booth Street, M2 4AW (831 3211, www.kingstreettownhouse.co.uk). Metrolink St Peter's Square, or City Centre buses, or Piccadilly rail. **££££**.

Another member of the boutique Eclectic Hotels clan, this one is housed in a Grade II-listed building dating back to 1864. It was originally a bank, but don't expect many original features as owners Sally and Eamonn O'Loughlin have gone wild with their eclectic decor; the group is well named. Forty individually furnished rooms and suites are joined by a bar and restaurant, tea rooms, and a rooftop spa pool and garden.

Macdonald Townhouse Hotel

101 Portland Street, M1 6DF (0844 879 9089, www.macdonaldhotels.co.uk). Metrolink Market Street, or City Centre buses, or Piccadilly rail. **££**.

Originally a cotton warehouse, this Grade II-listed property has been a

Great John Street Hotel

hotel since 1982. On the exterior, it's all Victorian splendour, but a recent £3.5-million makeover has left the interior looking far more cutting-edge. Its 85 boutique-style rooms offer free Wi-Fi, laptop safes and flatscreen TVs. 101 Brasserie, on the ground floor, serves contemporary British cuisine in stylish surroundings, including choices from Macdonald's signature Scottish Steak Club. A handy location for Canal Street, Chinatown and the City Centre.

Malmaison

Piccadilly, M1 1LZ (278 1000, www. malmaison.com). Metrolink Piccadilly, or City Centre buses, or Piccadilly rail. **£££**.
A favourite with visiting bands and celebs, the Mal is first choice for those who like to think of themselves as possessors of style. The old Joshua Hoyle textile mill's facelift introduced a dark-toned red, brown and black colour scheme to many of the suites. One of the stars is the sexy Moulin Rouge room; the freestanding bath in

the lounge takes around half an hour to fill, such is its depth. Other facilities include the meaty Smoak Grill and a popular bar.

Manchester Marriott Victoria & Albert

Water Street, M3 4JQ (832 1188, www. marriott.com). Metrolink Deansgate-Castlefield, or City Centre buses, or Salford Central rail. **£££**.
Originally a textile warehouse, this Grade II-listed building now houses 129 rooms, a conference centre, and a bar and restaurant. The corporate feel is softened by exposed wooden beams, bare brickwork and quirkily shaped rooms, while photographic reminders of Manchester in the olden days line the mezzanine gallery of the reception.

Midland Hotel

Peter Street, M60 2DS (236 3333, www.qhotels.co.uk). Metrolink St Peter's Square, or City Centre buses, or Oxford Road rail. **££££**.

ESSENTIALS

Radisson Blu Edwardian

This grand old Manchester dame opened in 1905. It's had its fair share of high-profile visitors over the decades and goes down in history as the place where Charles Stewart Rolls and Frederick Henry Royce met. The feel is modern classic throughout, from the marble-floored reception to richly furnished rooms. In a bold move, double Michelin-starred chef Simon Rogan took over the catering in 2013. The star-seeking French restaurant serves Rogan's tasting menus, while leafy bistro Mr Cooper's House & Garden is more relaxed. Herb-infused cocktails make this a destination, as does the spa, revamped in 2015.

Novotel Manchester Centre

21 Dickinson Street, M1 4LX (235 2200, www.novotel.com). Metrolink St Peter's Square, or City Centre buses, or Oxford Road rail. **£££**.
As a new-generation Novotel, this hotel does have more to offer than similarly branded accommodation in the city. The 164 rooms may be a set size, but effort has gone into funking up the decor, and a decent gym, steam room and sauna add to the appeal. There are busy bars in the vicinity, or head to nearby Chinatown.

Palace Hotel

Oxford Street, M60 7HA (288 1111, www.palacehotelmanchestercity.co.uk). Metrolink St Peter's Square, or City Centre buses, or Oxford Road rail. **£££**.
This well-loved, historic hotel is housed in the old Refuge Assurance Building (p118) and has just had a £22-million overhaul. The restored glass dome over the vast reception makes for an impressive entrance, while the bar and restaurant mix original Victorian flooring and tiles with contemporary lines.

Radisson Blu Edwardian

Free Trade Hall, Peter Street, M2 5GP (835 9929, www.radissonblu-edwardian. com). Metrolink St Peter's Square, or City Centre buses, or Oxford Road rail. **££££**.

ESSENTIALS

The Radisson Blu Edwardian is housed in the historic Free Trade Hall. The building dates back to 1856, and the hotel has retained many of the original features. The 263 deluxe bedrooms are mostly housed in a large extension, with king-size beds, lots of sleek technology and marble bathrooms. Suites are named after those who have performed or spoken at the hall, with Dylan and Fitzgerald making penthouse appearances, and Gladstone and Dickens patronising the meeting rooms. The underground spa is one of the city's finest. Pending planning permission, the hotel is mooted to be taking over the adjacent Theatre Royal in 2016.

Northern Quarter

Abel Heywood

38 Turner Street, M4 1DZ (819 1441, www.abelheywood.co.uk). Metrolink Shudehill, or City Centre buses, or Victoria rail. **£££**.

This pub and boutique hotel is named after the eccentric, radical Victorian ex-mayor of Manchester, Abel Heywood. The name is fitting, as unlike many larger branded hotels in the area, it has just 15 bedrooms and a quirky style. Features include original brickwork, wooden furnishings and patterned floors. The bar serves gastropub classics and hearty breakfasts, as well as ales from nearby Hydes Brewery.

Crowne Plaza Manchester City Centre

70 Shudehill, M4 4AF (828 8600, www.cpmanchester.com). Metrolink Shudehill, or City Centre buses, or Victoria rail. **£££**.

This comfortable, business-oriented 228-room hotel is a little at odds with the hip, happening Northern Quarter. Starting with the glass and slate entrance hall, a contemporary theme runs through the hotel, taking in floor-to-ceiling windows and a bold colour scheme. The restaurant serves plenty of locally sourced fare. The hotel is well placed for Manchester Arena.

Hatters

50 Newton Street, M1 2EA (236 9500, www.hattershostels.com). Metrolink Piccadilly Gardens, or City Centre buses, or Piccadilly rail. **£**.

A short walk from Piccadilly Station, Hatters offers hostel accommodation for backpackers and budget travellers. Rooms and facilities are basic, but added extras such as complimentary tea, coffee and toast, and quality mattresses on the bunk beds, make a stay here more comfortable. An open kitchen and canteen area gives guests somewhere sociable to warm up their soup. Friendly staff lead regular pub crawls and tours around the area. The nautical-themed bar (called Hold Fast) is better than it sounds, with craft beer and nightly movie screenings.

There's another Hatters-owned hostel (Hilton Chambers) with three-star facilities, just around the corner on Hilton Street.

Gay Village

New Union Hotel

111 Princess Street, M1 6JB (228 1492, www.newunionhotel.com). Metrolink St Peter's Square, or City Centre buses, or Oxford Road rail. **£**.

Pink, but not exclusively so, the New Union has a great position on the corner of Canal and Princess streets. It's ideal for travellers who prefer to spend money on having a good time while saving on accommodation. Groups are well catered for with triple and quad rooms. Karaoke takes place in the venue below.

Velvet

2 Canal Street, M1 3HE (236 9003, www.velvetmanchester.com). Metrolink Piccadilly, or City Centre buses, or Piccadilly rail. **££££**.

This boutique hotel offers 19 individual rooms, including three penthouse suites and three King Balcony Rooms, which overlook the throngs on Canal Street. REN toiletries, bathrobes and slippers are included in each high-spec room. Huge, ornately carved beds and opulent soft furnishings contrast with the exposed brick walls. Downstairs, there's a Moulin Rouge-style bar and restaurant with canalside terrace.

Castlefield

Oxnoble

71 Liverpool Road, M3 4NQ (839 7760, www.theox.co.uk). Metrolink Deansgate-Castlefield, or City Centre buses, or Deansgate rail. **£**.

This established gastropub (p131) has ten comfortable en suite rooms, each with its own funky style; the overall feel is retro-cool. There's no breakfast available, but there are plenty of places nearby to grab a cappuccino. Within easy walking distance of the city centre, the hotel is great value.

Oxford Road & around

Innside by Melia

1 First Street, M15 4RP (0808 234 1953, www.innside.com). Metrolink Deansgate-Castlefield, or City Centre buses, or Deansgate rail. **£££**.

While the arrival of a Euro-business hotel wouldn't normally be of note, this opening is welcome thanks to its Brit-meets-pan Asian restaurant menu and its airy, purpose-built design in the city's cultural heartland. The HOME theatre, art gallery and cinema is just next door, while rooms are plush and four-star with flawless Wi-Fi. Innside by Melia also offers long-stay options.

Salford

Hotel Football

99 Sir Matt Busby Way, M16 0SZ (751 0430, www.hotelfootball.com). Metrolink Old Trafford, or bus X50, 250, 251, 255, 256, 263. **£££**.

Lowry

This brilliantly conceived hotel, right opposite the entrance to Old Trafford football stadium, is owned and run by former players Gary Neville and Ryan Giggs. In the airy bar and restaurant – which is dominated by big-screen football – food director and Michelin-starred chef Michael Wignall has come up with a menu of affordable pies and bangers. Rooms are bright and family-friendly.

Islington Mill

James Street, M3 5HW (07917 714369, www.islingtonmill.com). Bus 36, 37, 38, 50, or Salford Central rail. £.
Not content with housing creative studios and a music venue, edgy Islington Mill is also a favourite place for visiting artists – and the artistically minded – to stay. An outbuilding facing the Mill has been converted into a B&B, and offers a six-bed dorm and two en suite doubles. Expect some noise if there's an event on (reduced-price tickets can be included in the cost of your stay), although the decent breakfast and courtyard garden (an oasis of calm in this less than leafy part of town) easily make up for it.

Lowry

50 Dearmans Place, Chapel Wharf, M3 5LH (827 4000, www.thelowry hotel.com). City Centre buses, or Salford Central rail. £££.
The accommodation of choice for visiting actors, politicians and Premiership footballers, the Lowry is Manchester's original five-star hotel. The address may be Salford, but it's located right on the edge of the city centre, on the banks of the murky River Irwell. Everything is as it should be – huge, achingly hip rooms with super-sized beds, original modern art, discreet service and clued-up staff. The swanky spa and afternoon teas are great, but the restaurant is a victim of the grill trend (though it does have great views).

Manchester Airport

Etrop Grange

Thornley Lane, M90 4EG (499 0500, www.etrophotel.co.uk). Metrolink Manchester Airport, or bus 43, 105, or Manchester Airport rail. ££.
At the other end of the airport accommodation scale from Radisson Blu, Etrop Grange is a traditional English hotel of the potpourri variety. Built in 1780, the country house offers 64 bedrooms with flowery or tartan designs. Choose from huge oak four-posters or polished iron bedsteads with layers of bedding. The hotel's restaurant maintains the atmosphere of traditional elegance with candelabra and big white tablecloths. After flirting with fine dining, it's now a bar and grill.

Radisson Blu

Chicago Avenue, M90 3RA (490 5000, www.radissonblu.com). Metrolink Manchester Airport, or bus 43, 44, 105, or Manchester Airport rail. £££.
The most convenient of Manchester's airport hotels is directly linked with the three terminals via a futuristic walkway, and is also connected to the railway station and Metrolink. The look is 21st-century, if somewhat airport-like. Rooms are comfortable and facilities good: there's a health club, beauty salon and pool; and for those in a rush, an express laundry service and checkout, plus a 'grab and run' breakfast.

Out of the city

Abbey Lodge

501 Wilbraham Road, Chorlton, M21 0UJ (862 9266, www.abbey-lodge.co.uk). Metrolink Chorlton, or bus 85. £.
A converted Victorian family home in the heart of bohemian Chorlton, the Abbey exemplifies the perfect English B&B. Pristinely kept and expertly run, it's decorated in a classical but unfussy way. Bedrooms are a good size and all

are en suite. One pleasant innovation is that, rather than breakfasting in a morning room, guests are invited to take a tray from a continental buffet to the comfort of their own rooms, all of which are furnished with generously sized dining tables.

Best Western Willow Bank

340 Wilmslow Road, Fallowfield, M14 6AF (224 0461, www.bestwestern.co.uk). Fallowfield buses. **££.**
If you like modern, minimal design, this place isn't for you. Willow Bank is from the more-is-more school of style, with 116 bedrooms busy enough to make you cross-eyed. If you can get past this, though, you'll find a pretty reliable hotel. It's also the only half-decent place that serves the student area of Fallowfield, otherwise dominated by rundown B&Bs and tatty hotels.

Didsbury House Hotel

11 Didsbury Park, Didsbury, M20 5LJ (448 2200, www.edectichotels.co.uk) Metrolink East Didsbury, East Didsbury buses, or East Didsbury rail. **£££.**
The second townhouse in Eamonn and Sally O'Loughlin's Eclectic Hotels collection, just up the road from Eleven Didsbury Park (see below), Didsbury House has the attractive look and style of its older sibling, with a few added extras, including a small but perfectly formed bar. There are more rooms here, 27 in all, including two stunning loft rooms with vaulted, beamed ceilings.

Eleven Didsbury Park

Didsbury Park, Didsbury, M20 5LH (448 7711, www.edectichotels.co.uk). Metrolink East Didsbury, East Didsbury buses, or East Didsbury rail. **£££.**
Eleven Didsbury Park was the first suburban townhouse hotel to open in Manchester. It remains one of the city's best-loved destinations and offers 20 great rooms and calm, quiet surroundings in the trendy 'burbs. Interior design credit goes to Sally O'Loughlin, who has created an undeniably hip but

welcoming hotel. The garden has a lovely decked area with white parasols and linen chairs, leading to a manicured lawn.

Lennox Lea

Irlam Road, Sale, M33 2BH (973 1764, www.lennoxlea.co.uk). Metrolink Sale, or bus 41, X41, 99. **£.**
This ivy-clad, red-brick house is family-run and prides itself on its friendly welcome and peaceful Sale location. Accommodation options are flexible, ranging from budget en suites to superior business rooms, family rooms sleeping up to six, and even a garden apartment with kitchen. You can dine in the popular Alexander's Bar & Bistro, and book a chauffeur-driven Bentley to the airport.

Whitehouse Manor

New Road, Prestbury, Macdesfield, SK10 4HP (01625 829376, www.the whitehousemanor.co.uk). Macdesfield rail. **£££.**
Leafy land of footballers' wives and long gravel drives, Prestbury is 20 miles from Manchester, but worth the journey if your destination is the Whitehouse. The lovingly restored Georgian townhouse has individually themed bedrooms, many with their own steam rooms. Options range from traditional four-posters swathed in fabric to contemporary alternatives such as the sparkling Crystal suite. Owner Ryland Wakeham is a trained chef, so breakfasts are something special.

Worsley Park Marriott Hotel & Country Club

Worsley Park, M28 2QT (975 2000, www.marriott.co.uk). Bus 25, or Walkden rail. **£££.**
This lush, green part of the city is ideal if you want fresh air and space without venturing too far from town. Just over ten miles from Manchester city centre, the hotel offers plush parkside rooms, two bars, a restaurant, an 18-hole golf course, leisure facilities and a spa.

Home comforts

Space to live, work and play.

If you're keen to experience the city at your own pace, Manchester's wide choice of serviced apartments could fit the bill. A good option for families or groups, apartments often offer better value than hotels. Most come with the kind of appliances you'd find (or dream of finding) in your own home, and while breakfast isn't made for you, there's also no room service knock on your door at 7am. And with spaces available in new, central residential developments, visitors have the chance to make themselves at home in some of the most fashionable addresses in town.

The **Place ApartHotel** (Ducie Street, M1 2TP, 778 7500, www. theplaceaparthotel.com) offers spacious four-star accommodation with DVD player, satellite TV and CD player as standard. As it's a converted Grade II-listed warehouse, there's plenty of exposed brickwork and original features. It's a stone's throw from Piccadilly Station too.

Elsewhere in the Northern Quarter, the swanky **Light Aparthotel** (20 Church Street, M4 1PN, 839 4848, www.thelight. co.uk) is a favourite with visiting celebrities thanks to the penthouse suites with rooftop jacuzzis. Another draw is the excellent family-owned French restaurant, 63 Degrees, at the base of the complex.

Bang in the heart of Chinatown, **Roomzzz Aparthotel** (36 Princess Street, M1 4JY, 236 2121, www.roomzzz.co.uk) offers 59 luxury apartments in a Grade II-listed building. There's free

Wi-Fi, a fully fitted kitchen in every room, 'grab and go' food available 24/7 in the lobby, plus a strong penchant for beige leather.

The **City Stop Apartments** (6-16 Dantzic Street, M4 2AD, 834 2963, www.citystop.co.uk), directly opposite the Printworks, sleep up to eight. Every apartment has a dishwasher, and some have a pool table in the living room.

The **City Warehouse Apartment Hotel** (6-14 Great Ancoats Street, M4 5AZ, 236 3066, www.thecity warehouse.com), just north of the Northern Quarter in quieter Ancoats, is a favourite with visiting film crews. The industrial-chic apartments have free Wi-Fi, plus tea- and coffee-making facilities. The penthouse suites (sleeping up to eight) also include satellite TV.

Light Aparthotel

Getting Around

Arriving & leaving

By air

Manchester Airport
0871 271 0711, www.manchester airport.co.uk. About 10 miles south of Manchester, junction 5 off the M56. The airport's three terminals are all accessible by train, bus, Metrolink tram and coach. All transport runs into one interchange, which is open 24 hours a day, with links to the terminals via Skylink walkways.

Airport trains
Up to eight direct trains an hour run to the airport from Piccadilly, taking about 20 minutes and costing £4.90 at peak times and £4.20 off-peak. Direct trains also run hourly from Stockport, at £5.60/£4.20 for peak/off-peak. Tickets must be purchased before you board. Visit www.nationalrail.co.uk or call 03457 484950 for departure times.

Airport buses
Buses leave the city centre every 30 minutes, 24 hours a day. **Stagecoach** operates the 43 service to the airport (around an hour, with buses departing every 10 minutes between around 9am and 6pm), while the 199 is the fastest service from Stockport (around 20 minutes). To check timetables, visit www.tfgm.com. Individual hotels may also offer shuttle bus services – check with your reception desk for details.

Airport parking
All three terminals have ample car parking. The cheapest option is the Jetpark car park, 15 minutes from the airport and accessible by a free bus. Discounted prices in advance start around £3 per day – and rise sharply. The Long Stay and Multi Storey car parks charge more. If money is no object, take the stress out of things entirely with the airport's Meet & Greet car-parking service. Book in advance for the best rates through www. manchesterairport.co.uk.

Airport Metrolink trams
Connect from the city centre via Cornbrook for services that run every 12 minutes from around 6am to 11.30pm on weekdays and Saturdays. On Sundays, trams run between 7am and 10.30pm. Journey time is 41 minutes from Cornbrook, but allow 55 minutes from the city centre. Tickets cost up to £4.20 for a single journey. Visit www.tfgm.com for timetables and ticket prices.

By rail

Manchester Piccadilly is the main rail station in the city centre, and most trains stop here. **Victoria**, **Oxford Road** and **Deansgate** stations also serve the centre. Smaller stations link the Greater Manchester suburbs with the centre. For timetables and ticket prices, call National Rail Enquiries on 03457 484950, or visit www.nationalrail.co.uk. Metrolink trams (p185) connect with trains at Piccadilly, Victoria and Deansgate stations, as well as **Manchester Airport**.

By coach

National Express
Manchester Central (formerly Chorlton Street Coach Station), Chorlton Street, M1 3JF (0871 781 8181, www. nationalexpress.com). Services to destinations around the UK.

Megabus
Shudehill Interchange, Shudehill, M4 2AF (0900 160 0900, http://uk.megabus.com). Services to destinations around the UK and Europe.

Public transport

Transport for Greater Manchester oversees all public transport. Most bus stations have a TfGM Travelshop, which provides general travel and timetable information, as well as selling multi-journey tickets. In the city centre, there are TfGM Travelshops at Piccadilly Gardens and at Shudehill interchange.

On trains and trams, fares cost less off-peak (after 9.30am on weekdays; all day Saturday, Sunday, public holidays). For service and timetable information, see www.tfgm.com or phone 0871 200 2233.

System One Travelcards

Day Saver tickets are available across the train, tram and bus networks. If you plan to do a lot of travelling, then the System One off-peak Day Saver is the best option. This allows you to travel on any bus, train and Metrolink tram between 9.30am and midnight any day of the week. The day ticket costs £8.60 and can be bought from bus drivers, at rail stations and from Metrolink ticket machines. For more fare information, see www.systemonetravelcards.co.uk.

Buses

Tickets can be bought from the driver on all buses – cash only, so it's advisable to have the correct change. **Stagecoach**, **Arriva** and **First Manchester** are the main operators in the centre. Fares vary depending on journey length. Stagecoach's Dayrider (£4.10) allows unlimited travel for a whole day, although travel is limited to the bus company you bought the ticket on, and in many cases it may be cheaper to buy a single or return ticket. Alternatively, a System One Day Saver can be bought from the driver for £5.60 (£5.20 off-peak) and applies to any buses for the whole day.

Metroshuttle

This free city centre bus service runs frequently on three routes, linking train stations to key areas. Visitors can hop on and off at stops all around the city centre.

Night buses

Night buses offer a cheap and safe alternative to getting a taxi home. Late services run from Piccadilly Gardens and other city centre stops, but most operate only on Fridays and Saturdays. Night buses run regularly until around 3.30am (check www.tfgm.com for timetables) and travel to many destinations in Greater Manchester. Fares are typically less than £5 per journey.

Trams

Metrolink (www.metrolink.co.uk) is a modern tram system running through the centre of Manchester and out to the suburbs, connecting with major train stations and key destinations across Greater Manchester. It runs seven days a week and is one of the most convenient and quickest ways to travel in the city. It also provides links to some of the city's main leisure and tourist attractions.

Lines run from the centre out as far as Altrincham, Bury and Eccles. As part of the network's £1.5-billion expansion programme, new lines to East Didsbury, Ashton and Manchester Airport, among others, have opened in recent years. A new line is planned for Trafford Park by 2019-2020, to link up with the Trafford Centre. The St Peter's Square stop is closed until late 2016.

Fares

Single, return and Saver tickets are available. Buy from the machines on the platform before you travel, as you cannot buy a ticket on the tram itself. Prices vary depending on journey length; for a fare calculator, visit www.metrolink.co.uk. Metrolink also has a range of travelcards available at ticket machines at all stops.

Timetable

Services run every six to 15 minutes, depending on route and time of day, across seven lines. Trams operate from around 6am until roughly 11.30pm Monday to Thursday, and until around 12.30am on Friday and Saturday and

ESSENTIALS

10pm on Sunday, although these times vary depending on the stop. 'Off-peak' applies to trams running from 9.30am onwards Monday to Friday and all day Saturday, Sunday and bank holidays.

Taxis

Hackney cabs ('black cabs') are licensed by the local council and can be hailed on the street or picked up at a taxi rank. Look out for cabs with their 'taxi' logo illuminated to show that they are free. There are many ranks around the city centre, including Piccadilly Gardens, Piccadilly station, St Peter's Square and Albert Square. You can also book a black cab (for example, Mantax, 230 3333); some accept credit cards, but it is best to confirm this before you start your journey. Taxi fares increase after midnight.

Minicabs

Private-hire cabs are usually saloon vehicles and are generally cheaper than black cabs. They cannot be hailed on the street and it is illegal for them to pick up customers on the road. Drivers touting for business on the street are often unlicensed, expensive and potentially dangerous. Book minicabs in advance over the phone; find taxi numbers on 118 500 or online. Legitimate drivers should display their licence in the car and on a plate on the back of the vehicle. Mini-cab smartphone apps that serve Manchester include Uber and StreetCars.

Driving

Manchester city centre has more than its fair share of one-way systems, although its outlying districts are relatively easy to navigate and tourist attractions are well signposted.

Parking

Always read the signs. The city-centre traffic wardens aren't shy of slapping on tickets or wheel-clamps, or even of towing offending vehicles away. As a general guide, you cannot park on a single yellow line between 8am and 8pm Monday to Sunday. Never park on a double yellow line, in a loading bay or on a space marked for residents or the disabled unless you have the appropriate permit.

There is both on-street and off-street parking in the city centre. On-street parking is often restricted to one, two or three hours maximum, depending on where in town you are. A ticket must be purchased from the machine on the pavement, over the phone (714 0140), online (www.paybyphone.co.uk) or via the Parker app (www.theparker app.com), with tariffs starting at £1.50 for up to 30 minutes. On-street parking charges in marked bays apply 8am to 8pm, seven days a week except on bank holidays, when parking is free. There are numerous NCP car parks (0345 050 7080, www.ncp.co.uk) around Manchester, many of which are 24-hour. These offer secure parking and charge up to a maximum of £4.50 for one hour.

Towed vehicles

Vehicles that are towed away are taken to the pound in Ardwick, which must be contacted to get your car back (234 4144). Proof of ownership and identity is needed – usually car keys, log book (V5) and two other forms of ID. The basic charge is £130, plus £12 for each day the car remains in the pound. After 14 days, the basic fee increases to a minimum of £155.

Vehicle hire

There are a number of companies around the city. **EasyCar** (www.easycar.com), allows you to rent privately owned cars at competitive prices. **City Car Club** (www.citycarclub.co.uk) and **Enterprise** (www.enterprise.co.uk) offer flexible solutions. Otherwise, try **Avis** (www.avis.co.uk) or, if you need something a bit bigger, **Salford Van Hire** (www.salfordvanhire.com).

Resources A-Z

Accident & emergency

The most central Manchester hospitals with 24-hour Accident & Emergency departments are listed below. The UK emergency number for police, fire and ambulance is **999**.

Manchester Royal Infirmary
Oxford Road, M13 9WL (276 1234). Oxford Road buses, or Oxford Road rail.
North Manchester General Hospital
Delauneys Road, Crumpsall, M8 5RB (624 0420). Metrolink Abraham Moss or Crumpsall.
Salford Royal
Stott Lane, Salford, M6 8HD (789 7373). Metrolink Ladywell, or Salford buses, or Eccles rail.

Credit card loss

American Express *01273 696933*
Diners Club *01244 470910*
MasterCard *0800 964767*
Visa *0800 891725*

Customs

For customs allowances, see www.hmrc.gov.uk.

Dental emergency

University Dental Hospital
Higher Cambridge Street, M15 6FH (275 6666). Oxford Road buses, or Oxford Road rail. **Open** 9am-5pm Mon-Fri.
A limited number of emergency patients can be seen (on a first come, first served basis) between 9am and noon Mon-Fri.

Arrive from 7.45am for registration between 9am and 10am. All patients are assessed to qualify for emergency care.

Disabled travellers

The majority of buses and trains have disabled access. Metrolink stations are equipped with ramps, lifts or escalators and most platforms have modified edges to help visually impaired travellers. **Shopmobility** (839 4060, www.shopmobility manchester.org.uk), at the Arndale Centre, provides free mobility aids and information for people with physical disabilities. **Ring & Ride** (200 6011, www.tfgm.com/ring andride) is a service aimed at local people, which works to connect those who might find it hard to get to public transport with their nearest hub.

Electricity

The UK uses the standard European 220-240V, 50 cycle AC voltage via three-pin plugs.

Embassies & consulates

For consular assistance, contact the relevant embassy or consulate in London:

Australian High Commission
020 7379 4334, www.uk.embassy.gov.au.
American Embassy
020 7499 9000, http://london. usembassy.gov.
Canadian High Commission
020 7004 6000, www.canada international.gc.ca.united_kingdom-royaume_uni.

ESSENTIALS

Irish Embassy
020 7235 2171, www.dfa.ie.
New Zealand High Commission
020 7930 8422, www.nzembassy.com.
South African High Commission
*020 7451 7299, http://
southafricahouseuk.com.*

Internet

Extensive free Wi-Fi access in cafés, bars and hotels means that dedicated internet cafés are few and far between in Manchester today. Most public libraries do, however, have terminals for public use.

There's a city-wide Wi-Fi network called the Cloud and there is also coverage on the Metrolink system.

Opening hours

Banks 9am-4.30pm (some close at 3.30pm, some 5.30pm) Mon-Fri; some also open Saturday mornings.
Offices The usual working day is 9am-5pm, with some variations.
Shops Most shops in the city are open 10am-6pm Mon-Fri, with some opening earlier, but many stores now stay open until 8pm. Most shops in the city centre are also open on Sunday, typically from around 11am to 4pm or 5pm.

Pharmacies

Britain's best-known pharmacy chain is **Boots**, with branches in the city centre and most of the surrounding town centres. The main branch in Manchester is on Market Street, open 8am-8pm Mon-Sat, 11.30am-5.30pm Sun. Pharmacists are able to give advice on simple injuries and ailments and suitable treatments.

There are no 24-hour pharmacies in Manchester, but **Cameolord** (7 Oxford Street, M1 5AE, 236 1445) is open 8am-midnight daily. It's near the Central Library in the city centre.

Police stations

Call **999** in an emergency and ask for the police, or call 101 or 872 5050 for non-emergencies.

The main police station is located two miles from the city centre at Central Park (Northampton Road, M40 5BP, 856 3529), but all suburbs are served by a local neighbourhood station. For details, call Directory Enquiries (118 118, 118 500, 118 888) or see the Greater Manchester Police website at www.gmp.police.uk.

Public Enquiry Counter – City Centre
Ground Floor, Mount Street Elevation, Town Hall Extension, M2 5DB (856 3129). Metrolink St Peter's Square, or City Centre buses, or Oxford Road rail. **Open** 24hrs daily.

Postal services

Post offices are usually open 9am-5.30pm Mon-Fri, 9am-noon Sat.

Manchester Post Office
26 Spring Gardens, M2 1BB (0845 722 3344). Metrolink Market Street, or City Centre buses, or Piccadilly rail. **Open** 9am-6pm Mon, Wed-Fri; 9.30am-6pm Tue; 9am-5.30pm Sat.

Safety

Manchester is generally a safe city to visit. However, the usual rules should be followed: remain vigilant in crowded areas – buses, busy streets, train stations – for petty criminals and keep your wits about you in deserted areas after dark. Keep your valuables in your hotel room or safe and make sure the cash and cards you carry are tucked away.

Smoking

Smoking is prohibited in all enclosed public places in the UK, including bars, restaurants and stations.

Telephones

The dialling code for Manchester, Greater Manchester, Salford and Stockport is **0161**.

If you're dialling from outside the UK, dial your international access code, then the UK code (44), then the full number omitting the first 0 from the code. To dial abroad from the UK, first dial 00, then the country code.

Public phones

Public payphones are pretty few and far between these days. If you do find one, it will take coins or credit cards. The minimum cost is 60p. International calling cards offering bargain minutes via a freephone number are widely available from newsagents.

Tickets

Most main venues in Manchester sell their tickets through third parties (and there's normally a booking fee involved). Sites to check include **Ticketmaster** (0844 844 0444, www.ticketmaster.co.uk), **ATG Tickets** (020 7206 1182, www.atgtickets.com) and **Gigs and Tours** (www.gigsandtours.com) for the major theatres and venues in the centre. **See Tickets** (www.seetickets.com), **Skiddle** (www.skiddle.com) and **Quay Tickets** (0843 208 0500, www.quaytickets.com) represent a good number, including small independent venues. **Piccadilly Records** (53 Oldham Street, M1 1JR, 839 8008) sells local gig tickets with no booking fee.

Time

Manchester operates on Greenwich Mean Time (GMT), which is five hours ahead of North America's Eastern Standard Time. In spring, the UK puts its clocks forward by one hour to British Summer Time. In autumn, clocks go back by one hour to GMT.

Tipping

You should tip in taxis, minicabs, restaurants, hotels, hairdressers and some bars (not pubs). Ten per cent is normal; note that some restaurants add on a service charge of up to 15 per cent. In this case it's not necessary to add any further tip.

Tourist information

Manchester's main tourist office offers a wide variety of information on accommodation and sights, and more general details on Manchester and the surrounding suburbs. The office is currently moving location, so check the website for the most up-to-date address. To book accommodation, call 0333 014 3701.

For information on Salford, see www.visitsalford.info. Stockport (and other towns) have their own tourist offices.

Manchester Visitor Information Centre
www.visitmanchester.com.
Stockport Tourist Information Centre
Staircase House, 30-31 Market Place, Stockport, SK1 1ES (474 4444, www.stockport.gov.uk). Stockport buses, or Stockport rail. **Open** 10am-5pm Tue-Sat; 11am-5pm Sun.

Visas

EU citizens do not require a visa to visit the UK; citizens of the USA, Canada, Australia, South Africa and New Zealand need only a passport for tourist visits. Check current status on www.ukvisas.gov.uk well before you travel.

ESSENTIALS

Index

ESSENTIALS

ESSENTIALS

Manchester
Visitor Information Centre

Piccadilly Plaza, Portland Street, Manchester, M1 4AJ
Monday - Saturday: 9.30am - 5.30pm
Sunday: 10.30am - 4.30pm

Tel: 0871 222 8223
Email: touristinformation@visitmanchester.com

Buy Manchester merchandise online at
visitmanchester.com/giftshop

Also available at
The Manchester Store
The Trafford Centre, M17 8AA